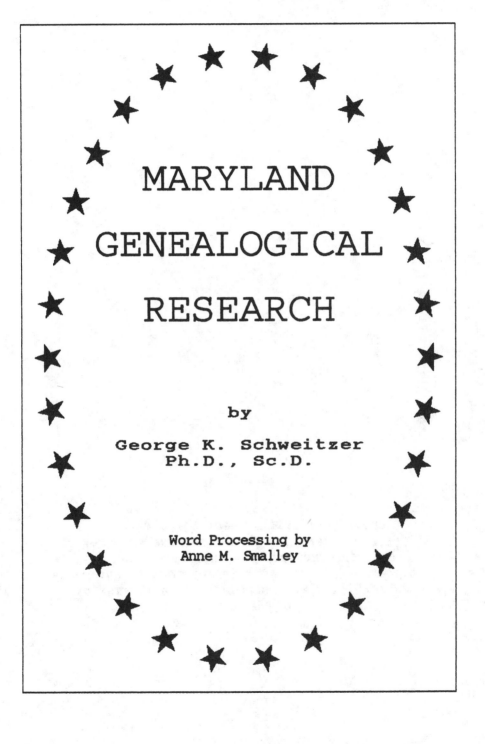

MARYLAND

GENEALOGICAL

RESEARCH

by

George K. Schweitzer
Ph.D., Sc.D.

Word Processing by
Anne M. Smalley

ISBN 0-913857-14-9

TABLE OF CONTENTS

Chapter 1

MARYLAND BACKGROUND

1. MD geography

The state of Maryland (hereafter abbreviated MD), one of the thirteen original colonies, is located in the central region of the eastern seaboard of the US. In shape the state resembles a sauce pan with a deep bowl on the right and a thin handle on the left. See Figure 1. Its longest length (at the top) is about 195 miles and its greatest depth (along the right edge) is approximately 125 miles. MD is bordered on the east by the Atlantic Ocean and DE, on the north by PA, on the west by WV, and on the south by the Potomac River, across which rests WV and VA. A large estuary, Chesapeake Bay, runs from the bottom of the bowl 180 miles north. It gives MD over 3600 miles of water frontage, many excellent sheltered harbors, and connects with the Atlantic Ocean. Since 1791, the District of Columbia has occupied a section of land in south central MD which was given to set up a national capital. The main metropolitan areas of MD are Baltimore and its environs, and the regions surrounding DC.

Figure 2 depicts the major rivers of MD. Only one river of MD drains westward, its water ending up in the MS River. This is the Youghiogheny River (Y) which is located in the extreme western part of MD. All other rivers drain into the Atlantic Ocean mostly through the Potomac River (Po) and/or Chesapeake Bay (CB). The Potomac River flows along the southern border of MD, its southern bank defining the MD state line. This river drains into the Chesapeake Bay (CB). The Monocacy River (M) and several large creeks empty into the Potomac River. On the Western Shore of Chesapeake Bay (CB), the Susquehanna (S), Patapsco (Pa), and Patuxent (Px) Rivers enter the Chesapeake Bay. And emptying into the Bay from its Eastern Shore are the Chesapeake (Ch), Nanticoke (N), Wicomico (W), and Pocomoke (P) Rivers. Most of the history of MD has been dominated by Chesapeake Bay and the numerous creeks and rivers flowing into it.

Figure 3 shows the population centers of MD, the largest cities (with populations in thousands) being Baltimore (787K), Rockville (51K), Bowie (37K), Hagerstown (35K), and Annapolis (35K), the last being the state capital. MD also has a number of sizable unincorporated communities. Those which are suburbs of Baltimore are Dundalk (75K), Columbia (54K), Towson (54K), Essex (41K), and Glen Burnie (33K). Those which are suburbs of Washington, DC, are Silver Spring (77K), Bethesda (77K), and Wheaton (58K). The map also shows towns and county seats. The three major land regions of MD are set forth in Figure 4. The Coastal Plain is the easternmost region. It consists of low-lying, relatively flat tidewater lands, and is heavily indented by the Chesapeake Bay (bays, estuaries, rivers).

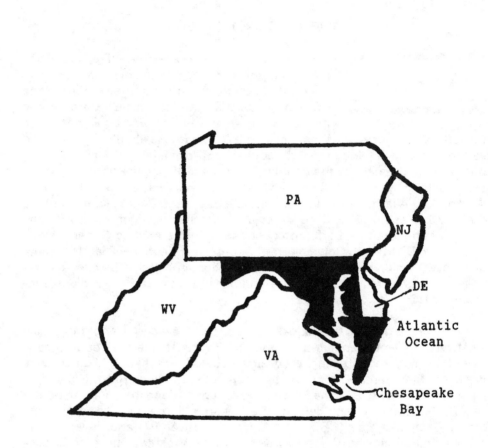

Figure 1. Maryland

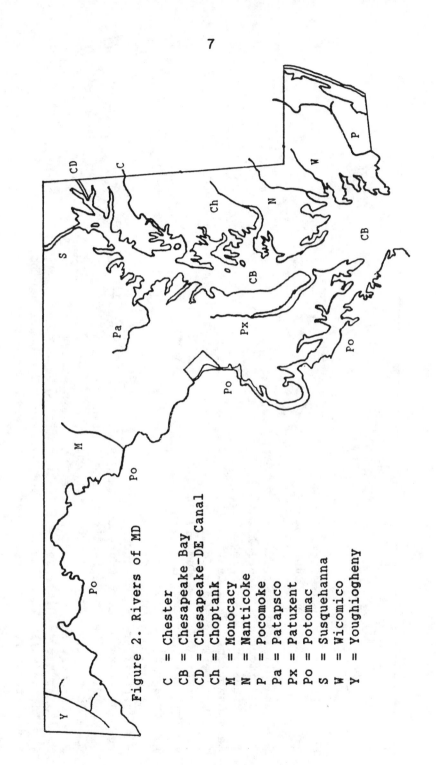

Figure 2. Rivers of MD

C = Chester
CB = Chesapeake Bay
CD = Chesapeake-DE Canal
Ch = Choptank
M = Monocacy
N = Nanticoke
P = Pocomoke
Pa = Patapsco
Px = Patuxent
Po = Potomac
S = Susquehanna
W = Wicomico
Y = Youghiogheny

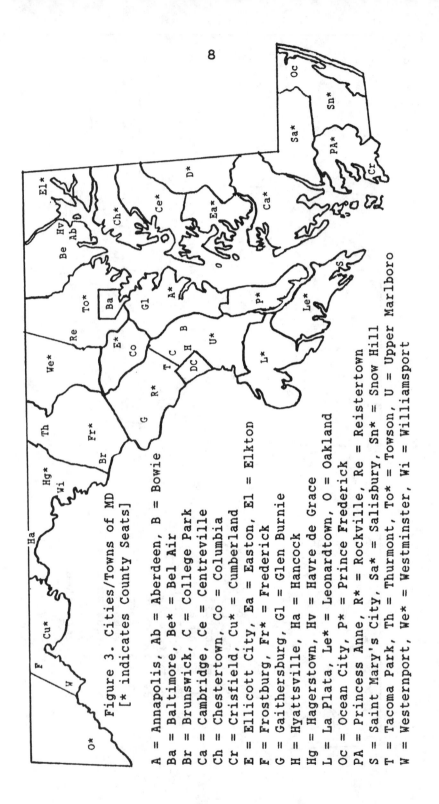

Figure 3. Cities/Towns of MD
[* indicates County Seats]

A = Annapolis, Ab = Aberdeen, B = Bowie
Ba = Baltimore, Be* = Bel Air
Br = Brunswick, C = College Park
Ca = Cambridge, Ce = Centreville
Ch = Chestertown, Co = Columbia
Cr = Crisfield, Cu* = Cumberland
E = Ellicott City, Ea = Easton, El = Elkton
F = Frostburg, Fr* = Frederick
G = Gaithersburg, Gl = Glen Burnie
H = Hyattsville, Ha = Hancock
Hg = Hagerstown, Hv = Havre de Grace
L = La Plata, Le* = Leonardtown, O = Oakland
Oc = Ocean City, P* = Prince Frederick
PA = Princess Anne, R* = Rockville, Re = Reistertown
S = Saint Mary's City, Sa* = Salisbury, Sn* = Snow Hill
T = Tacoma Park, Th = Thurmont, To* = Towson, U = Upper Marlboro
W = Westernport, We* = Westminster, Wi = Williamsport

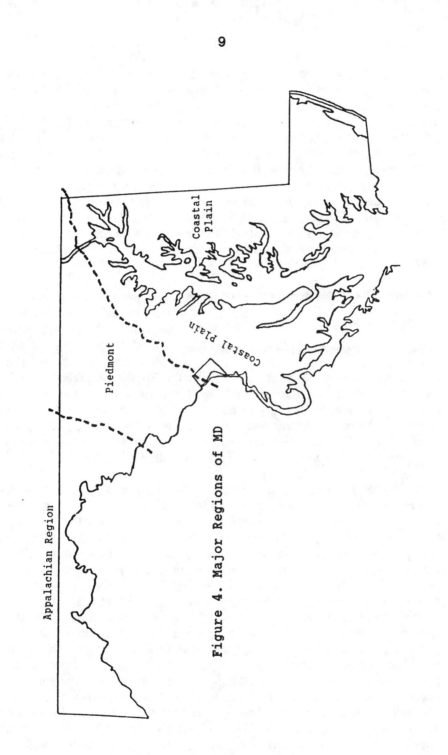

Figure 4. Major Regions of MD

The Coastal Plain is divided by the Chesapeake Bay into two sub-regions: the Western Shore and the Eastern Shore, which is part of the Delmarva (DE-MD-VA) Peninsula. Just west of the Coastal Plain is the Fall Line which makes up the border between the Coastal Plain and the Piedmont. At the Fall Line the land rises rapidly (up to about 100 feet), and west of it (in the Piedmont), the land is broadly rolling hills, rising to about 1000 feet at its western extreme. Beyond the Piedmont, one enters the Appalachian Region. This mountainous area consists of ridges and valleys in the eastern and central portions, which give way to a rugged plateau in the western part. The mountains and valleys rest in a northeasterly to southwestwardly direction. The highest point in MD (3360 feet) is Backbone Mountain in the northwest. The deep valleys which streams have cut into the plateau provided early trails to the west.

2. The early proprietorship, 1634-89

The area which today is MD was known to early explorers including the Englishman Cabot (1498), an Italian da Verrazano sailing for France (1524), the Spaniard Marques (1574), and the Englishman Gilbert (1603). It was charted by Captain John Smith, working out of VA, in 1608. William Claiborne, also from VA, set up a trading post on Kent Island in 1631. The island is in Chesapeake Bay just off the Eastern Shore and just opposite Annapolis. This Chesapeake Bay area was considered by some leaders in VA to belong to their colony, which had been settled since 1607.

In 1625, George Calvert, who had faithfully and effectively served King James I as secretary of state, converted to Catholicism. In spite of this, the King recognized Calvert's many years of dedicated service by giving him the title Baron of Baltimore. Then in 1632, the King began the process of granting Lord Baltimore (George Calvert) what is now MD plus some adjacent land. Before the paper work could be completed George Calvert died, and the charter went to Cecilius Calvert, his son, the second Lord Baltimore. Cecilius Calvert thereby became the first proprietor of MD, and was given power over the area equal to the power of a king. He could establish a government, raise an army, wage war, collect taxes, establish towns and ports, appoint officials, grant land, and enact laws with the consent of the freemen of the proprietorship. With this large territory and his extensive governing powers, Cecilius Calvert set about colonizing MD. Every settler was to receive 100 acres of land and 50-to-100 acres for each person he brought in. Those who brought working men received 1000 acres for every five men. The colonists were expected to farm and collect furs to earn money for themselves and Lord Baltimore, and were required to pay him a quit rent or tax on their land. Calvert also insisted that the colony exercise religious tolerance, admitting and extending religious freedom to all Christians.

Cecilius Calvert, the second Lord Baltimore, Proprietor (absolute owner of MD), appointed his brother Leonard Calvert as Governor of the Proprietorship. He led about 200 settlers who sailed from England in November 1633 on two small ships, the Ark and the Dove. The passengers were mostly men, mostly Protestants, and mostly indentured servants, although there were also numerous Catholics, including the leaders. The group arrived in Chesapeake Bay in early March 1634, and after peaceful agreement with the native Indians, settled at a site on the southern Western Shore which they named St. Mary's City. The Bay provided abundant seafood sustenance, and tobacco farming became the major source of revenue. The large investors who had brought many laborers took their manor plots of land along the shores of the bay and its rivers. The freemen took their smaller farm plots in between. By 1642, the population had grown to about 400.

During the earliest years, 1634-8, there were continual acts of aggression between MD and the Virginians on Kent Island, who resisted Lord Baltimore's rule. In 1638, MD took the island and added it as Kent County to the original St. Mary's County. The government at first consisted of a governor, a council of several advisors, a secretary to keep records, all being appointed by Lord Baltimore. The governor and his council acted as the Provincial Court and sat as the upper house of the legislature. The lower house of the legislature was made up of delegates elected by the landowners in each county. As time went on, the governor appointed county officials as needed. The lower house of the legislature had few powers at first, but they gradually began challenging Lord Baltimore's authority, and he slowly and usually reluctantly gave them greater rights.

In 1642, Civil War between the King and the Parliament broke out in England. By about 1645, the parliamentary interests (chiefly Puritans) won out, but warfare was resumed in 1647, with the king's supporters again losing. The King, Charles I, was beheaded by Parliament in 1649, and the Puritans ruled England until 1660, when the monarchy was restored. The turmoil in England was reflected in MD. With a Catholic proprietor and a population chiefly non-Catholic, religious tensions developed. In 1645, a Puritan ship attacked MD, forced the governor to flee to VA, and took over. In the year following, the governor returned with troops and regained the province. To attempt to settle the religious conflicts, Lord Baltimore appointed a Protestant governor in 1647, and in 1649 about 300 VA Puritans settled on the Severn River near the site of Annapolis. The Assembly passed an act in that year granting toleration to all Christian denominations. The continuing settlements led to the formation of Anne Arundel and Calvert Counties as of 1650. Two years later, a treaty with Indians on the Eastern Shore opened it up, and colonization began. Puritan opposition to religious tolerance led to their taking control of MD in 1654, and the repeal of toleration. They held on until 1657, when Lord Baltimore regained control and restored toleration. Population growth necessitated the establishment of Charles County (1658) and Baltimore County (1659). In 1660, when royal rule returned to England, about 8000 people were in MD. Kent County (Eastern Shore) split off Talbot County in 1661, and Somerset and Dorchester Counties in 1668-9. The population in 1670 had risen to approximately 16,000.

During this time (1634-80), the lower house of the assembly had been gaining legislative power, and was becoming more influential in managing the society. Justices of the peace in the counties were holding court and administering county affairs. The farmers and planters raised tobacco for sale to Europe, and grew corn and vegetables and apples, raised livestock, and fished the Bay for their own benefit. Initially labor was provided by indentured servants, but they were slowly being replaced by imported slaves. Most of the immigrants to MD were English, but others came, including Scots-Irish (Eastern Shore, 1680 and after), and a few Germans, French, Dutch, and Italians. The settlers represented many religious faiths: English Anglicans (Episcopalians), English Catholics, English Puritans, Scots-Irish Presbyterians, and English Quakers (Anne Arundel County, and the Eastern Shore). The natives (Indians) in MD gradually moved away as settlers occupied more land, and the bringing of smallpox by the immigrants took a sizeable toll among them. As of 1675, a few Germans were moving out of PA into central MD.

3. The royal colony, 1689-1715

During the 1680s, the growing numbers of Protestants in MD showed increasing resentment to Lord Baltimore's nepotism, his favoritism toward the Catholic Church, and in 1688-9 the delay in recognizing the switch-over of the English monarchy from Catholic to Protestant. In the middle of 1689, a group of Protestant leaders gathered a force and seized control of MD. The new government called itself the Protestant Association, and they asked the King to send a royal governor. The King agreed to constitute MD as a royal colony, and a governor arrived in 1692. The land in MD was still considered to belong to Lord Baltimore and rents were due him, but he no longer ran the government. The Anglican (Episcopalian) Church was made the official religion, the capital was moved from St. Mary's to Arundel Town (renamed Annapolis), and King William's School (a public school) was founded in Annapolis. Quakers were forbidden to become legislators, and Catholics were not allowed to hold any public office.

During this period (1689-1715), England and France fought two wars: King William's War (1689-97) and Queen Anne's War (1702-13). These conflicts caused interruption of the tobacco trade and created periods of economic depression. But in between these periods, MD advanced both socially and economically. The larger planters bought up more land, imported more slaves, and began to develop into an elite moneyed class which was influential in local and MD government. In general, living standards improved during the time of the royal colony, and MD became stable and prosperous. When Lord Baltimore converted to Protestantism in 1715, the King was persuaded to restore his proprietorship. The years of royal governance had markedly altered MD. There was an established church (Anglican), religious discrimination, a much larger population (43,000 in 1710), strong local leaders, and a larger part being played in the government by the colonists. They had growing expectations of having the same rights as people living in England. Finally, the forms of power in the province had moved from the governor/council to the lower house of the legislature.

4. The restored proprietorship, 1715-63

As mentioned above, Lord Baltimore faced a radically changed situation in his restored proprietorship of MD. He and the lower house of the legislature were in for over 5 decades of controversy. The representatives of the colonists claimed that they should be governed as all other Englishmen and not under a proprietor who could veto their legislative acts. They also objected to high fees which Lord Baltimore permitted officials to collect, to duties which were levied on tobacco, and to taxes paid to support the Anglican church. In 1732, the proprietor visited MD and did away with the tobacco duties, replaced them with the old quit rents, and regulated officials' fees. The changes helped the situation for a few years, but Lord Baltimore was challenged again in 1738 and after by assertive colonists and legislators. Gradually the proprietor lost his ability to keep the citizens in a subordinate role. They increasingly insisted on a greater and greater degree of self-government.

In spite of the colonist-proprietor controversies, MD underwent extensive development during this period. Previously, a one-crop economy (tobacco), MD began to diversify: growing wheat and corn, raising livestock, producing timber products, cultivating orchards, fishing, producing craft articles, and developing merchant trade. The people of MD also began some technological endeavors: iron works in Cecil and Baltimore Counties, shipbuilding in Somerset and Anne Arundel Counties, and craftsmen of various sorts (such as tanners, blacksmiths, woodworkers) and professional people (clergymen, lawyers, physicians) increased. The population grew and settlers began to move into the Piedmont where they joined Germans who had come down from PA.

The development of the economy was accompanied by the growth of towns to act as trade centers and ports. At first there had been only St.

Mary's, never very large. When the capital was moved to Annapolis in 1694, St. Mary's declined and Annapolis grew, but slowly. Around the turn of the century, the government began to establish numerous towns in addition to the few very small ones that had previously gathered. Many of these had only short existences, but some prospered, including Baltimore which was set up in 1729. Baltimore's prosperity was due to its growth as a wheat processing and exporting center and as an iron shipping port. In the 1750s Baltimore began to function as an entry port for Germans, and many came. As wheat cultivation spread westward, towns developed there, Frederick (1747) and Hagerstown (1762) being notable. As of 1755, 98% of the MD population lived on farms. Annapolis was the largest town (about 1000 people). The only MD newspaper at that time was the Maryland Gazette which had started continuous publication in 1745.

A census taker in 1755 reveals the structure of MD society at that time. About 153,000 people were in the colony. At the very top were the proprietor and his officials and advisors. Just beneath the top were the gentry (7% or about 11,000). These men owned half of the land, about 65% of the colony's wealth, and about 60% of the slaves. They were planters, merchants, lawyers, and government officials. They ran the colony, regulated its trade, supervised its commercial activities, and made its laws. By this date, they had wrested considerable power from the proprietor and were governing the people in many matters, especially at the local or county level. Next in the ranking, just under the gentry were the middle-class planters (16% or about 24,000). Most of them owned land, on average about 200 acres. They raised tobacco, corn, wheat, and/or oats, and also horses, cattle, sheep, and/or hogs. They owned a few slaves, ordinarily two, three, or four. Beneath the middle-class planters were the small planters, tenant farmers, and hired laborers (48% or about 73,000). Some of the hired laborers were indentured servants and some were transported convicts. And at the bottom of the structure were slaves (29% or about 44,000).

In 1754, the French and Indian War broke out. The British had settled in the eastern coastal areas (the 13 colonies), and the French had entered what is now part of Canada and had come into the country behind (west) the colonies. Early in the conflict (1754-8), the French successfully defended the back country with the aid of the Indians. But the tide turned in 1759, and the British began a series of successful campaigns. In 1760, Canada was conquered and most of the French outposts behind the colonies were taken. In the next year, the one remaining conflict, between the British and the Cherokees behind the southern colonies, was resolved in the British favor. The war ended in 1763 with the Treaty of Paris and the British receiving Canada and the back county all the way to the MS River. MD contributed very little to the war in terms of manpower or supplies. The colony was locked into a three-cornered power struggle between the assembly, the proprietor, and the British government over the defense of the frontier.

During this restored proprietorship period (1715–63), MD entered into controversies with other colonies over its borders. These disagreements were produced by the expanding and spreading populations of the colonies. The resolution of boundary quarrels with PA and VA in 1732 entailed the loss of much territory by MD. In the 1760s further disputes with PA were settled by the survey of the DE–MD–PA boundaries by two surveyors, Mason and Dixon.

5. The American Revolution, 1763–89

The end of the French and Indian War saw Britain with newly acquired land and deep in debt. In order to govern their enlarged empire and to help pay this debt, the British government began to enact stricter regulations, enforce previously neglected taxation laws, and to levy new taxes. The members of the gentry, whose prerogatives and profits were threatened by this policy, became leaders in protesting. The first of the new moves was an act of 1763 forbidding settlement beyond the Appalachian Mountains. This was regarded as unfair and oppressive, especially by land speculators. Two acts of 1764 forbade the issuing of paper money by any colony and levied a tax on imported sugar. In 1765 came a quartering act requiring colonists to house British troops and the Stamp Act requiring all documents, licenses, and newspapers to bear a tax stamp. The protests in all the colonies were vigorous, and they claimed they could only be taxed by their own elected representatives. While this went on, Lord Baltimore was enforcing the tax to support the Anglican Church. To quell the furor, the British Parliament repealed the Stamp Act in 1766, but replaced it with taxes on tea, paper, glass, and painter's colors. Further protests ensued, but Parliament passed more regulations. Boycotts against British imports resulted, and all the taxes except the one on tea were removed in 1770. Things went well until 1773, when the British government passed the Tea Act which gave special treatment to the East India Company to undersell all other companies in the colonies. Many colonies, in protest, turned away the ships carrying the tea, but citizens of MA reacted by throwing the cargo overboard.

The British promptly closed Boston harbor, cutting off all imports. MA sent letters to the other colonies asking for help, and food and clothing was sent to them. A convention of delegates from 12 of the colonies met in 1774 in Philadelphia to discuss the situation. This First Continental Congress pleaded with the King to grant them their rights and liberties and not to tax them without letting their representatives make the decision. Political leaders from the MD counties also met in Annapolis, took over the government, and formed governing committees in the counties. When a tea-bearing ship arrived in Annapolis, citizens threatened the owner of the vessel to the point that he set it on fire. Having taken the government away from the proprietor, MD was reluctant to sever its ties with the King. As late as May of 1776, MD would not let its delegates to the Continental Congress vote for independence, hoping for a reconciliation. But in June things had gotten so bad, MD sent 2000 men to the Continental army and joined the other colonies in moving toward a declaration of independence. Such occurred on 02 July 1776.

MD sent many men into the fighting as Britain tried to force them back into the Empire. The American troops in the first year of the war threw the British out of Boston and Charleston, and unsuccessfully invaded Canada. But in 1776, the British along with German mercenaries invaded NY with the capture of NY City as their goal. After several battles in which MD troops fought valiantly, NY was lost. The Americans won two minor surprise-attack battles in late 1776 at Trenton and in early 1777 at Princeton, which renewed their hopes. Then in the Spring, the British set out to take Philadelphia, which was accomplished in the early Fall after the American losses at Brandywine and Germantown. A large British force then started moving down the Hudson Valley from Canada. After an initial success at Fort Ticonderoga, the British were dealt a defeat at Bennington, were blocked at Bemis Heights and Freeman's Farm, and then were surrounded, defeated, and forced to surrender at Saratoga. When the news reached France, they declared war on Britain as an American ally. The American troops went into winter quarters near Philadelphia 1777-78, and suffered greatly from exposure, disease, and hunger.

The British then moved the war to the south. Savannah was captured in late 1778, and Augusta fell in early 1779, the entire colony of GA being occupied soon thereafter. An attempt by the Americans and the French to retake Savannah failed in October of 1779. In May of 1780, Charleston fell to the British, and much of SC was occupied. At Camden, an American army was routed, and NC was exposed to invasion. As the British forces entered NC, they got news that the backwoods militia had defeated Loyalist forces at Kings Mountain, so they returned to SC. In 1781, Americans began intensive guerilla warfare against the British outposts in SC and GA. A large British group was defeated at Cowpens, and then the two combatants met at Guilford Courthouse where the British won the field, but the Americans exacted a heavy toll on their forces, 25% dead or wounded. In weakened condition, the British moved to Wilmington on the NC coast, then northward into VA. The Americans took advantage of this and began operations in SC and GA which drove the British back into Charleston and Savannah. The British troops which had gone into VA took up a position at Yorktown where they were trapped and defeated by a combined American-French force. The surrender of the British on 19 October 1781 virtually ended the war, with a preliminary treaty recognizing an independent United States being signed in 1782 and a final one in 1783.

No battles of the war were fought in MD. However, troops of both sides repeatedly crossed MD, often looting farms, stealing supplies, and taking food. Inflation and scarcity of goods were severe. MD supplied wheat, cannon, shot, and salt to the troops. During the conflict Baltimore became the largest city in MD and the third largest in the US, chiefly due to increased trade, manufacturing, and shipbuilding. MD had numerous Loyalists who sided with the British, especially on the Eastern Shore, where they rebelled against the Revolutionary government several times. Some Loyalists left the state, others kept a low profile, the property of many of them was confiscated and sold. When MD declared independence in 1776, the old proprietary government was ended. A state constitution was written and a new government was set up by the gentry. This was a government which made them the ruling class, with only landowners having a vote, and with only rich men qualifying to hold office. A legislature with upper and lower houses was established, with the voters choosing the legislators, and with a governor being elected by the legislature. State support for the Anglican Church was terminated, and religious freedom was granted to all Christians.

The new federal congress chose to hold its first session in Annapolis in 1783. They accepted Washington's resignation as military commander, and in early 1784 approved the peace treaty with Britain. In 1787, a convention of the 13 states met in Philadelphia and framed a new federal constitution which would create a strong national government. MD was the seventh state to ratify the new document, which was approved. Ten important amendments, the Bill of Rights (freedom of speech, assembly, worship, and the press, and the right to jury trial), were added in 1791. To solve the problem of deciding among the many cities that offered to be the national capital, a new town called Washington City was located on land on the north side of the Potomac River. This land was donated by MD and consisted of an area just across the river from Alexandria, VA. Congress first met there in 1800.

Tremendous changes, both in MD and the US took place during 1763-89. Baltimore grew from about 6000 to about 12,000. Many merchants had gotten rich by supplying the army, and numerous persons speculated in land by buying large tracts in western MD. The removal of the British prohibition to settlement in the west had profound effects. A great westward movement of MD people took place after the war, many going southwest down the back country of VA (VA, NC, SC, KY, TN), and many going west down the OH River valley (OH, KY, IN, IL). Opposition to slavery grew during the war, chiefly among Quakers and Methodists, and there was an increase in the number of manumissions (freeing of slaves). MD ended the war badly in debt, and this brought about a depression with many problems, but the crisis began to ease in 1787 when good prices for tobacco enhanced the economy. The government remained in the hands of the rich, and they were strongly opposed to a full democracy. Hence the struggle between them and the majority of MD's people continued. The revolution had given the common people a good taste of freedom and they continued to press for more democracy.

---

6. Early statehood, 1789-1850

The early years of this period saw continuing movements by the common people to take power away from the elite and to democratize MD. With the election of Jefferson in 1800, the federal government took a turn in this direction. This encouraged the people of MD and they were able to abolish the property requirement for voting, to reform the court system, and to lower the requirements for holding office. They were not able to replace indirect election of the governor, the upper house of the legislature, and some county officers with direct election. Very large strides were made economically in the early 1800s. Baltimore, which had superseded Annapolis as MD's metropolitan center, continued to expand. The city merchants traded with England, France, and the West Indies, shipping them grain, flour, tobacco, and lumber products. These products were sent all over the world by fleets of clipper ships, many of which were built in MD.

In 1793, France and Britain went to war once again. Americans traded with both sides, and they prospered, since their produce brought high prices. Both countries opposed the trading with its enemy, and began taking action against American ships carrying material to the other. The British actions were more extreme involving stopping and searching American vessels, blockading French ports, removal of sailors from American ships and putting them in the British navy, and inciting and arming Indians on the frontier.

In 1812, the US declared war on Britain, seeing the conflict as a second war of independence, an opportunity to force British forces out of some western outposts which they had never left, and an occasion to add Canada to the US. The country was badly split over the war, and this division was reflected by the clash of angry mobs in 1812 in Baltimore. The year 1812 brought US losses in land battles at Detroit and Niagara River. These defeats were balanced by several notable victories on the water, and many successful forays by privateers. However, in 1813, Britain reasserted her rule of the seas, a number of American ships were captured, and many others were bottled up in harbors along the Atlantic coast. Chesapeake Bay was essentially blockaded, British ships moved freely in it, and raided towns on its shores. On land, American troops were defeated at the

Raisin River (south of Detroit), but American sailors won an important sea battle on Lake Erie. This victory permitted US forces to drive the British out of Detroit, pursue them into Canada, and defeat them at the Thames River. When 1814 came, it brought bleak prospects for the US. There was strong opposition to the war in New England, and Napoleon had been defeated, freeing the British military forces to concentrate on America. But Americans rose to the occasion. British troops were held in Canada, especially by stand-off battles at Chippawa and Lundy's Lane. Then in September a combined land-water attack by the British along and on Lake Champlain was turned back near Plattsburgh.

In August 1814, the British had turned their attention to Chesapeake Bay as they planned an attack on the US capital. The British moved up the Patuxent River, then proceeded on land toward Washington. They defeated American forces at Bladensburg, then occupied and burned Washington. Their next goal was Baltimore, and the city threw up defenses and dug in for the attack. The British landed troops at North Point (just SE of Baltimore), and their navy came up the Patapsco River to attack Fort McHenry. The Americans put up a stubborn defense, and after two days the British withdrew. On Christmas Eve of 1814, a treaty of peace was signed by the US and Britain in Ghent, Belgium. However, before news of the peace reached the US, the British attacked New Orleans in January 1815, and were dealt a stunning defeat by the Americans.

Following the War of 1812, sizeable changes came to MD. There was a strong westward movement, and many immigrants came from Europe. The population of the state grew from about 320,000 in 1790 to about 583,000 in 1850. The people of MD continued to move toward a more democratic government as more officials came to be directly elected. The Eastern Shore continued to be an agricultural area, with wheat replacing tobacco as the chief crop. Travel continued to be mainly by water, so there was not much road development. In 1829, the Chesapeake and Delaware Canal was opened so the farmers of the Eastern Shore could send produce to Philadelphia, in addition to Baltimore where they had previously sent it. Very few European immigrants came to the Eastern Shore, its people remaining primarily British with the Catholic or Anglican faith. Southern MD also continued as a predominantly agricultural area, with tobacco as the chief crop. Again, few European immigrants settled here, and the good river systems provided transportation routes so little road development occurred. Southern MD's tobacco culture used many slaves, unlike the wheat production on the Eastern Shore. The people of Southern MD were mainly British, and their religious orientations were Anglican or Catholic. Western MD grew very rapidly, receiving people from more easterly sections of MD, from PA, and from Europe. The pressing back of the MD frontier can be seen readily by noting the creation of new counties in the west: Allegany (1789), Carroll (1837), Howard (1851). The people of western MD were quite diverse: British (Anglican, Catholic), Scots–Irish (Presbyterian), and German (Lutheran, Pietistic sects, Catholic). The rich soil of western MD was used largely to grow wheat. In order to ship it back east, road and turnpike development began to occur early. And regional towns grew larger as their trade–center activity increased, for example, Frederick, Hagerstown, and Cumberland.

Baltimore City continued to grow as the major commercial city of MD. It functioned as the region's grain center, increased its shipbuilding activities, developed much new industry (boots, shoes, oyster packing, sugar refining, clothing, foundries, furnaces), and expanded its trade with more and more foreign ports. All of this increased the population of the city, with merchants, artisans, professional people, and unskilled workers coming in. Banks, insurance companies, and business corporations were set up bringing Baltimore to be the financial center for the region. Baltimore was connected to the Eastern Shore and Southern MD by water routes, and very quickly roads were built going out north and west of the city. One of the best routes from the Atlantic coast to the midwestern frontier (OH, KY, IN, IL, and on) cut across MD to the Ohio River valley. So the leaders of MD recognized the importance of transportation along this route.

In order to improve the state's economy, MD encouraged and supported the building of roads, canals, and railroads. The federal government in 1815 began building a road, the National Road, from Cumberland westward. This road was extended to St. Louis (after 1840) and became the major land route to the west (follows Highway 40). Private companies in MD built roads from Baltimore and other towns to Cumberland. Three major canals were constructed: the Chesapeake and Ohio Canal (along the Potomac River), the Susquehanna and Tidewater Canal (along and on the Susquehanna River), and Chesapeake and Delaware Canal (connecting northern Chesapeake Bay and the DE River). The Baltimore and Ohio Railroad was laid from Baltimore to Ellicott Mills in 1830, extended to Frederick in 1831, to Cumberland in 1842, and to Wheeling, VA, in 1853. During this time other rail lines connected Baltimore with Washington, DC, York, PA, and Philadelphia, PA. In the middle of this period, in 1825, the Erie Canal was opened in NY, connecting NY City, the Hudson River, and central and western NY with the Great Lakes. This route to the west took much of Baltimore's trade and moved it to NY City.

When MD became a state, the Anglican Church ceased to be the established church. Methodists separated from Anglicanism in 1784 and soon became the predominant religious group. The Catholic denomination also increased and the first US Catholic bishop took his seat in Baltimore in 1790. Both the Methodists and the Quakers opposed slavery, the use of slaves declined as crops other than tobacco came to be grown, and slavery was not too useful in towns. As a result, a number of slaves were freed, but

MD still did not afford them equal rights, most not having the vote. In 1817, the MD Colonization Society was organized to assist free blacks to emigrate to Liberia in Africa. Not many blacks went. Baltimore started public schools in 1829, and some other towns did so a little later, but there was no state-wide system until after 1865. Most counties, however, had private acade-mies requiring tuition and some churches sponsored free schools. For higher education, Washington College was established in Chestertown in 1782, St. John's College in Annapolis in 1784, and the Medical College of MD in Baltimore in 1807.

During this period (1789–1850) many immigrants came to MD from Britain (England, Scotland, Wales), Ireland, and the Germanic states. There were not too many Irish immigrants at first, but the potato famines in the 1840s sent many to MD. Most of them were Catholic and they settled in Baltimore. Many Germans remained in Baltimore, but lots of them also went to western MD. They were Lutheran, Catholic, German Reformed, and Pietistic. Especially large numbers came in 1848–50 as refugees from the German revolutions. In 1850, 70% of MD's foreign-born people lived in Baltimore. Most of the others were in western MD, since very few had gone to Southern MD or the Eastern Shore. As this period closed, the US en-tered into the Mexican War. The quota for MD was two regiments, these being filled by volunteers. The total number that served was about 2000.

7. The Civil War era, 1850-70

In the 1850's, MD was in consid-erable change, sometimes with turmoil, politically, economically, and sociologically. The arrival of numerous immigrants, many of which were Catholics, stirred up a strong political reaction against Catho-lics and foreigners, and led to fraudulent and violence-ridden elections and state government which was often demagogic. The traditional small-farm economy of MD was slowly giving way to large farms operated with new technology and as commercial enterprises. Crops were being moved to markets by improved transportation (roads, railroads, canals, rivers, and Chesapeake Bay). About 30% of MD's citizens now lived in Baltimore, which was a center for industry, much of it shipbuilding, iron milling, sugar refining, tanning, and textiles manufacturing. Baltimore was the port and trade center of the region with large international connections. The aver-age life expectancy was about 35, with many children dying young, and with epidemics and fatal illness being common. There was no statewide school system, but more communities were taxing people to support elementary schools. A large part of the population had become Catholic, but Protes-tants still were a majority. The largest denominations were Methodist, Lu-theran, and Presbyterian.

There were, as of 1860, about 84,000 free blacks and about 87,000 slaves in MD. The slaves were largely in Southern MD and on the Eastern Shore. The largest group of free blacks (29,000) were those working in Baltimore. MD, as was the US, was split over the issue of slavery, with the south and north (in both the US and MD) differing. Abolitionists and free blacks helped slaves escape to PA, which was a free state. At the national level, prior to 1860, compromises between the many differences that separated the northern states and the southern states were worked out, chiefly by moderates in the Congress. The people of MD were largely of this view, being divided over slavery, but strongly supporting the Union. From about 1856 forward, the north–south compromises became increasingly unsatisfactory, particularly to the south, and as 1860 approached, the potential for war loomed large. When Lincoln was elected that year, southern states began seceding. MD had given Lincoln only 2% of its vote, throwing its support almost equally to Democrat Breckenridge and Constitutional Unionist Bell, both of whom supported the Union, but probably would not go to war to preserve it. The southern states SC, AL, FL, GA, LA, MS, and TX had seceded by April 1861. When US Fort Sumter in Charleston, SC, harbor fell to Confederate forces, and Lincoln called for troops to put down the rebellion, four other southern states seceded (NC, VA, AR, TN). The two sides, Union and Confederate, mobilized their men and resources, and four years of horrible conflict began.

On Lincoln's call, MD men volunteered to save the Union, but others organized Confederate military companies. However, the governor decided to take no action, hoping for a peaceful resolution. Lincoln, however, recognizing the importance of the border states (MD, KY, MO) began political and military action to keep them in the Union. MD was particularly important, since it surrounded Washington on three sides. So when a Baltimore mob of southern sympathizers attacked MA and PA soldiers travelling to Washington, Lincoln declared martial law and began placing Union troops at sites in MD where Confederate sympathies were strong. Soon a majority sentiment for the Union emerged, but many men went south to enlist in the Confederate cause. By the close of the war, over 47,000 MD men had fought for the Union and about 22,000 for the Confederacy, many of the latter under military units of other states. The position of MD in between the North and South, the position of the Union capital in MD, and the nearness of the Confederate capital Richmond made MD into a critical military area.

Thirty-one military engagements were fought in MD, three of them major, and in addition there were hundreds of skirmishes and raids. In September 1862, a large Confederate force crossed the Potomac River into MD, and on the 14th clashed with Union troops at South Mountain. The Confederates were driven back a few miles, then on the 16th and 17th, the armies fought the war's bloodiest battle. At this Battle of Antietam, 12,000 Union soldiers were wounded or killed, and 11,000 Confederates. The

Confederates withdrew to VA after the conflict, but the Union solders were too exhausted to follow them. In June 1863, Confederate troops entered MD, then went into PA, where they were defeated at Gettysburg in a 3-day engagement 1–4 July. A third advance by Southern troops into MD toward Washington was made in July 1864. This advance was delayed on the 9th by a Union force at the Battle of Monocacy, which permitted the fortification of Washington, and the successful defense by Union soldiers. The Confederates then withdrew. By the fall of 1864 the Union was putting strong pressure on Richmond, and were also moving through GA and heading north. Finally in April 1865, Confederate surrenders at Appomattox, VA, and Durham, NC, effectively ended the war.

Reconstruction in MD was rather smooth as compared to that in states that had seceded. In MD, the process began in 1861 with the Union occupation, then a new state constitution of 1864 emancipated slaves. This constitution also penalized people who had supported the Confederacy by denying them the vote. Shortly after the end of the war, Democrats regained control of the state and redid the constitution to remove the penalties on Confederate supporters. MD's economy suffered greatly during the war largely because ties between the port of Baltimore and the South and the OH Valley were disrupted. Recovery was fairly rapid, although NY City took some of the trade away from Baltimore, and shipbuilding never recovered. The freed slaves did not become the social, economic, or political equals of whites. Much antiblack opinion remained, and discrimination was broadly practiced. Industry, commerce, and manufacturing continued to center in Baltimore and several towns in northwest MD, with most rural Marylanders still farming, now with black laborers rather than with slaves. In 1870, the 15th Amendment to the US Constitution gave the vote to black males, and within the year 35,000 had registered.

8. After the Civil War, 1865–

Four major movements set in and accelerated once the wounds of war began to heal: immigration, industrialization, urbanization, and reform. In 1868, about 10,000 foreigners landed in Baltimore, rising to over 42,000 in 1882, and to 67,000 in 1907. Just after the war the chief immigrants were German and Irish, but beginning in the early 1870s people from central, eastern, and southern Europe came in increasing numbers (Austrian Empire, Poland, Russia, Italy, the Balkans). Many immigrants passed through MD to the west, but many also stayed in Baltimore. Very few went into eastern and southern MD. Accompanying this immigration, and supplying jobs for numerous immigrants, was the progressive industrialization and commercial activity of MD. This centered in Baltimore where factories and plants proliferated for making clothing, shoes, iron, copper, steel, tin, metal products, grain products, canned food, fertilizer, lumber products, paper, and for meat processing and packing. By 1900 Baltimore was the third largest US port. Starting in the 1880s, industrial development spread to other towns in the state, especially towns in western MD. All of these advances brought notable improvements in the transportation system, particularly roads and railroads.

The industrial and commercial activities of MD, which centered in Baltimore and other towns, drew people into cities and towns. These people came from rural MD, other states, and overseas. Many problems resulted in the cities: slums, child labor, poor wages, long working hours, unhealthy labor conditions, lack of water and sewer systems, fire hazards, racial and ethnic discrimination, and inadequate education facilities. In 1910 the number of city people exceeded the number of rural people for the first time. In the rural areas, there was a marked move from the prewar tobacco culture to wheat raising, dairy farming, and animal husbandry. When the midwestern US began to raise cheaper wheat, MD farmers responded by switching to truck gardening to raise produce for the cities. Coal mining prospered in western MD, and the seafood industry continued apace in Chesapeake Bay. From 1867 for about 30 years a Democrat patronage machine governed and misgoverned MD.

As the last third of the century moved along, numerous reform movements took shape in MD. They challenged the political system, the poor working conditions, the lack of health and safety measures, the poor educational facilities, and discrimination. Immigrant societies, private charities, churches, labor unions, and several private philanthropists worked to change the conditions, to induce the government to take action, and to quicken the awareness of the public. Notable success was achieved in practically all of these areas except in the area of black discrimination which got worse.

In 1898, the US entered into the Spanish-American War, and two MD regiments were called into service. Neither went overseas, their duty being confined to stations in the US. A very bad fire ravaged Baltimore in 1904, and when the city was rebuilt, it was greatly improved: waterfront facilities, sewer system, water system, gas, electricity, and other items. Progressive legislation in the early 1900s led to political reforms, anti-corruption laws, and labor reforms. About 65,000 MD servicemen fought in World War I (1917-8). The supplying of war materials caused Baltimore's economy to prosper during the conflict, its industries functioning full-time. This prosperity continued into the 1920s, except for coal mining, and then the Great Depression of the 1930s brought hardship all over the US. As did World War I, World War II (1939-5) enhanced the economy of MD, again because of Baltimore's industrial prowess. War workers poured into Baltimore and governmental and military employees came to the MD suburbs of Washington. After the war, MD's industry and population continued to grow, and numerous improvements in its transportation system were made. In the late

1950s and early 1960s federal court action against segregation was taken, and MD responded slowly but favorably.

The growth of MD through the years is illustrated by these population figures: 1634 (200), 1660 (12,000), 1671 (20,000), 1701 (25,000), 1715 (30,000), 1748 (130,000), 1756 (154,000), 1760 (167,000), 1770 (200,000), 1775 (225,000), 1782 (254,000), 1790 (320 000), 1800 (342,000), 1810 (381,000), 1820 (408,000), 1830 (447,000), 1840 (342,000), 1810 (381,000< 1820 (408,000), 1820 (447,000), 1840 (470,000), 1850 (583,000), 1860 (687,000), 1870 (781,000), 1880 (935,000), 1890 (1,042,000), 1900 (1,188,000), 1910 (1,295,000), 1920 (1,450,000).

9. MD counties

The state of MD is today made up of 23 counties and one independent city, Baltimore City. These counties are depicted in Figure 5. The counties (and independent city) along with their dates of establishment (or separation as an independently-governed city) are as follows: Saint Mary's (1637), Kent (1642), Anne Arundel (1650), Calvert (1654), Charles (1658), Baltimore County (1659), Talbot (1662), Somerset (1666), Dorchester (1668), Cecil (1674), Prince George's (1695), Queen Anne's (1706), Worcester (1742), Frederick (1748), Caroline (1773), Harford (1773), Montgomery (1776), Washington (1776), Allegany (1789), Carroll (1837), Howard (1851), Baltimore City (1851), Wicomico (1867), and Garrett (1872). By following the location of the earlier counties, you can trace the movement of settlement in MD: Saint Mary's (1st settlement, southwestern shore of Chesapeake Bay), Kent (island and east central shore of the Bay), Anne Arundel (west central shore of the Bay), Calvert (filling in between Saint Mary's and Anne Arundel), Charles (behind Saint Mary's), Baltimore (northwestern shore of the Bay), Talbot (south of Kent on the eastern shore), Somerset (southeastern shore of the Bay), Dorchester (filling in between Talbot and Somerset), Cecil (northern reach of the Bay), Prince George's (behind Anne Arundel), Queen Anne's (on east central shore of the Bay), Worcester (behind Somerset), Frederick (going west), Caroline (behind Talbot), etc. Do not fail to notice the counties going up the Potomac River: Saint Mary's (1637), Charles (1658), Prince George's (1695), Frederick (1748), Montgomery (1776), Washington (1776), Allegany (1789).

The development of MD's counties is depicted chronologically in Figures 6-12. The settlement pattern of MD is shown in Figure 13. A few notes on the early years of county formation will be helpful. In 1642, Kent Island (off the east central coast of Chesapeake Bay) was recognized as the second county. However, as people settled on the coast, they were counted as being in Kent County. In 1650, Old Charles County was erected, and in 1654 became Calvert County. This Old Charles County must not

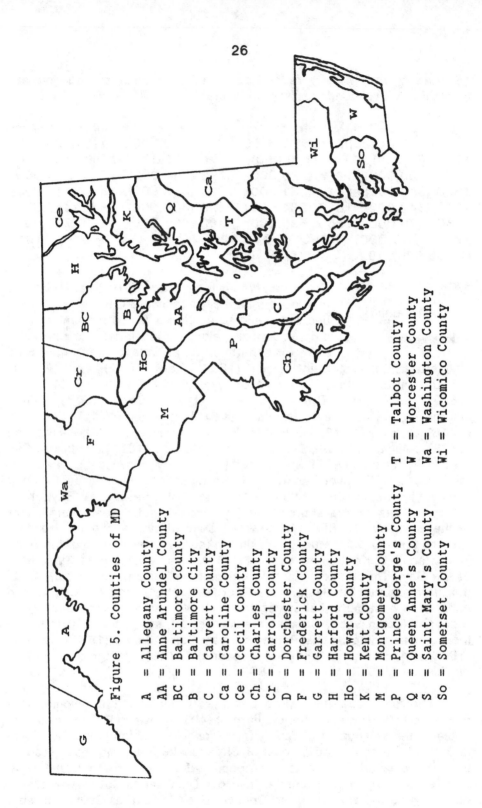

Figure 5. Counties of MD

A = Allegany County
AA = Anne Arundel County
BC = Baltimore County
B = Baltimore City
C = Calvert County
Ca = Caroline County
Ce = Cecil County
Ch = Charles County
Cr = Carroll County
D = Dorchester County
F = Frederick County
G = Garrett County
H = Harford County
Ho = Howard County
K = Kent County
M = Montgomery County
P = Prince George's County
Q = Queen Anne's County
S = Saint Mary's County
So = Somerset County
T = Talbot County
W = Worcester County
Wa = Washington County
Wi = Wicomico County

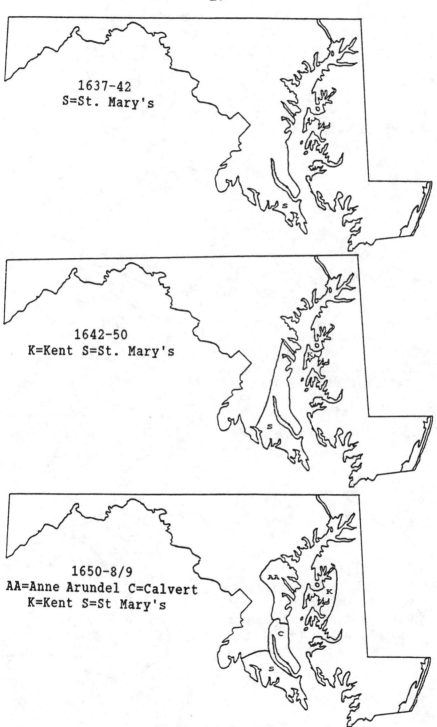

1637-42
S=St. Mary's

1642-50
K=Kent S=St. Mary's

1650-8/9
AA=Anne Arundel C=Calvert
K=Kent S=St Mary's

Figure 6. MD Counties

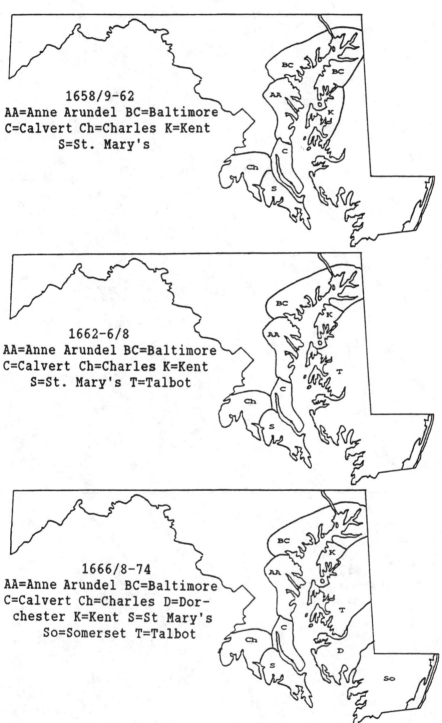

Figure 7. MD Counties

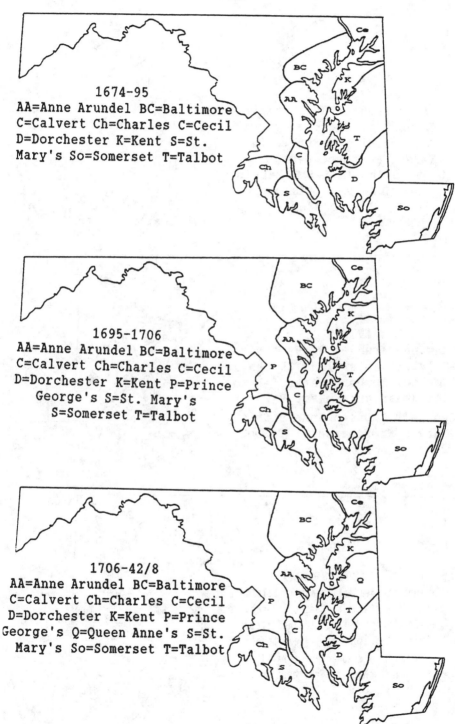

1674-95
AA=Anne Arundel BC=Baltimore
C=Calvert Ch=Charles C=Cecil
D=Dorchester K=Kent S=St.
Mary's So=Somerset T=Talbot

1695-1706
AA=Anne Arundel BC=Baltimore
C=Calvert Ch=Charles C=Cecil
D=Dorchester K=Kent P=Prince
George's S=St. Mary's
S=Somerset T=Talbot

1706-42/8
AA=Anne Arundel BC=Baltimore
C=Calvert Ch=Charles C=Cecil
D=Dorchester K=Kent P=Prince
George's Q=Queen Anne's S=St.
Mary's So=Somerset T=Talbot

Figure 8. MD Counties

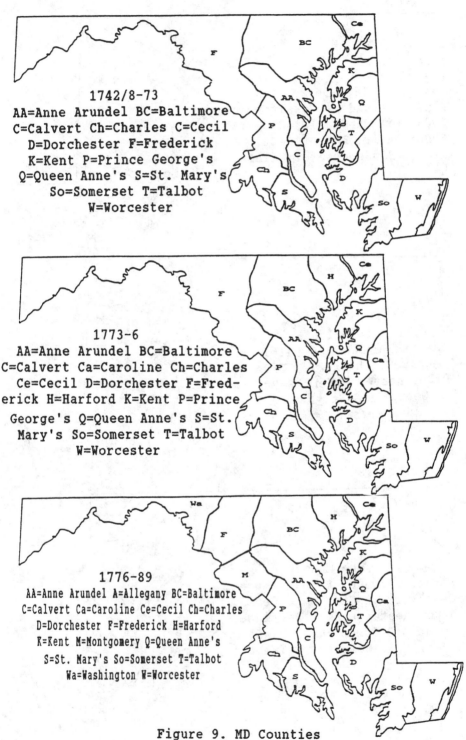

Figure 9. MD Counties

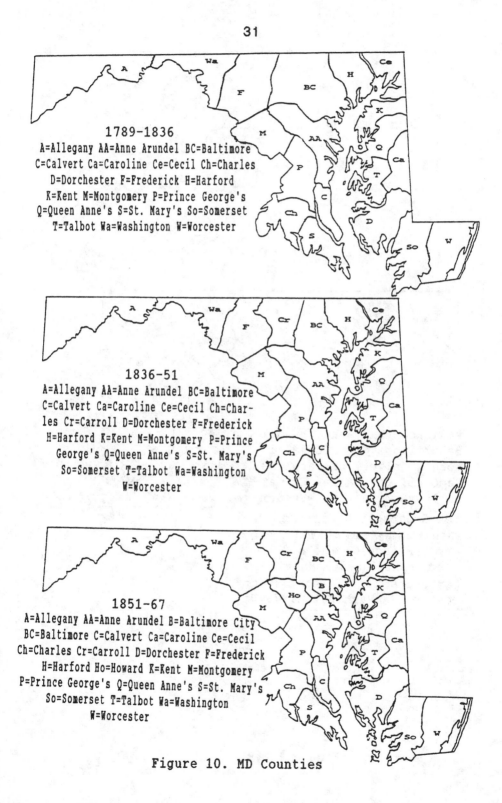

1789-1836
A=Allegany AA=Anne Arundel BC=Baltimore
C=Calvert Ca=Caroline Ce=Cecil Ch=Charles
D=Dorchester F=Frederick H=Harford
K=Kent M=Montgomery P=Prince George's
Q=Queen Anne's S=St. Mary's So=Somerset
T=Talbot Wa=Washington W=Worcester

1836-51
A=Allegany AA=Anne Arundel BC=Baltimore
C=Calvert Ca=Caroline Ce=Cecil Ch=Char-
les Cr=Carroll D=Dorchester F=Frederick
H=Harford K=Kent M=Montgomery P=Prince
George's Q=Queen Anne's S=St. Mary's
So=Somerset T=Talbot Wa=Washington
W=Worcester

1851-67
A=Allegany AA=Anne Arundel B=Baltimore City
BC=Baltimore C=Calvert Ca=Caroline Ce=Cecil
Ch=Charles Cr=Carroll D=Dorchester F=Frederick
H=Harford Ho=Howard K=Kent M=Montgomery
P=Prince George's Q=Queen Anne's S=St. Mary's
So=Somerset T=Talbot Wa=Washington
W=Worcester

Figure 10. MD Counties

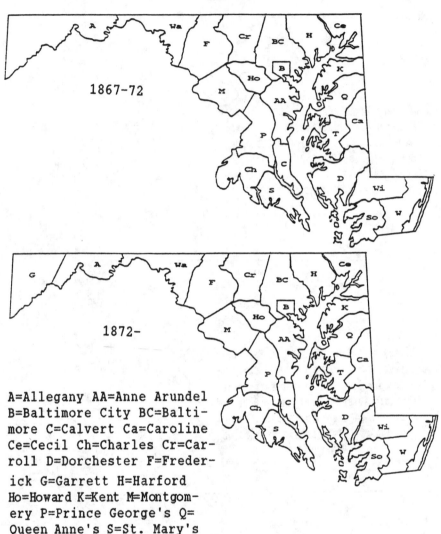

A=Allegany AA=Anne Arundel
B=Baltimore City BC=Balti-
more C=Calvert Ca=Caroline
Ce=Cecil Ch=Charles Cr=Car-
roll D=Dorchester F=Freder-
ick G=Garrett H=Harford
Ho=Howard K=Kent M=Montgom-
ery P=Prince George's Q=
Queen Anne's S=St. Mary's
So=Somerset, T=Talbot, W=Wor-
cester, Wa=Washington, Wi=Wi-
comico

Figure 11. MD Counties

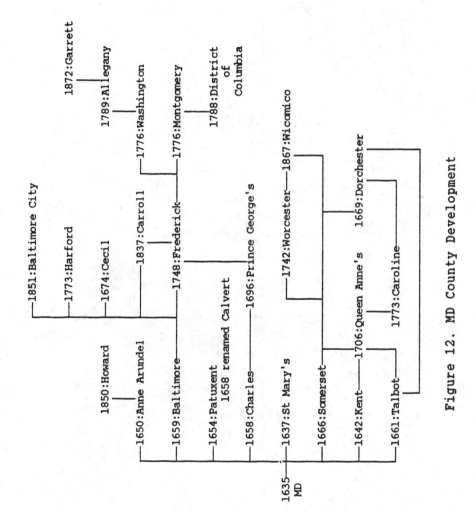

Figure 12. MD County Development

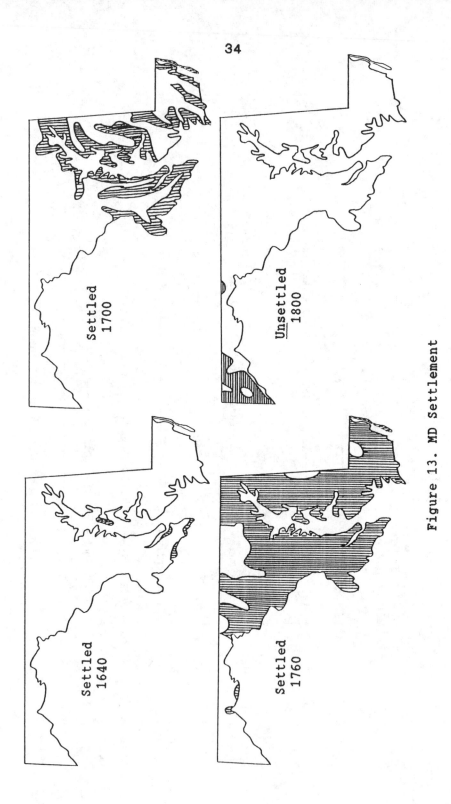

Settled 1640

Settled 1700

Settled 1760

Unsettled 1800

Figure 13. MD Settlement

be confused with the Charles County which was established in 1658. The Puritan government of 1654-6 temporarily changed the name of Saint Mary's County to Potomac, of Anne Arundel County to Providence, and of Calvert County to Patuxent. It is well to remember that the borders between the early counties were sometimes incompletely defined or ill-defined. This means that in searching for ancestors, adjacent counties must always be investigated. For considerably more detail on county formations and boundary changes see:

_E. B. Mathews, THE COUNTIES OF MD, THEIR ORIGIN, BOUNDARIES, AND ELECTION DISTRICTS, MD Geological Survey, Volume 6, 1906, pages 417-572.

_M. R. Brown, AN ILLUSTRATED GENEALOGY OF THE COUNTIES OF MD AND THE DC, French-Bray, Baltimore, MD, 1967.

The counties of MD are very important to genealogical researchers because of the many records they have kept. These records refer to individuals who have lived in the county and often give a great deal of detailed information. The record-keeping agencies in the counties and the records of genealogical importance which they have will now be indicated. The county court (or circuit court) kept records on births (1865-), bonds, court proceedings, deaths (1865-), detailed original papers of court activities, divorces, land (deeds, mortgages, plats), manumissions, marriages (1777-), naturalizations (declarations of intent, petitions, certificates of naturalization), oaths, and voter registrations. The orphans' court kept (from 1777) records of court proceedings, equity records, estate records (accounts, administrations, appraisals, claims, inventories, letters testamentary, petitions, releases, sales), guardian records (accounts, bonds, dockets), indentures, and wills. The records of the county commissioners (and their predecessors the levy court and the commissioners of tax) included commissioners of tax records, county commissioners tax records, levy court taxation records, and tax assessment records. Because of the large population which collected in and around Baltimore City, it was split in 1851 from Baltimore County, and became an independently-governed unit. Other courts, all of which kept records, were set up in the city: court of common pleas, superior court, criminal court, Baltimore circuit courts 1 and 2, and the city court.

Many of the county records mentioned in the previous paragraph will be discussed in detail in Chapter 2. You will be told exactly what years they cover, how they may be obtained, what information they contain, and how to discover if they have been published, either in printed or microfilm form. Chapter 3 will inform you about the major genealogical collections (libraries and archives) in and out of MD, and will indicate to you which of the county records are available there. The fourth chapter lists all the MD counties and tells you what records (books, microfilms, originals) are available for each and where they can be found. In addition, you are told where the county seat is, when the county was created, and the county or counties from which it was formed. These county formation data are very important to you because sometimes you will need to trace an ancestor back into a county out of which a new county came. This occurs when your predecessor lived on a piece of property which was in land split off from an old county to form a new county.

10. MD government

Throughout most of its history, MD has had three major branches of government: executive, legislative, and judicial. Each of these will be treated in turn. When MD was chartered, it was completely, totally given to Lord Baltimore, its proprietor. He was given almost absolute right to constitute the government, to assemble and command the military, to make and enforce laws, to appoint judges, justices, magistrates and officers, to establish counties, incorporate cities, and set up ports, to found churches, to grant land, to naturalize foreigners, to levy taxes, rents, and duties, and to control the disbursement of all funds. The only restrictions laid on the proprietor were that all laws he enacted had to have the approval of the freemen of the province or their delegates. And all free people of the colony were to be treated as English citizens with all the rights, privileges, and freedoms of the British Empire. Hence, the proprietor had to set up and call into session a citizens' legislature, which was called the General Assembly. This assembly and the governor of MD (appointed by the proprietor) were in constant conflict throughout most of the pre-Revolutionary period. The assembly used its approval power and its claim to Englishmen's rights to gradually take governing powers away from the governor (and the proprietor).

The executive branch of MD government until 1776 was made up of a governor (appointed by the proprietor) and his council (or his cabinet of advisors and assistants). At first, in 1637, the governor also had a secretary who was clerk to the governor and council, recorder of land grants, supervisor of surveying, recorder of appointments, collector of taxes, rents, and duties, justice of the peace, probate officer, marriage license clerk, and attorney general. As the years went on and the population increased these duties were assigned to separate officers. And for some offices, deputies were placed on the Eastern Shore, and then in each county. The proprietary governor and his council functioned 1635-89, then Puritan governors took charge 1689-92, followed by royal governors and their counselors 1692-1715. With the restoration of proprietary rule, proprietary governors and their counselors held forth 1715-76, followed by the Revolutionary government's Council of Safety 1776-7. In accordance with the new state constitution, state governors and their councils (both elected by the legislature) operated 1777-1838, and since 1838, the governor (popularly elected) has headed the executive branch. Figure 14 shows the history of the executive branch in diagrammatic form.

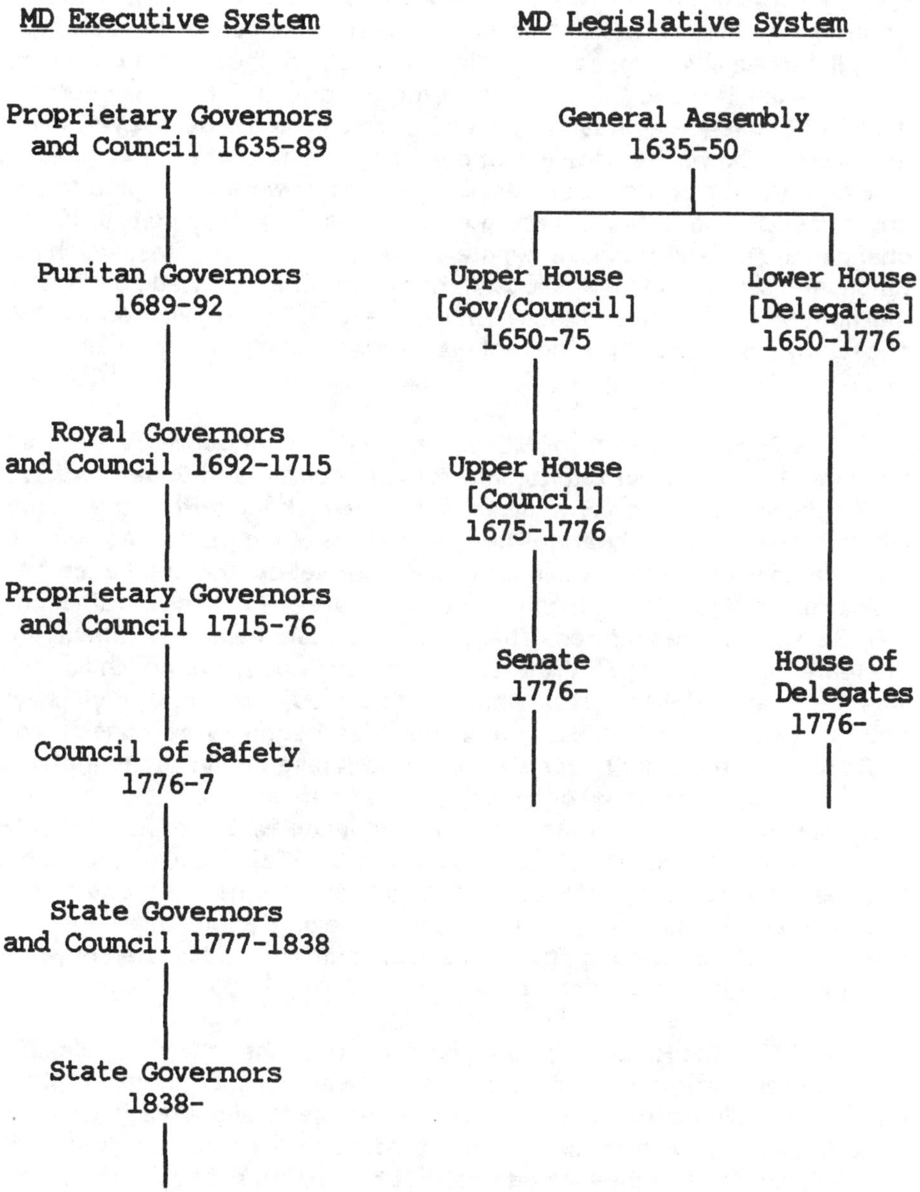

MD <u>Executive</u> <u>System</u>   MD <u>Legislative</u> <u>System</u>

Proprietary Governors   General Assembly
and Council 1635-89   1635-50
        | _____|_____
        | | |
Puritan Governors   Upper House   Lower House
    1689-92   [Gov/Council]   [Delegates]
        | 1650-75   1650-1776
        | | |
Royal Governors   Upper House
and Council 1692-1715   [Council]
        | 1675-1776
        | |
Proprietary Governors |
and Council 1715-76   Senate   House of
        | 1776-   Delegates
        | | 1776-
Council of Safety | |
    1776-7 | |
        | | |
        |
State Governors
and Council 1777-1838
        |
        |
State Governors
    1838-
        |
        |

Figure 14. MD Executive and Legislative Systems

The legislative branch of MD government came into being as an assembly of MD freemen, but quickly became an assembly of delegates elected by the freemen. This General Assembly in 1650 was joined by the governor and his council who operated as an upper house, thus giving MD an upper and a lower house of legislators. In 1675, the upper house membership was altered to that of the governor's council. From the beginning, the lower house (delegates, burgesses) gradually and progressively wrested governing power from the governor and his council. They demanded and obtained greater and greater decision-making powers and rights to self-government. The Revolutionary government and constitution of 1776/7 changed the legislature into a senate and a house of delegates, which have functioned since. Unlike previously, the voters of MD elected both houses, the house of delegates directly, but the senate by an electoral college chosen by the voters. This indirect election was altered to direct election in 1838.

The judiciary branch of MD government can be conveniently divided into three groups: lower courts, intermediate courts, and upper courts. At the beginning of the colony, minor cases were handled by lower courts which were essentially hearings before a justice of the peace. As time went on, other lower (or petty or minor courts) were set up, the chief ones being police magistrates (1882), city peoples' court (1912), city traffic court (1918), and trial magistrates. These lower courts are shown in the diagram presented in Figure 15. At the start of the province, the provincial court was the intermediate court at which more serious crimes, civil suits, and equity matters were treated. When counties began to be constituted in 1637/8, county (circuit) courts were set up, these continuing to the present. In 1669, a provincial chancery court was established, and in 1670 a provincial prerogative court to handle estate matters. In 1692, prerogative deputies were placed in each of the counties, but they had to submit all their records to the provincial office. An admiralty court to handle maritime matters was put in place in 1694. Sometime along about this time a city mayor's court operated in St. Mary's City, but few details are known. In Annapolis, such a city mayor's court operated from 1708-1818.

In 1776, the Revolutionary government abolished the provincial court and provincial prerogative court, and in 1777 established county orphans' courts to handle estates. In 1776, an eastern general court and a western general court were established on the respective shores to replace the provincial court, and they lasted until 1806. The admiralty court was disbanded in 1789 when the federal government took over such matters. The court system in Baltimore County expanded fairly early from the handling of all cases in the County (Circuit) Court. Provisions for the population increase In Baltimore City led to the establishment of the Court of Oyer and Terminer and Gaol Delivery in 1789, this being replaced by the Baltimore City Court in 1817. Two very important changes occurred in 1851. One

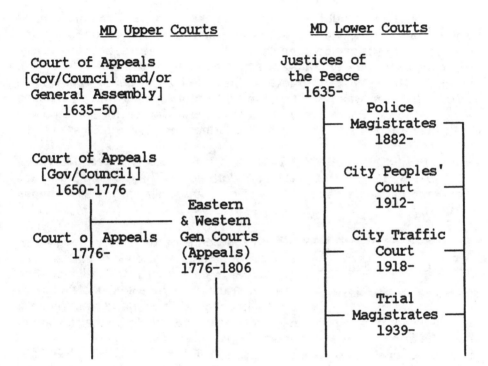

Figure 15. MD Upper and Lower Courts

was the termination of the chancery court during 1851–4 when its equity cases were transferred to the county courts. The second was the establishment of some special Baltimore city courts: court of common pleas, superior court, criminal court, circuit court. These were followed by other Baltimore intermediate level courts, Baltimore city court (1867), and a second circuit court (1888). A chart presented in Figure 16 succinctly shows the chronological progression of the intermediate courts.

Figure 15 sets out the history of the upper courts which are essentially appeals courts, that is, courts to which decisions of the lower and intermediate courts can be appealed. In the earliest years, both the governor/council and the General Assembly functioned in this way (1635–50). Then from 1650–1776, the governor and his council heard appeals. In 1776, jurisdiction was transferred to a Court of Appeals which continues today, and to the Eastern and Western General Courts (for some cases) during their existence 1776–1806. For further details on the courts of MD, see:

_G. Skordas, MD GOVERNMENT, 1634–1866, and J. B. Hively, MD GOVERNMENT, 1867–1956, in M. L. Radoff, editor, The Old Line State, Hall of Records Commission, State of MD, Annapolis, MD, 1971, pages 308–87.

---

11. Recommended reading

A knowledge of the history, geography, government, and laws of MD and its local regions is of extreme importance for tracing the genealogies of its former inhabitants. This chapter has been a brief treatment of some of these. Your next step should be the reading of one of the following, relatively short one–volume works:

_S. E. G. Chapelle and several others, MD, A HISTORY OF ITS PEOPLE, Johns Hopkins Univ. Press, Baltimore, MD, 1986.
_V. Rollo, YOUR MD, MD Historical Press, Lanham, MD, 1985.
_R. Wilson and E. L. Bridner, MD, ITS PAST AND PRESENT, MD Historical Press, Lanham, MD, 1981.
_C. Bode, MD, A BICENTENNIAL HISTORY, Norton, New York, 1978.
Then, if you care to extend your knowledge, there is an absolutely essential volume. This work has chapters by experts on MD history, the regions of MD (southern, eastern, western), Annapolis, Baltimore, military MD, MD government, and blacks in MD.
_M. L. Radoff, editor, THE OLD LINE STATE, A HISTORY OF MD, MD Hall of Records Commission, Annapolis, MD, 1971.
For Baltimore, the major population center of MD, the following are recommended histories:
_J. T. Scharf, HISTORY OF BALTIMORE CITY AND COUNTY, Genealogical Publishing Co., Baltimore, MD, 1971, 2 volumes. With biographies.

MD Intermediate Courts

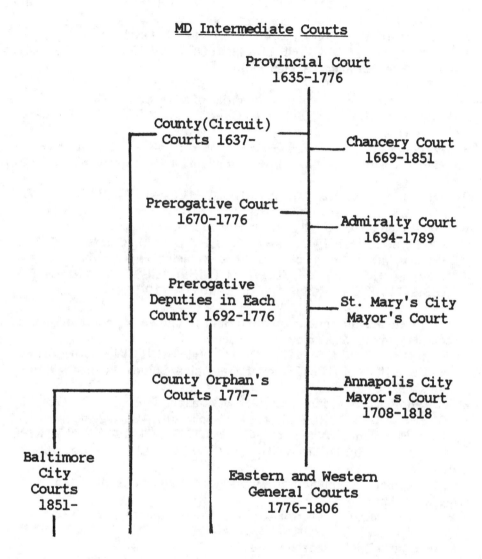

Figure 16. MD Intermediate Courts

_C. C. Hall, BALTIMORE, ITS HISTORY AND ITS PEOPLE, Lewis Historical
    Publishing Co., New York, New York, 1912.
_H. E. Shepherd, HISTORY OF BALTIMORE, 1729–1898.
_S. H. Olson, BALTIMORE, THE BUILDING OF AN AMERICAN CITY, Johns
    Hopkins Press, Baltimore, MD, 1985.

Other useful single–volumed histories of MD are:
_M. P. Andrews, HISTORY OF MD, PROVINCE AND STATE, Gale Research
    Co., Detroit, MI, 1965.
_R. J. Brugger, MD, A MIDDLE TEMPERAMENT, 1634–1980, Johns Hop-
    kins Press, Baltimore, MD, 1988. Excellent bibliography on pages 712–
    69.
_R. Walsh and W. L. Fox, MD, A HISTORY, 1632–1972, Baltimore, MD,
    1974.
Two multi–volumed historical works which could be of help to you are:
_M. P. Andrews, TERCENTENARY HISTORY OF MD, Clarke Publ. Co.,
    Baltimore, MD, 1925, 4 volumes. Three volumes biographical.
_J. T. Scharf, HISTORY OF MD FROM THE EARLIEST PERIOD TO THE
    PRESENT DAY, Gale Research Co., Detroit, MI, 1967, 3 volumes.

For detailed information on the formation and early characteristics of
MD counties, these works may be consulted:
_E. B. Mathews, THE COUNTIES OF MD, THEIR ORIGIN, BOUNDARIES,
    AND ELECTION DISTRICTS, in MD Geological Survey, Volume 6, 1906,
    pages 417–572.
_M. L. Radoff, G. Skordan, and P. R. Jacobsen, THE COUNTY COURT-
    HOUSES AND RECORDS OF MD, Annapolis, MD, 1963, 2 volumes
_MD State Planning Department, THE COUNTIES OF MD AND BALTIMORE
    CITY, THEIR ORIGIN, GROWTH, AND DEVELOPMENT, The Department,
    Baltimore, MD, 1968.
For geographical information on MD, a good start will be provided by the
following books:
_J. E. DiLision, MD, A GEOGRAPHY, Westview, Baltimore, MD, 1983.
_M. J. Kaminkow, MD FROM A TO Z, A TOPOGRAPHICAL DICTIONARY,
    Magna Carta Book Co., Baltimore, MD, 1985
_E. C. Papenfuse and J. M. Coale, III, ATLAS OF HISTORICAL MAPS OF
    MD, 1608–1908, Johns Hopkins University Press, Baltimore, MD,
    1982.
In order to understand genealogical data from many governmental sources,
it is well to have some knowledge of MD law. The following volumes are
recommended:
_L. C. Davis, AN INTRODUCTION TO MD STATE PUBLICATIONS FOR THE
    LAW LIBRARIAN, American Association of Law Libraries, Washington,
    DC, 1981.
_CONSTITUTIONS OF MD: 1776, 1851, 1864, 1867, MD Secretary of
    State, Annapolis, MD, 1870.

_LAWS OF MD, 1637–1763, Jonas Green, Annapolis, MD, 1765.
_LAWS OF MD, 1692–1818, Frederick Green, Annapolis, MD, 1799–1818, 7 volumes.
_LAWS OF MD, 1810–, MD State Government, Annapolis, MD, 1810–.

In order to locate books and articles dealing with certain time periods of MD history, certain regions or counties or towns of MD, certain trends, movements or developments in MD history, the following historical bibliographies can be consulted:
_BIBLIOGRAPHIES OF ARTICLES AND BOOKS ON MD (annually since 1975) and BOOK REVIEWS (most issues) in MD Historical Magazine, MD Historical Society, Baltimore, MD, 1906–.
_BIBLIOGRAPHY in R. J. Brugger, MD, A MIDDLE TEMPERAMENT, 1634–1980, MD Historical Society, Johns Hopkins Univ. Press, Baltimore, MD, 1988, pages 711–69.
_M. J. Kaminkow, US LOCAL HISTORIES IN THE LIBRARY OF CONGRESS, Magna Carta Book Co., Baltimore, MD, 1975 ff., 5 volumes.
_P. W. Filby, BIBLIOGRAPHY OF AMERICAN COUNTY HISTORIES, Genealogical Publishing Co., Baltimore, MD, 1985.
_NY Public Library, US LOCAL HISTORY CATALOG, Hall, Boston, MA, 1974, 2 volumes, with BIBLIOGRAPHIC GUIDE TO NORTH AMERICAN HISTORY, Hall, Boston, MA, annual supplements, 1977–.
_National Society of the DAR, DAR LIBRARY CATALOG, VOLUME 2, STATE AND LOCAL HISTORIES AND RECORDS, The Society, Washington, DC, 1988.
_B. S. Giles, SELECTED MD BIBLIOGRAPHY AND RESOURCES, The Author, Seattle, WA, 1988, 2 volumes.
A very important MD historical periodical which you might want to consult because of its excellent articles on all phases of MD history is:
_MD Historical Magazine, MD HISTORICAL SOCIETY, Baltimore, MD, 1906–.

Key to Abbreviations

A	=	Agricultural census records
AGLL	=	American Genealogical Lending Library
B	=	Baltimore police census
BCA	=	Baltimore City Archives (Baltimore)
C	=	Civil War Union veterans census
DAR	=	Daughters of the American Revolution
E	=	Early census–like lists
FHC	=	Family History Center(s)
FHL	=	Family History Library (Salt Lake City)
FHLC	=	Family History Library Catalog
I	=	Industrial census records
IGI	=	International Genealogical Index
LGL	=	Large genealogical libraries
LL	=	Local library(ies) in MD
LR	=	Local repositories
M	=	Mortality census records
MHS	=	MD Historical Society (Baltimore)
MSA	=	MD State Archives (Annapolis)
MSLL	=	MD State Law Library (Annapolis)
NA	=	National Archives (Washington)
NARB	=	National Archives, Regional Branch(es)
P	=	Revolutionary War pensioner census
R	=	Regular census records
RL	=	Regional library(ies) in MD
S	=	Slaveholder census
SASE	=	Long, self–addressed, stamped envelope

Chapter 2

TYPES OF RECORDS

1. Introduction

The state of Maryland (MD) is relatively rich in genealogical source material, even though there have been some sizable losses of records. A great deal of work has been done by many people in accumulating, preserving, photocopying, microfilming, transcribing, abstracting, printing, and indexing records. Among the most important genealogical records of MD are the local county governmental records (birth, bond, circuit court, death, divorce, equity, estate, guardian, indenture, land, manumission, marriage, naturalization, oaths, voter, tax, will). The originals of these records are largely in the county courthouses, the Baltimore City Archives, or the MD State Archives (MSA). A number of these records have been microfilmed by the MD State Archives (MSA) and/or the Family History Library (FHL) in Salt Lake City, UT. Those microfilmed by the FHL are available at their Library, as well as on loan through their over 270 branches (known as Family History Centers, FHC) in the US. A number of the original records have been transcribed and published (books, manuscripts, typescripts, articles), most being available in large genealogical libraries in MD, and many being available in large genealogical libraries elsewhere.

In addition to the local governmental records, there are several other categories of records which are of immense use genealogically: state (and colony) governmental records (birth, census, colonial, court, death, divorce, immigration, land grants and patents, marriage, military, probate, tax, will), national governmental records (census, immigration, military, naturalization, tax), and private records (Bible, biography, cemetery, church, city directory, city and county histories, manuscripts, maps and atlases, mortuary, newspaper, regional histories). Most of the state and national records are available in microfilm and/or published form in the MD State Archives (MSA), in the MD Historical Society Library (MHS), in other large genealogical libraries, and in Salt Lake City at the Family History Library (FHL), and through its branch Family History Centers (FHC). Private records are available in published, microfilmed, manuscript, and original forms in the MD Historical Society (MHS), in various MD county libraries, and at the Family History Library (FHL), which makes them available through its branch Family History Centers (FHC). Local private record repositories which must not be overlooked are churches, mortuaries, newspaper offices, and organization headquarters. Some of the state, national, and private records will be available in large genealogical libraries outside of MD, and the national records can be found at the National Archives and its eleven regional field Branches (NAFB). Many of the national and state, and some

of the county records can be borrowed by mail from the American Genealogical Lending Library (AGLL) in Bountiful, UT.

The best overall centralized collection of genealogical materials for
MD are to be found in Baltimore and Annapolis, just 25 miles apart on the
eastern coast of western MD. In <u>Baltimore</u>, the principal repository is the
library of the MD Historical Society (MHS). In addition, there are the Baltimore City Archives, the Enoch Pratt Free Library, and the George Peabody
Library of Johns Hopkins University. In <u>Annapolis</u>, the primary repository is
the Hall of Records of the MD State Archives (MSA). Not to be overlooked in
Annapolis is the MD State Law Library (MSLL).

The library of the <u>MD Historical Society</u> (MHS) has an exceptionally
large genealogical and historical collection. It holds over 75,000 books,
over 2700 microfilm rolls, over 1400 volumes of bound newspapers, and
about 2 million manuscripts. Included are atlases, Baltimore city directories, Bible records, biographies, biography compilations, cemetery inscriptions, censuses, church records, county and city histories, genealogical
indexes, genealogical journals, genealogical manuscripts, genealogical
reference works, genealogies, family histories, historical journals, historical manuscripts, maps, military records, newspapers, passenger lists,
unpublished genealogies, and wills and estate records. The <u>Baltimore City
Archives</u> (BCA) holds governmental records pertaining to Baltimore City
dating from about 1729. Records of the following types are available there:
board of health, city commissioner, city council, city court, Civil War, coro-
ner's inquests, county court, land, manumission, mayoral, naturalization,
passenger lists, plats, superior court, tax, voter registration.

The Hall of Records at the <u>MD State Archives</u> (MSA) makes available
an exceedingly voluminous collection of state and county governmental
records. The main types of records which are to be found there are: black,
birth, court, death, divorce, estate, federal census, colonial, freedom, land,
map, marriage, military, municipal, naturalization, plat, probate, tax, and
will. The MSA has most MD governmental records up to about 1850, and
many after that date. In addition, the MSA has goodly numbers of non-
governmental records, chiefly church records and newspapers. The records are readily accessed by over 140 major indexes (card, volume, microform), hundreds of smaller indexes, and numerous other finding aids.
The nearby <u>MD State Law Library</u> (MSLL) has a collection of over 240,000
volumes, many of them making up a large reference collection on MD genealogy and MD state and local history. The library is also strong, as you
might realize from its name, in MD law and governmental holdings, and
holds many MD journals and newspapers.

Other repositories which have MD materials include these located in
Baltimore: Enoch Pratt Free Library (the MD Room for Baltimore city direc-

tories, Baltimore histories, biographical file, black histories, maps, MD state, regional, and county histories, newspapers, published genealogies, and general genealogical references), George Peabody Library of Johns Hopkins University (genealogy, MD state, regional, and county histories, maps). Another library of note is the McKeldin Library of the University of MD located at College Park (historical, geographical, legal, governmental, and genealogical materials).

There is a sizable collection of books and microfilm copies of MD genealogical materials (especially colonial, state, and county records) in the largest genealogical library in the world, namely, the Family History Library (FHL) of the Genealogical Society of UT, which is located in Salt Lake City, UT. Not only are these abundant sources available at the FHL in Salt Lake City, but the microfilms may be borrowed through the numerous branch libraries known as Family History Centers (FHC), which are located all over the US and beyond. Included among these branches are several in the state of MD: Annapolis, Baltimore (Lutherville), Ellicott City, Frederick, and Kensington (Silver Spring). There are also some other branches just over MD's borders: Wilmington, DE (just beyond northeastern MD), Annandale, VA, and Falls Church, VA (just southwest of Washington, DC), Fairmont, WV (just beyond western MD), and York, PA (north of Baltimore County). Each branch FHC has microform copies of several major genealogical indexes and of the major indexes which list the holdings of the FHL in Salt Lake City, from which record microfilms can be borrowed.

Many records pertaining to MD which were accumulated by the federal government [after 1775/6] are available in the National Archives (NA) in Washington, DC (just 45 miles southeast of Baltimore). These records include the following types: census, passenger arrival, naturalization, military (service, pension, bounty land), Indian, black, land, claims, federal court, maps. Many of the most useful of these materials have been microfilmed. These microfilms are available in many of the MD libraries mentioned previously, and sizable numbers of them will be found in the eleven National Archives Regional Branches (NARB), the nearest one of them to MD being the one in Philadelphia. Many may also be borrowed personally or through your local library from AGLL (American Genealogical Lending Library, PO Box 244, Bountiful, UT 84010).

In addition to the above collections, there are MD record collections in a number of large genealogical libraries (LGL) around the country, especially those in states near MD. Finally, local libraries (LL) in county seats and some other towns and cities often have good materials relating to their own areas. These local libraries may be county, city, town, or private (such as ones sponsored by local historical or genealogical societies). All of the archives, libraries, and repositories mentioned above will be discussed in detail in Chapter 3 (Record locations).

In this chapter, the many types of records which are available for MD genealogical research are discussed. Those records which are essentially national or state-wide in scope will be treated in detail, both governmental and private (non-governmental). Records which are basically county records (both governmental and non-governmental, and including city records), will be named and described generally. Detailed lists of them will be given in Chapter 4, where the major county (and city) records available for each of MD's 23 counties and Baltimore City will be presented.

2. Bible records

During the past 200 years it was customary for families with religious sympathies to keep vital statistics on their members in the family Bible. These records vary widely, but among them the items that may be found are names, dates, and places of birth, christening, confirmation, baptism, marriage, death, burial, and sometimes military service. Although most Bibles containing recorded information probably still remain in private hands, some of the information has been submitted for publication and some has been filed in libraries and archives throughout MD. You should inquire about such records at every possible library and archives in or near your ancestor's county, especially the LL. These repositories will be listed in Chapter 4 under the counties and Baltimore City.

You should also seek Bible records in the larger archives and libraries in MD: MSA, MHS, MSLL. Also the indexes at FHC (FHL) should be consulted. In these repositories, there may be a special alphabetical record file, or as is more often the case, data from Bibles may be listed in indexes or alphabetical files labelled something other than Bible Records. The most likely labels are family records, genealogies, manuscripts, names, and surnames. Also, do not fail to look in the major card or computer index in each of these repositories for the names you are seeking. It is also important to use the locality and surname indexes at the nearest FHC.

Among the published Bible records and Bible record indexes for MD are the following:
_R. W. Barnes, supervisor, INVENTORY OF MD BIBLE RECOREDS, Family Line Publications, Westminster, MD, 1989-.
_DAR Chapters of MD, DAR GENEALOGICAL RECORD VOLUMES, typescripts, various MD DAR Chapters, several MD cities and towns, numerous volumes. Arranged by county, most with a surname index. Contain Bible, birth, cemetery, church, death, marriage, and will records.
_National Society, DAR, DAR LIBRARY CATALOG, The Society, Washington, DC, 1982/6. Many family, local, and state records are listed. Some contain MD Bible records.

_FHL CATALOG, LOCALITY SECTION, FHL, Salt Lake City, UT. Also at every FHC. Look under MD–Bible records, MD–[County]–Bible records, and MD–Baltimore (Independent City)–Bible records.
_INDEX 32, FAMILY BIBLE AND TOMBSTONE RECORDS INDEX, MSA, Annapolis, MD.
_E. K. Kirkham, AN INDEX TO SOME OF THE FAMILY RECORDS OF THE SOUTHERN STATES, Everton, Logan, UT, 1979. Contains some MD Bible records.
_Genealogical Council of MD, MD BIBLE RECORDS, The Council, Baltimore, MD, 1991. Over 2500 MD Bible records.
_HOLDCRAFT MD COLLECTION, 59 microfilms, FHL, Salt Lake City, UT. Over 250,000 entries from MD Bible, cemetery, county, family, and newspaper (obituary) records. Chiefly Frederick County and neighboring areas.
_E. P. Passano, AN INDEX TO THE SOURCE RECORDS OF MD: GENEALOGICAL, BIOGRAPHICAL, HISTORICAL, Genealogical Publishing Co., Baltimore, MD, 1967. Over 20,000 entries, some Bible material.
_M. E. Stuart, BIBLE RECORDS, UPPER EASTERN SHORE OF MD, typescript, MHS, Baltimore, MD, also on microfilm at FHL, Salt Lake City, UT.

Bible records also appear in genealogical periodical articles and in published family genealogies. These two record sources will be discussed in later sections of this chapter.

3. Biographies

There are several major national biographical works which contain sketches on nationally-prominent Marylanders of the past. If you suspect or know that your ancestor was that well known, consult:

_NATIONAL CYCLOPEDIA OF AMERICAN BIOGRAPHY, White Co., New York, NY, 1893–present, over 54 volumes, cumulative index for volumes 1–51.
_DICTIONARY OF AMERICAN BIOGRAPHY, Scribners, New York, NY, 1928–37, 20 volumes, cumulative index.
_THE 20TH CENTURY BIOGRAPHICAL DICTIONARY OF NOTABLE AMERICANS, Gale Research Co., Detroit, MI, 1968, 10 volumes.
_AMERICAN BIOGRAPHY: A NEW CYCLOPEDIA, American Historical Society, New York, NY, 1916–33, 54 volumes, cumulative index for volumes 1–50.
_ENCYCLOPEDIA OF AMERICAN BIOGRAPHY, NEW SERIES, American Historical Co., West Palm Beach, FL, 1934–present, 4 volumes.
_WHO WAS WHO IN AMERICA, 1607–1896, Who's Who, Chicago, IL, 1967.
Most of these works and over 500 more have been indexed in a large microfiche/computerized set containing more than 6 million entries. This set is available in numerous large libraries, and is added to annually:

_BIOBASE, Gale Research Co., Detroit, MI, latest issue.

Several extensive biographical compilations for the state of MD exist. These volumes list persons who have attained state-wide prominence in the fields of law, agriculture, business, politics, medicine, engineering, industry, science, military, manufacturing, teaching, government, public service, or philanthropy. Included among the better ones are:

_M. P. Andrews, TERCENTENARY HISTORY OF MD, Clarke Publ. Co., Baltimore, MD, 1925, 4 volumes. Volumes 2-4 biographical.

_THE BIOGRAPHICAL CYCLOPEDIA OF REPRESENTATIVE MEN OF MD AND THE DC, National Biographical Publishing Co., Baltimore, MD, 1879.

_E. Boyle, BIOGRAPHICAL SKETCHES OF DISTINGUISHED MARYLAND-ERS, Kelly, Piet, Baltimore, MD, 1877.

_E. F. Cordell, THE MEDICAL ANNALS OF MD, 1799-1899, Williams and Wilkins, Baltimore, MD, 1903. Biographies of physicians.

_DISTINGUISHED MEN OF BALTIMORE AND MD, Baltimore American Publishers, Baltimore, MD, 1914.

_W. G. Helmes, NOTABLE MD WOMEN, Tidewater, Cambridge, MD, 1977.

_F. A. Kummer, THE FREE STATE OF MD, Historical Record Association, Baltimore, MD, 1942, 4 volumes. Volumes 2-4 biographical.

_M. H. Luckett, MD WOMEN, The Author, Baltimore, MD, 1931.

_MD HISTORICAL MAGAZINE, MD Historical Society, Baltimore, MD, 1906-, Volume 1-. Many biographies.

_F. S. McGrath, PILLARS OF MD, Dietz Press, Richmond, VA, 1950.

_H. W. Newman, THE FLOWERING OF THE MD PALATINATE, 1634-54, Genealogical Publishing Co., Baltimore, MD, 1985. Biographies of people on the Ark and the Dove.

_D. M. Owings, HIS LORDSHIP'S PATRONAGE OFFICES FOR PROFIT IN COLONIAL MD, MD Historical Society, Baltimore, MD, 1953. Biographical data on early office holders.

_E. C. Papenfuse and others, A BIOGRAPHICAL DICTIONARY OF THE MD LEGISLATURE, 1634-1789, Johns Hopkins University Press, Baltimore, MD, 1979/85, 2 volumes.

_C. W. Sams, THE BENCH AND BAR OF MD, A HISTORY, 1634-1901, Lewis Publishing Co., Chicago, IL, 1901, 2 volumes. Biographical data on judges and attorneys.

_R. and V. Schaun, MD: BIOGRAPHICAL SKETCHES, MD Historical Press, Lanham, MD, 1984.

_R. H. Spencer, GENEALOGICAL AND MEMORIAL ENCYCLOPEDIA OF THE STATE OF MD, American Historical Society, New York, NY, 1919, 2 volumes.

_B. C. Steiner, MEN OF MARK IN MD, Johnson-Wynne, Washington, DC, 1907-12, 4 volumes.

_P. Winchell, MEN OF MD SINCE THE CIVIL WAR, Arnold Publishing Co., Baltimore, MD, 1934.

In addition to the state-wide biographical works, there are also a number of biographical collections for sections or regions of the state. Among those with the largest number of names are:

_C. C. Hall, BALTIMORE, ITS HISTORY AND ITS PEOPLE, Lewis Historical Publishing Co., New York, NY, 1912, 3 volumes. Volumes 2-3 biographical.

_G. W. Howard, THE MONUMENTAL CITY, ITS PAST HISTORY AND PRESENT RESOURCES, Ehlers and Co., Baltimore, MD, 1873.

_S. A. Mallick, SKETCHES OF CITIZENS OF BALTIMORE CITY AND BALTIMORE COUNTY, Baltimore, MD.

_B. Mayer, BALTIMORE, PAST AND PRESENT, Richardson and Bennett, Baltimore, MD, 1871.

_PORTRAIT AND BIOGRAPHICAL RECORD OF THE EASTERN SHORE OF MD, Chapman, New York, NY, 1898, 2 volumes.

_J. T. Scharf, HISTORY OF BALTIMORE CITY AND COUNTY, Genealogical Publishing Co., Baltimore, MD, 1971, 2 volumes.

_J. T. Scharf, HISTORY OF WESTERN MD, Regional Publ. Co., Baltimore, MD, 1968.

There are, for MD, several large, important indexes of biographical data which should not be overlooked by any researcher. These are:

_S. M. Andrusko, MD BIOGRAPHICAL SKETCH INDEX, The Author, Silver Spring, MD, 1986. Over ten thousand names from MD local histories.

_BIOGRAPHY FILE, Enoch Pratt Free Library, Baltimore, MD. A huge card index to biographical materials taken from newspapers, periodicals, and history books of the 1800s and 1900s.

_DIELMAN-HAYWARD FILE, MHS, Baltimore, MD. Over 250,000 biographical, death, and marriage items from MD newspapers, 1780 to the present.

_E. P. Passano, AN INDEX OF THE SOURCE RECORDS OF MD, GENEALOGICAL, BIOGRAPHICAL, HISTORICAL, Genealogical Publishing Co., Baltimore, MD, 1974, reprint of a 1940 volume. An older bibliography of MD genealogical and biographical works. Over 20,000 names.

_Indexes to MD HISTORICAL MAGAZINE, see indexes in the magazine and the integrated index for 1906-60 in MSA, Annapolis, MD.

Not only are there national, state, and regional biographical works for MD, and some important indexes, there are also a number of local biography compilations and local histories containing biographical data. Most of the biographical books mentioned above are available in MHS, as are many local volumes. Some are also to be found in MSLL and in FHL (FHC). The local publications will also be found in LL of the places of interest. When you seek biographical compilations in a library, look under these headings in their catalogs: US-Biography, MD-Biography, [County Name]-Biography, [City Name]-Biography. Listings of biographical materials for MD will often be found in the following sources. These will be especially helpful for what is available at the local level, where you are most likely to find references to your ancestor.

_M. J. Kaminkow, US LOCAL HISTORIES IN THE LIBRARY OF CONGRESS, Magna Carta, Baltimore, MD, 1975, 5 volumes.

_CATALOGS (CARD, COMPUTER, PRINTED) IN MHS, MSLL, MSA, and FHL (FHC), Baltimore and Annapolis, MD, and Salt Lake City, UT.

_F. Rider, AMERICAN GENEALOGICAL [-BIOGRAPHICAL] INDEX, Godfrey Memorial Library, Middletown, CT, 1st Series, 1942-52, 48 volumes; 2nd Series, 1952-, in progress, over 170 volumes so far.

Biographical information is also sometimes found in ethnic publications, genealogical compilations, genealogical periodicals, manuscripts, military records, newspapers, published genealogies, regional records, and historical works (state, regional, local). All of these sources will be discussed in sections to follow.

4. Birth records

In 1640, just 6 years after the initial settlement, the MD Assembly mandated the keeping of birth records. Because of non-compliance, erratic record keeping, and losses, very few early records survived. Those which are known are all in the MSA: Charles County (1654-96, 1702-6), Kent County (1650-1793), Somerset County (1649-1720), Talbot County (1657-91). In 1692, the Anglican (Episcopalian) Church was made the established church of MD, and the parishes were ordered to keep birth records. The establishment remained in place until 1776. A number of these parish records have been preserved, and they will be discussed in a later section entitled Church records. During 1776-1865, very few governmental birth records were kept, except for some that appear in land and other types of records. An index for Anne Arundel County births (1801-77) is also available.

In 1865, MD passed a law mandating birth recording by the counties, but only slightly more than half the counties complied, and even these kept erratic, incomplete, and/or sporadic records. During this record period, 1865-98, the counties and dates of the records are as follows: Allegany (1865-84), Anne Arundel (1804-77), Caroline (1865-84), Carroll (1865-85), Cecil (1865-91), Charles (1865-70), Frederick (1865-73), Kent (1865-73), Montgomery (1865-99), Prince George's (1865-7), Queen Anne's (1865-81), Somerset (1865-94), Talbot (1865-73), Washington (1865-7, 1876), Wicomico (1868-75), and Worcester (1865-89). Most of these are in MSA, a few in CH. These are indexed.

Baltimore City began recording births in 1875 and a state law required all births in the counties to be registered with the state from 1898 forward. The MD Division of Vital Records (PO Box 13146, Baltimore, MD 21203-3146) holds these records, and issues official certified copies to the individuals who are named in the records or to their authorized representatives or their parents. The MSA has microfilm copies of most of the records and indexes to them. They will abstract genealogical information from them for anyone for a small fee.

There are several indexes and published birth record compilations which are important to MD genealogical searchers:

_CARD FILE OF COLONIAL BIRTH RECORDS, MSA, Annapolis, MD.

_INDEX 30, BIRTH RECORD INDEX, 1649-1715, 1898-1923, incomplete, MSA, Annapolis, MD.

_H. Chance, WESTERN MD PIONEERS, LISTS OF MARRIAGES, BIRTHS, AND DEATHS OF 8000 EARLY SETTLERS, Library of the PA Historical Society, Philadelphia, PA, 1968.

_C. Torrence, OLD SOMERSET ON THE EASTERN SHORE, Regional Publishing Co., Baltimore, MD, 1966.

_F. W. Wright, MD EASTERN SHORE RECORDS, 1648-1825, Family Line Publications, Silver Spring, MD, 1982-6, 5 volumes.

_ARCHIVES OF MD, VOLUME 54, MSA, Annapolis, MD, 1937, early Kent County birth records.

_INTERNATIONAL GENEALOGICAL INDEX (IGI), on microfiche and CD disk, FHL, Salt Lake City, UT, look under MD. Also available at every FHC.

_MD DAR, MD DAUGHTERS OF THE AMERICAN REVOLUTION COLLECTION OF TYPESCRIPT VOLUMES, MD Chapters of the DAR, Baltimore, MD, various dates, numerous volumes. Arranged by county, most of them with a surname index, contain Bible, birth, cemetery, church, death, marriage, and will records.

_FHL CATALOG, LOCALITY SECTION, on microfiche and CD disk, FHL, Salt Lake City, UT, look under MD-Vital records, MD-[County]-Vital records, and MD-Baltimore (Independent City)-Vital records. Also available at every FHC.

_E. P. Passano, INDEX OF THE SOURCE RECORDS OF MD, Genealogical Publishing Co., Baltimore, MD, 1974, reprint of a 1940 volume. An older bibliography listing many birth records.

Since MD is so short on birth records before 1865, other types of records often have to be consulted. Among the better sources of birth data are these record types: Bible, biography, cemetery, census, church, death, genealogical periodicals, manuscripts, marriage, military, mortuary, naturalization, newspaper, and published genealogies. All of these are treated in other sections of this chapter. When you are seeking birth date and place information in archives and libraries, be certain to explore all the above mentioned sources, and do not fail to look under the county listings and the following heading in library catalogs: Register of births, etc. A few of the records mentioned in this section are available on microfilm at FHL (FHC).

5. Cemetery records

If you know or suspect that your ancestor was buried in a certain MD cemetery, the best thing to do is to write the caretaker of the cemetery, enclose an SASE, and ask if the records of tombstone inscriptions or the records of burials show your forebear. Gravestones often display names, ages, dates of death and birth, and sometimes family names of wives. Tombstones of children may bear the initials of the parents. In order to locate the caretaker try writing the local historical society, the local genealogical society, or the LL. If you do not find your progenitor is buried there, then you should ask the above organizations about records for other cemeteries in the area. The addresses of these organizations will be given in Chapter 4. As you consider possible burial sites, please remember that many early cemeteries were in conjunction with churches. Therefore, if you know your ancestor's religious affiliation, this could be of help. Another valuable item is a listing of MD cemeteries which gives locations, addresses, names of caretakers or contact persons, whether the tombstone inscriptions have been copied and indexed, and where these copied data may be found.

_Genealogical Council of MD, DIRECTORY OF MD CEMETERIES, The Council, Baltimore, MD, latest edition.

Another important cemetery record source is provided by the numerous collections of cemetery records which have been made by the DAR, by state, regional, and local genealogical and historical societies, and by individuals. Some of these have been published (in journals and as books), some are in typescript, and some are in hand-written form. Many have been microfilmed. Notable among them is a large series of volumes put together by various MD chapters of the DAR.

_MD DAR, MD DAUGHTERS OF THE AMERICAN REVOLUTION COLLECTION OF TYPESCRIPT VOLUMES, MD Chapters of the DAR, Baltimore, MD, various dates, numerous volumes. Arranged by county, most of them with a surname index, contain Bible, birth, cemetery, church, death, marriage, and will records.

Other finding aids for, indexes to, and compilations of cemetery records are:

_FHL CATALOG, LOCALITY SECTION, on microfiche and CD disk, FHL, Salt Lake City, UT, look under MD-Cemetery records, MD-[County]-Cemetery records, and MD-Baltimore (Independent City)-Cemetery records. Also available at every FHC.

_INDEX 32, FAMILY BIBLE AND TOMBSTONE RECORDS INDEX, MSA, Annapolis, MD.

_MAIN CARD CATALOG, MHS, Baltimore, MD. Look under the pertinent county for cemetery records.

_H. W. Ridgely, HISTORIC GRAVES OF MD AND THE DC, Genealogical Publishing Co., Baltimore, MD, 1967.

_M. d. F. Zacharias, INSCRIPTIONS COPIED FROM VARIOUS GRAVE-YARDS IN VA, PA, AND MD, The Compiler, on microfilm at FHL, Salt Lake City, UT. Available through FHC.

_J. M. Holdcraft, NAMES IN STONE, CEMETERY INSCRIPTIONS FROM FREDERICK COUNTY, MD, Genealogical Publishing Co., Baltimore, MD, 1985. About 78,000 names.

_E. P. Passano, AN INDEX OF THE SOURCE RECORDS OF MD, GENEA-LOGICAL, BIOGRAPHICAL, HISTORICAL, Genealogical Publishing Co., Baltimore, MD, 1974. Reprint of a 1940 volume. An older volume, but helpful references to many tombstone inscriptions.

Not to be overlooked are the numerous cemetery records that have been published in MD historical and genealogical periodicals. The most important ones are THE MD AND DE GENEALOGIST, MD GENEALOGICAL SO-CIETY BULLETIN, MD HISTORICAL AND GENEALOGICAL BULLETIN, MD HISTORICAL MAGAZINE, and MD MAGAZINE OF GENEALOGY. These should be sought in MHS, MSLL, LGL, and FHL (FHC). Use the indexes in the volumes and the card index (1906-60) to the MD HISTORICAL MAGA-ZINE located in MSA. LL sometimes have records of cemeteries in their own counties. The major LL are listed in Chapter 4. In these, and other libraries, cemetery records may be located by looking in their catalogs under the surname, county, city, and town, the church, the denomination, the ethnic group, and the cemetery name. Also look under the headings Epitaphs-MD and Cemeteries-MD. Further, you should not forget to inquire about any special cemetery record indexes or files.

Several other important sources for cemetery records must not be overlooked. These include church records, manuscripts, mortuary records, newspaper obituaries, and fraternal organization records (such as a Masonic Lodge). These will be discussed in detail in later sections of this chapter.

6. Census records

Excellent ancestor information is available in eight types of census reports which have been accumulated for MD: some early census-like lists before 1790 (E), the regular federal censuses 1790-1800-10-20-30-40-50-60-70-80-1900-10 (R), slaveholder censuses 1850-60 (S), agricultural censuses 1850-60-70-80 (A), industrial or manufactures censuses 1820-50-60-70-80 (I), mortality censuses 1850-60-70-80 (M), the special 1840 Revolutionary War pensioner census (P), and the special 1890 Union Civil War veteran census (C).

For the colonial period and for the state period before 1790, a number of lists of MD inhabitants are available. Some of these early lists (E) are colony- or state-wide, most are local (regional, county, city, town), but all are incomplete. They are of various kinds, the main categories being lists of residents, freemen, petitioners, oath-takers, taxpayers, and persons for whom tobacco assessments were made (1637/8, 1641/2, 1652, 1678, 1681/2/3/4/6/8/9, 1692/6, 1710/3, 1738/9, 1740/1/2/4/5/7/8/9, 1750/1/3/5/6/8/9, 1760/1/3/5/6/8). The published Archives of MD contain many of these, most during the colonial period:

_ARCHIVES OF MD, MD Historical Society, Baltimore, MD, 1883 ff; Volume 1, pages 28-31, 116-20, 142-6, 167-80; Volume 4, page 21; several places in Volume 5; Volume 7, pages 66-104, 208-14, 248-52, 326-7, 438-44, 610-2; Volume 8, pages 110-1, 129-47, 315-6, 411; Volume 11, page 194; Volume 13, pages 129-32, 225-7; Volume 17, page 409; Volume 20, pages 539-46.

In addition, the calendar of MD papers refers to a number of others:

_CALENDAR OF MD STATE PAPERS, MD Hall of Records Commission, Annapolis, MD, 1943-58; Volume 1, pages 15-8, 22-4, 37-44, 53-6, 59-79, 83-5, 95, 103-4, 112, 119-20, 125-8, 134-9, 141-58, 162-4, 183-9, 192-5; Volume 10, pages 195-6, 232, 235, 242; Volume 11, pages 113-31.

Other similar lists will be found in MSA, MHS, and some of them are available at FHL (FHC). Quite a number also appear in:

_R. J. Cox, A PRELIMINARY LIST OF EARLY BALTIMOREANS, 1729-66, MD Genealogical Society Bulletin, Volume 21, Nos. 2-3, 1980.

_R. V. Jackson and others, EARLY MD, 1700-9, 1740-9, Accelerated Indexing Systems, Bountiful, UT, 1980. Over 25,000 names.

Not to be overlooked are some useful indexes:

_CARD INDEXES TO CENSUS OF 1776, OATHS OF FIDELITY, AND CENSUS OF 1778, MSA, Annapolis, MD.

_CARD INDEX TO PERSONS WHO TOOK THE OATH OF FIDELITY, 1778, MHS, Baltimore, MD. About 14,000 names.

There are also two important British lists:

_1708 CENSUS OF MD, Public Records Office, London, England, Reference CO5/716/54.

_1762 CENSUS OF MD, Public Records Office, London, England, Reference CO5/1276/25.

In 1776 a census of MD was taken to ascertain the population in the new state, and in 1778 a list of those who took an oath of fidelity to the new government, and a census of those who did not were taken. These incomplete compilations, or portions of them, have been published in:

_G. M. Brumbaugh, MD RECORDS, COLONIAL, REVOLUTIONARY, COUNTY, AND CHURCH, FROM ORIGINAL SOURCES, Genealogical Publishing Co., Baltimore, MD, 1975, 2 volumes. Includes 1776/8 censuses and many other early records.

_B. S. Carothers, 1776 CENSUS OF MD, The Author, Lutherville, MD, 1972. For the counties of Anne Arundel, Baltimore, Caroline, Dorchester, Frederick, Harford, Prince George's, Queen Anne's, and Talbot.

_B. S. Carothers, MD OATHS OF FIDELITY, The Author, Lutherville, MD, 1980, 2 volumes.

_B. S. Carothers, 1778 CENSUS OF MD, The Author, Lutherville, MD, 1972. For the counties of Caroline, Charles, and Queen Anne's.

Other compilations of names of individuals of MD during the early period (1634–1790) will be referred to in other sections of this chapter. Of particular value are those dealing with church records, colonial record compilations, court records, emigration and immigration lists, ethnic records, genealogical periodicals (especially MD Historical and Genealogical Bulletin, MD Genealogical Society Bulletin, MD Historical Magazine, MD and DE Genealogist, MD Original Research Society of Baltimore Bulletin, and Western MD Genealogy), land records (especially patents), military records (colonial and Revolutionary), naturalization records, and regional compilations.

Regular census records (R), taken by the federal government are available for MD in 1790, 1800, 1810, 1820, 1830, 1840, 1850, 1860, 1870, 1880, 1900, and 1910. The 1790, 1800, and 1830 schedules are incomplete, with these portions missing in 1790 (Allegany, Calvert, Somerset, and part of Dorchester Counties), in 1800 (all of Baltimore County outside of Baltimore City), and in 1830 (Montgomery, Prince George's, Queen Anne's, St. Mary's, and Somerset Counties). The 1840 federal census and all before it listed the head of the household by name plus a breakdown of the numbers (not names) of persons in the household according to age brackets and gender. Beginning in 1850, the names of all persons were recorded along with age, sex, occupation, real estate, marital, and other information, including the US state or foreign country of birth. With the 1880 census and thereafter, the birthplaces of the father and mother of each person are also shown. With the 1900 census and thereafter, the year of immigration is shown for each foreign-born individual. Chapter 4 lists the regular federal census records (R) available for each of the 23 MD counties and Baltimore City.

Census data for 1790 are available in both a published transcript and two microfilms, the first and third items being indexed:

_US Bureau of the Census, HEADS OF FAMILIES AT THE FIRST CENSUS OF THE US TAKEN IN 1790 IN MD, Genealogical Publishing Co., Baltimore, MD, 1952. Indexed.

_US Bureau of the Census, FIRST CENSUS OF THE US, 1790, MD, The National Archives, Washington, DC, Microfilm M637, Roll 3. Unindexed.

_US Bureau of the Census, FIRST CENSUS OF THE US, 1790, MD, The National Archives, Washington, DC, Microfilm T498, Roll 1. Indexed.

Microfilms of the remaining original census records (1800–1910) are available as:

_US Bureau of the Census, SECOND CENSUS OF THE US, 1800, MD, The National Archives, Washington, DC, Microfilm M32, Rolls 9–12.

_US Bureau of the Census, THIRD CENSUS OF THE US, 1810, MD, The National Archives, Washington, DC, Microfilm M252, Rolls 13–16.

_US Bureau of the Census, FOURTH CENSUS OF THE US, 1820, MD, The National Archives, Washington, DC, Microfilm M33, Rolls 40–46.

_US Bureau of the Census, FIFTH CENSUS OF THE US, 1830, MD, The National Archives, Washington, DC, Microfilm M19, Rolls 53–58.

_US Bureau of the Census, SIXTH CENSUS OF THE US, 1840, MD, The National Archives, Washington, DC, Microfilm M704, Rolls 157–172.

_US Bureau of the Census, SEVENTH CENSUS OF THE US, 1850, MD, The National Archives, Washington, DC, Microfilm M432, Rolls 277–302.

_US Bureau of the Census, EIGHTH CENSUS OF THE US, 1860, MD, The National Archives, Washington, DC, Microfilm M653, Rolls 456–485.

_US Bureau of the Census, NINTH CENSUS OF THE US, 1870, MD, The National Archives, Washington, DC, Microfilm M593, Rolls 566–599.

_US Bureau of the Census, TENTH CENSUS OF THE US, 1880, MD, The National Archives, Washington, DC, Microfilm T9, Rolls 493–518.

_US Bureau of the Census, TWELFTH CENSUS OF THE US, 1900, MD, The National Archives, Washington, DC, Microfilm T623, Rolls 604–630.

_US Bureau of the Census, THIRTEENTH CENSUS OF THE US, 1910, MD, The National Archives, Washington, DC, Microfilm T624, ROLLS 549–570.

The 1790 census records are indexed in the published volume mentioned above and in the microfilm (T498) of the printed volume. Indexes have been printed for the 1800, 1810, 1820, 1830, 1840, 1850, and 1860 census records. Chief among these indexes are:

_R. V. Jackson, MD 1800 CENSUS, Accelerated Indexing Systems, Bountiful, UT, 1978. About 32,000 entries.

_MD Genealogical Society, MD 1800 CENSUS, The Society, Baltimore, MD, 1965–75.

_L. M. Volkel and others, AN INDEX TO THE 1800 FEDERAL CENSUS OF MD, Heritage House, Thomson, IL, 1967/8.

_R. V. Jackson, MD 1810 CENSUS, Accelerated Indexing Systems, Bountiful, UT, 1976. About 45,000 entries.

_R. V. Jackson, MD 1820 CENSUS, Accelerated Indexing Systems, Bountiful, UT, 1977. About 57,000 entries.

_G. W. Parks, INDEX TO THE 1820 CENSUS OF MD AND WASHINGTON, DC, Genealogical Publishing Co., Baltimore, MD, 1980.

_R. V. Jackson, MD 1830 CENSUS, Accelerated Indexing Systems, Bountiful, UT, 1976. About 79,000 entries.

_R. V. Jackson, MD 1840 CENSUS, Accelerated Indexing Systems, Bountiful, UT, 1977. About 132,000 entries.

_R. V. Jackson, MD 1850 CENSUS, Accelerated Indexing Systems, Bountiful, UT, 1976. About 200,000 entries.

_R. V. Jackson, MD 1860 CENSUS, Accelerated Indexing Systems, Salt
  Lake City, UT, 1990, 2 volumes, 1 for Baltimore, 1 for rest of state.
There is as yet no state-wide index to the 1870 census, even though a few
county indexes are now available.

In addition to the above bound indexes, there is a microfilm index
which contains only those families with a child aged 10 or under in the
1880 census. There is also a complete microfilm index to the 1900 MD
Census. These two census indexes are arranged according to a phonetic
code called Soundex. Librarians and archivists can show you how to use it.
Nothing from the 1890 census survives for MD.
_US Bureau of the Census, INDEX (SOUNDEX) TO THE 1880 POPULATION
  SCHEDULES OF MD, The National Archives, Washington, DC, Microfilm
  T753, Rolls 1-47.
_US Bureau of the Census, INDEX (SOUNDEX) TO THE 1900 POPULATION
  SCHEDULES OF MD, The National Archives, Washington, DC, Microfilm
  T1050, rolls 1-127.
No index to the 1910 MD Census exists.

The indexes listed in the two previous paragraphs are exceptionally
valuable as time-saving devices. However, few indexes of any sort are
perfect, and therefore you need to exercise a little caution in using them. If
you do not find your progenitor in them, do not conclude that she or he is not
in the state; this may only mean that your forebear has been accidentally
omitted, or that the name has been misspelled, misread, or misprinted.
Once you have located a name in the indexes, you can go directly to the
reference in the census microfilms and read the entry. When indexes are
not available (for all 1870 and partially for 1880), it is necessary for you to
go through the census listings entry-by-entry. This can be essentially
prohibitive for the entire state, so it is necessary for you to know the county
in order to limit your search. In Baltimore, census searches in these years
(1870/80, 1910) can be greatly aided by city directory information (see
later section). Addresses obtained from city directories can lead to proper
sections of the census schedules. Both the census records and the indexes are available in MHS, MSA, FHL (FHC), and many are held by LGL and
RL. Ones pertaining to specific counties are often in LL. Both the NA and
the eleven NARB have the microfilms and the printed indexes. Also, the
microfilmed census records and the microfilmed indexes may be borrowed
by you or by your local library from AGLL (American Genealogical Lending
Library, PO Box 244, Bountiful, UT 84010). There is a charge of a few
dollars per roll.

Slaveholder censuses (S) are in existence for MD for the years 1850
and 1860. The census records show the names of the slave owners and
the numbers of the slaves held with their ages, genders, and colors given.
Most of the schedules do not give names of slaves, but once in a while, they

are found. The slave owner census schedules for MD are in with the regular census schedules. As you will recall, they have been microfilmed:

_US Bureau of the Census, SEVENTH CENSUS OF THE US, 1850, MD, SLAVEHOLDER SCHEDULES, The National Archives, Washington, DC, Microfilm M432, Rolls 300–302.

_US Bureau of the Census, EIGHTH CENSUS OF THE US, 1860, MD, SLAVEHOLDER SCHEDULES, The National Archives, Washington, DC, Microfilm M653, Rolls 484–485.

An index for the 1860 slaveholder schedules has been published:

_R. Clayton, JR., INDEX TO 1860 MD SLAVE CENSUS SCHEDULES, MD Genealogical Society Bulletin, Volume 25 (1984), pages 92–112.

The slaveholder censuses may be located exactly as the regular censuses. See the previous paragraph for the locations.

Agricultural census records (A), also known as farm and ranch censuses, are available for 1850, 1860, 1870, and 1880 for MD. These federally–gathered records list the name of the owner, size of farm or ranch, value of the property, crops, livestock, and other details. If your ancestor was a farmer, it will be worthwhile to seek him in these records. No indexes are available, but you will probably know the county and the area in the county (from the regular censuses), so your entry–by–entry searches should be fairly easy. The agricultural census are at the MSA.

Industrial census records (I), also known as manufactures censuses, were taken by the federal government in a number of years. Those of value to MD genealogists are the ones accumulated in 1820, 1850, 1860, 1870, and 1880 for MD. The records list manufacturing businesses (in 1850/60/70/80 only those with over $500 of product), owner's name, product, machinery, number of employees, and other details. Indexes accompany the 1820 microfilmed records, but the others are unindexed. The records can be found at the MSA. The 1820 microfilm is also available at the NA.

_US Bureau of the Census, RECORDS OF THE 1820 CENSUS OF MANU-FACTURES, The National Archives, Washington, DC, Microfilm M279, 27 Rolls. With indexes.

Mortality census records (M) are available for MD for the one–year periods 01 June (1849/59/69/79) to 31 May (1850/60/70/80), respectively. The federal records give information on persons who died in the year preceding the 1st of June of the census years 1850/60/70/80. The data contained in the compilations include name, month of death, age, sex, occupation, place of birth, and other information. The records and indexes are available in MSA, MSLL, and the records may be found at FHL (FHC). A published index to the 1850 records is:

_R. T. Dryden, 1850 STATE OF MD MORTALITY SCHEDULE, The Author, San Diego, CA, no date shown.

Revolutionary War pensioners (P) were included in the data collected in the 1840 regular federal census. An attempt was made to list all pension holders, however, there are some omissions and some false entries. The list has been copied out, indexed, and published:

_US Bureau of the Census, A CENSUS OF PENSIONERS FOR REVOLU-
TIONARY OR MILITARY SERVICES, Genealogical Publishing Co., Baltimore, MD, 1965.

This volume is present in MHL, MSA, FHL (FHC), in most LGL, in many RL, and in some LL.

Civil War Union veterans (C) of MD were included in a special federal census taken in 1890, as were widows of the veterans. These records display the veteran's name, the widow's name (if applicable), rank, compa-ny, regiment or ship, and other pertinent military data.

_US Veterans Administration, SPECIAL SCHEDULES OF THE ELEVENTH
CENSUS, 1890, ENUMERATING UNION VETERANS AND WIDOWS OF
UNION VETERANS OF THE CIVIL WAR, The National Archives, Wash-
ington, DC, Microfilm M123, Rolls 8-10.

These special schedules have been indexed in the following microfiche:

_B. L. Dilts, 1890 MD CENSUS INDEX OF CIVIL WAR VETERANS OR THEIR
WIDOWS, Index Publishing, Salt Lake City, UT, 1985.

The above microforms are available in MSA, MHS, FHL (FHC), some LGL, and some RL.

One final census list which is very important is a police census which was taken in Baltimore in 1868 (B). Since Baltimore was the major urban center of the state at that time, the listing can be of use. It is located in the Baltimore City Archives.

_1868 POLICE CENSUS OF SOME CITY WARDS OF BALTIMORE, Balti-
more City Archives, Baltimore, MD.

The census records of all the above types (E, R, S, A, I, M, P, C, B) available for each of the 23 counties and Baltimore City will be shown in the county listings in Chapter 4. For a county for which all the above censuses are available, the listing will read: Pre-1790E, 1790R, 1800R, 1810R, 1820RI, 1830R, 1840RP, 1850RSAIM, 1860RSAIM, 1870RAIM, 1880 RAIM, 1890C, 1900R, 1910R. For Baltimore City, 1868B will also appear to remind you of the 1868 police census. Do not forget that there are other types of listings of people which can function as census substitutes. Most notable among them are city directories and tax lists, both of which will be treated in detail later.

7. Church records

The first ships of settlers to MD (1634) were Roman Catholic and Protestant, the latter being slightly greater in number. Among them were two Jesuit priests who celebrated mass shortly after landing. The Catholic proprietor of MD prohibited any religious intolerance, the assembly of 1638 passed laws affirming this, and freedom of worship characterized the early colony. Prior to 1634, an Anglican (Church of England, Episcopalian) minister had been present at a trading post on Kent Island since 1631. In 1639, Puritans from VA came in, and since they tended to intolerance, freedom of religion was reasserted in a law passed in 1649. However, reflecting the civil war in England, Puritans took control, and in 1654 forbid the practice of Roman Catholicism and Anglicanism. In 1657, the Puritans were removed, and religious tolerance was reintroduced. Friends (Quakers) came into MD about 1657/8, and their MD Yearly Meeting was organized in 1672. Enough Presbyterians had entered by 1683 that they brought in a minister who organized these congregations on the lower Eastern Shore.

After a resurgence of intolerance, especially against Roman Catholics, the MD government was taken in 1692 from the Catholic proprietor, the Anglican Church was established, and public worship by Catholics was forbidden. Thirty Anglican parishes were laid out, and they were assigned vital record keeping duties. In 1718, both Catholics and Friends were disenfranchised, and this persisted until the Anglican disestablishment in 1776. The first Baptist Church was organized in Baltimore County in 1742, and the denomination grew rapidly thereafter. As Germans came into western MD from PA, beginning about 1729, they brought in the Lutheran, Reformed, and Moravian faiths. The earliest German church was built near Creagerstown in 1733. In 1760, a small log chapel in Carroll County became the first Methodist house of worship. They, like the Baptists, grew very rapidly to become the predominant faith in MD during the 1800s.

After the Revolution, the remaining Anglicans constituted a new denomination, the Protestant Episcopal Church, retaining almost all of the Anglican tradition. In 1790, the Roman Catholic Church consecrated a Bishop of Baltimore with the entire US as his diocese. Many blacks became Baptist following the admission of slaves to Baptist Churches, which began about 1780. The first black Baptist Church was organized in 1836, the first black Methodist Church in 1802, and there were numerous black Catholics by 1810. Unitarians date to 1819. In 1829, the Hebrew congregation in Baltimore received its charter.

Because of the deficiency of early governmental vital records, the church records of MD are very important. The vital records kept by the Anglican churches during their establishment (1692-1776) were quite good and many of them are extant. For 1718-76, the period of the Catholic and Quaker disenfranchise, there are only a few of their records which survive. In general, Catholic, Anglican (Episcopal), Lutheran, Reformed, Moravian, and Friends records are very good, those of Presbyterians and early Unitarians good, and those of Methodists and Baptists only fair to poor.

Church records in MD are to be found in many forms and places: original records in the churches; original records in LL, RL, MHS, MSA, and denominational archives; manuscripts in LL, RL, MHS, MSA, and denominational archives and libraries; microfilmed records in LL, RL, MHS, MSA, FHL (FHC), and denominational archives; records published in books; and records published in genealogical periodicals. Fortunately, there is an exceedingly useful volume which serves as the indispensable key to MD's church records:

_E. A. Kanely, DIRECTORY OF MD CHURCH RECORDS, Family Line Publns., Silver Spring, MD, 1988.

This volume lists a large number of enduring MD churches which were organized before 1910, over 2500 in all. It gives the years of operation, the years for which records exist, and the locations of the records. The largest centralized collections of church records are in MHS, MSA, and FHL (FHC). Access to them is facilitated by the following finding aids:

_NORRIS HARRIS CHURCH REGISTER INDEX, CHURCH RECORD INDEX, GENEALOGY INDEX, CARD INDEX TO MD HISTORICAL MAGAZINE, MAIN CARD CATALOG (See county), MICROFORMS REFERENCE LISTS, and LOOSELEAF REGISTRY OF CHURCH RECORDS, in MHS, Baltimore, MD.

_CHURCH RECORDS-MARRIAGE INDEX, CHURCH RECORDS-BIRTHS AND BAPTISMS INDEX, CHURCH RECORDS-DEATHS AND BURIALS INDEX, and GUIDE TO MICROFORM CHURCH RECORDS in MSA, Annapolis, MD.

_LOCALITY SECTION, FHL CATALOG (See county), in FHL, Salt Lake City, UT, and in every FHC.

The MD DAR members have collected many typescript volumes of genealogical information. Some of these contain church records. They may be found in the DAR Library in Washington, DC, in MHS, in MSLL, and some in FHL (FHC).

_MD DAR, MD DAUGHTERS OF THE AMERICAN REVOLUTION COLLECTION OF TYPESCRIPT GENEALOGICAL RECORD VOLUMES, MD Chapters of the DAR, Baltimore, MD, various dates, numerous volumes. Arranged by county, most of them with a surname index. Contain Bible, birth, cemetery, church, death, marriage, and will records.

Listed in this paragraph and in several to follow will be the major denominations of MD, their repositories, and pertinent genealogical and historical volumes (volumes which cover all or large parts of the state). Baptists, originated in England about 1607-11 in Puritan (Congregational) circles. They first emerged as a denomination in the colonies in 1639 in RI. Later the center of colonial Baptist activity came to be Philadelphia. Beginning about 1750, Baptist membership rose rapidly so that by 1800 they were the largest denomination in the US. The first Baptist church in MD was organized in 1742 in Baltimore County. Some records are in MHS. Baptist repositories and publications include:

_(Archives) Historical Room, Baptist Convention of MD, 1313 York Road, Lutherville, MD 21093; Southern Baptist Historical Commission, 127 Ninth Avenue North, Nashville, TN 37234; American Baptist Historical Society, 1106 South Goodman St., Rochester, NY 14620.

_ENCYCLOPEDIA OF SOUTHERN BAPTISTS, Broadman Press, Nashville, TN, 1958, 3 volumes. See article on MD.

_E. C. Starr, A BAPTIST BIBLIOGRAPHY, BEING A REGISTER OF PRINTED MATERIAL BY AND ABOUT BAPTISTS, American Baptist Historical Society, Rochester, NY, 1947-, continuing.

_R. C. Torbet, A HISTORY OF BAPTISTS, Judson Press, Valley Forge, PA, 1963.

_J. F. Weishampel, THE BAPTIST CHURCH IN MD, 1742-1885, MD Baptist Union Association, Baltimore, MD, 1885.

Brethren (Church of the Brethren) originated in the German Pietistic movement of the 1600s as Lutherans who turned to the simple life. Their major period of migration to the colonies was 1719-40, almost all of them initially settling in PA. They are sometimes called Dunkers because of their baptismal practice of triple immersion. When Germans came into western MD from PA, Brethren were among them. Both MHS and MSA have records. Repositories and publications are:

_(Archives) Brethren Historical Archives, 1451 Dundee Ave., Elgin, IL 60120; Juniata College Library, Huntingdon, PA 16652; Bethany Theological Seminary, Butterfield and Meyers Rds., Oak Brook, IL 60521.

_J. M. Henry, HISTORY OF THE CHURCH OF THE BRETHREN IN MD, Brethren Historical Society, Elgin, IL, 1936.

_F. S. Weiser, MD GERMAN CHURCH RECORDS, Noodle-Doosey Press, Manchester, MD, 1986.

_M. G. Brumbaugh, A HISTORY OF THE GERMAN BAPTIST BRETHREN, AMS Press, New York, NY, 1971, with INDEX, Bookmark, Knightstown, IN, 1977.

As you will recall, Catholic (Roman Catholic) services were celebrated upon the settlement of MD in 1634. During the colonial period, the highest concentration of Catholics in the English colonies was in MD, even though the Episcopal Church (Anglican Church, Church of England, Protestant Episcopal Church) as the established church replaced religious freedom in 1692. Catholics were disenfranchised in 1718, and doubly-taxed in 1740, they being often forced to operate underground. After the Revolution, religious freedom was gradually restored, and Baltimore became the early center of Roman Catholicism in the US. From 1790-1865, over 2 million Catholics came to the US, chiefly Irish and German. From 1865-1900, over 3 million more came, these being mostly Italian, Austro-Hungarian, and Polish. MSA has microfilmed Catholic record church records. Repositories and publications include:

_(Archives) Archives of the Archdiocese of Baltimore, 320 Cathedral St., Baltimore, MD 21201; Library, Georgetown University, Washington, DC 20057; St. Mary's Seminary Library, 5400 Rowland Ave., Baltimore, MD 21210.

_T. J. O'Rourke, COLONIAL SOURCE RECORDS, SOUTHERN MD CATHOLIC FAMILIES, The Author, Venice, CA, 1980.

_T. J. O'Rourke, CATHOLIC FAMILIES OF SOUTHERN MD, RESIDENTS OF ST. MARY'S COUNTY IN THE 18TH CENTURY, Genealogical Publishing Co., Baltimore, MD, 1985. About 9000 names.

_J. P. Dolan, THE AMERICAN CATHOLIC EXPERIENCE, A HISTORY FROM COLONIAL TIMES TO THE PRESENT, Doubleday, New York, NY, 1985.

_J. T. Ellis, CATHOLICS IN COLONIAL AMERICA, Helicon Press, Baltimore, MD, 1963.

The Episcopal Church (Anglican Church, Church of England, Protestant Episcopal Church) was one of the two major denominations in the colonies in the 1600s, the other being the Puritans (Congregationalists). Episcopalians were among the original settlers of MD, and the first church was constituted in 1658 in St. Mary's County. In 1692, the Episcopal Church became the established church and continued so until 1776. In 1692, MD was divided into 30 parishes, and from then forward, the records are fairly good, and most have been preserved. All people were supposed to have birth, baptism, marriage, and death information recorded in the Episcopal Church books. Very good collections will be found at MHS and MSA. Archives and publications are:

_(Archives) MD Diocesan Library of the Episcopal Church, 105 West Monument St., Baltimore, MD 21404; MHS, Baltimore, MD.

_Historical Records Survey, INVENTORY OF THE CHURCH ARCHIVES OF MD, PROTESTANT EPISCOPAL CHURCH, DIOCESE OF MD, The Survey, Baltimore, MD, 1940.

_Historical Records Survey, INVENTORY OF THE CHURCH ARCHIVES OF MD, PROTESTANT EPISCOPAL CHURCH, DIOCESE OF WASHINGTON, The Survey, Baltimore, MD, 1940.

_N. W. Rightmyer, MD'S ESTABLISHED CHURCH, Church Historical Society for the Diocese of MD, Philadelphia, PA, 1956.

_E. Ingle, PARISH INSTITUTIONS IN MD, Johns Hopkins University Press, Baltimore, MD, 1883.

_G. Partie, CHURCH AND STATE IN EARLY MD, Johns Hopkins University Press, Baltimore, MD, 1892.

_P. G. Skirven, THE FIRST PARISHES OF THE PROVINCE OF MD, HIS-
TORICAL SKETCHES OF THE TEN COUNTIES AND THIRTY PARISHES
IN 1692, Remington Co., Baltimore, MD, 1923.

Friends (Quakers) came into MD early, about 1657, shortly after they
developed in England. They were good record keepers, and many of their
records are extant. Sizable collections are located in MHS and MSA.
Archives, guides, and other publications which will be of assistance to you
are:
_(Archives) Friends Historical Society, Swarthmore College, Swarthmore,
PA 19081; Magill Historical Library, Haverford College, Haverford, PA
19041; Baltimore Yearly Meeting of Friends, Stony Run Meeting House,
5114 North Charles St., Baltimore, MD 21218.
_P. R. Jacobsen, QUAKER RECORDS IN MD, Hall of Records State Com-
mission, Annapolis, MD, 1966. Guide to record locations.
_W. W. Hinshaw, ENCYCLOPEDIA OF AMERICAN QUAKER GENEALOGY,
Genealogical Publishing Co., Baltimore, MD, 1969.
_K. L. Carroll, JOSEPH NICHOLS AND THE NICHOLITES, THE NEW
QUAKERS OF MD, DE, NC, AND SC, Eastern Publishing Co., Easton,
MD, 1962. Many births, marriages, and deaths.
_K. L. Carroll, QUAKERISM ON THE EASTERN SHORE, MD Historical
Society, Baltimore, MD, 1970. Births, deaths, membership lists.
_R. G. Kelly, QUAKERS IN THE FOUNDING OF ANNE ARUNDEL COUNTY,
Prentice-Hall, Baltimore, MD, 1963.

Only a few Jewish people were in colonial MD, and they were not
bothered. However, until 1825, they were excluded by law from holding
political office. In 1828, the Baltimore Hebrew Congregation received its
charter. For Jewish records consult:
_(Archives) American Jewish Historical Society, 2 Thornton Rd., Waltham,
MA 02154; American Jewish Archives, 3101 Clifton Ave., Cincinnati,
OH 45220; Judaic Museum, 6125 Montrose Rd., Rockville, MD 20851;
JEWISH HISTORICAL SOCIETY OF MD, 15 Lloyd Street, Baltimore, MD
21215.
_M. H. Stern, FIRST AMERICAN JEWISH FAMILIES, 600 GENEALOGIES,
1654-1977, American Jewish Archives, Cincinnati, OH, 1978.
_I. Rosenwaike, THE JEWS OF BALTIMORE, in American Jewish Historical
Quarterly, Volume 64, No. 4, June 1975; Volume 67, No. 2, December
1977; Volume 67, No. 3, March 1978.

Lutheran people, along with Germans of other denominations, began
coming into western MD from PA about 1730. Their first church was organized in 1733. Archives and books relating to Lutherans which will serve
you well are:
_(Archives) Archives of the MD Synod, Evangelical Lutheran Church in
America, 7604 York Road, Towson, MD 21204; MHS, Baltimore, MD

21201; Lutheran Archives Center, 7301 Germantown Ave., Philadelphia, PA 19119; Archives of the Evangelical Lutheran Church in America, 8765 West Higgins Road, Chicago, IL 60631; Wentz Library, Lutheran Theological Seminary, Gettysburg, PA 17325; Historical Society of York County, 250 East Market Street, York, PA 17401.
_F. S. Weiser, MD GERMAN CHURCH RECORDS, Noodle-Doosey Press, Manchester, MD, 1986, 3 volumes.
_A. R. Wentz, HISTORY OF THE EVANGELICAL LUTHERAN SYNOD OF MD, Evangelical Lutheran Press, Harrisburg, PA, 1920.

The Methodist (Methodist Episcopal) denomination had its origin in England during the 1720s as a movement within the Episcopalian Church (Church of England). The first Methodist worship service in MD was held in 1760 in Carroll County. Formal organization of the sect proceeded slowly, two meeting houses being constructed in Baltimore 1773-4. In 1784, a final separation from the Episcopal Church occurred as the Methodist Church in America was formed in Baltimore. The archives and good reference volumes are:
_(Archives) United Methodist Historical Society, Baltimore Conference, 2200 St. Paul Street, Baltimore, MD 21218; MHS, Baltimore, MD 21201; MSA, Annapolis, MD 21404; United Methodist Archives Center, Drew University, Madison, NJ 07940.
_T. H. Lewis, HISTORICAL RECORD OF THE MD ANNUAL CONFERENCE OF THE METHODIST PROTESTANT CHURCH, 1829-1939, Baltimore, MD, 1939. Numerous biographies.
_R. W. Todd, HISTORY OF THE METHODIST CHURCH IN THE MD AND DE PENINSULA, Methodist Episcopal Book Rooms, Philadelphia, PA, 1886.

Moravians were Protestants who took their origin in 1457 in Moravia (now central Czechoslovakia). They first came to America (PA) in 1735, and some of them moved into western MD shortly thereafter. Archives and published information are as follows:
_(Archives) Archives of the Moravian Church, 41 West Locust St., Bethlehem, PA 18018; MHS, Baltimore, MD 21201; Historical Society of York County, 250 East Market Street, York, PA 17401.
_E. A. DeSchweinitz, HISTORY OF THE CHURCH KNOWN AS UNITAS FRATRUM, Moravian Publishing Concern, Bethlehem, PA, 1901.

Presbyterian people entered the lower Eastern Shore of MD very early and the first congregation was formed about 1683. In 1715 a Presbyterian church was organized in Baltimore. Record repositories and published works on Presbyterians include:
_(Archives) Presbyterian Historical Society, 425 Lombard Street, Philadelphia, PA 19147; MHS, Baltimore, MD 21201.
_J. W. McIlvain, EARLY PRESBYTERIANISM IN MD, Johns Hopkins University Press, Baltimore, MD, 1890.

The Reformed (or German Reformed) people were among the various German groups which came into western MD from PA in the 1740s and 1750s. The denomination remained separate until 1934, when it united with the German Evangelical Church to constitute the Evangelical and Reformed Church. This church then in 1957 joined the Congregational Christian Churches to form the United Church of Christ. The major reposi- tories and books which can assist you are:
_(Archives) Evangelical and Reformed Historical Society, Franklin and Marshall College, 555 West James St., Lancaster, PA 17603; MHS, Baltimore, MD 21201.
_G. P. Bready, HISTORY OF THE REFORMED CHURCH IN MD AND THE US, Carroll Record Printing, Tanneytown, MD, 1938.
_K. Pfeiff, REFORMED CHURCH RECORDS, MD, Reformed Church Soci- ety, Lancaster, PA, 1958.
_F. S. Weiser, MD GERMAN CHURCH RECORDS, Noodle-Doosey Press, Manchester, MD, 1986.

The United Brethren (United Brethren in Christ) denomination was formed in 1800 near Frederick by some members of the Reformed Church who had been strongly influenced by Methodism. In 1946, it merged with the Evangelical Church to form the Evangelical United Brethren Church. This church, in turn, combined with the Methodist Church in 1968 to give the United Methodist Church. The archives is:
_(Archives) Evangelical United Brethren Archives, 140 South Perry Street, Dayton, OH 45401; MHS, Baltimore, MD 21201.
_F. S. Weiser, MD GERMAN CHURCH RECORDS, Noodle-Doosey Press, Manchester, MD, 1986.
The FHL has some MD church records on microfilm, especially those of Episcopal, Friends, and Presbyterian churches. Do not fail to check the indexes at FHC, from which the microfilms can be borrowed. A valuable volume for early MD clergymen is:
_F. L. Weis, THE COLONIAL CLERGY OF MD, DE, AND GA, Genealogical Publishing Co., Baltimore, MD, 1978.

When you are seeking MD church records, first consult the book by Kanely (5th paragraph of this section). Then, inquire at all these reposito- ries: MHS, MSA, FHL (FHC), RL, and LL. Finally, check with the individual church and the pertinent church archives. When looking for church re- cords in a library or archives catalog, you should look under the county name, the church name, and the denomination name. Church records are often found in several other sources, which are discussed in different sections of this chapter: cemetery, city and county histories, colonial, DAR, ethnic, genealogical indexes and compilations, genealogical periodicals, manuscripts, mortuary, newspaper, published genealogies, regional re- cords, and WPA records.

---

8. City directories

In 1752, a city directory was issued in Baltimore, and then another in 1796, and again in 1799. Beginning in 1800/01, city directories appeared erratically, but on the average about every 2 years up to 1835/6. From then on, there is a city directory almost every year, with a few exceptions. Washington, DC, directories appeared first in 1822, then erratically on the average every 3 or 4 years up to 1860, then annually. Frederick, MD, began issuing city directories in 1859/60, and other MD urban areas began later. The first directories for various MD cities were as follows: Cumberland (1876), Hagerstown (1884), Havre de Grace (1857). MD state business directories were published in 1878, 1880, and 1899, and in several years thereafter. City directories usually list heads of households and workers, plus their home addresses, and sometimes the names and addresses of their places of employment. Also often listed in city directories are businesses, professions, institutions, churches, and organizations (sometimes with officers, rarely with all members).

City directories are available in MHS, MSLL, LL in the pertinent cities, and in the Library of Congress. The Baltimore city directories for 1752–1901 have been put on microfiche or microfilmed:
_BALTIMORE CITY DIRECTORIES, 1752–1901, Research Publications, New Haven, CT, volumes 1752–1860 on microfiche, volumes 1861–1901 on microfilm.
These microforms are available in some LGL, and in some state and large private university libraries.

---

9. City and county histories

Histories for all MD counties and several MD cities, including Baltimore, have been published. These volumes usually contain biographical data on leading citizens, details about early settlers, histories of organizations, businesses, trades, and churches, and often lists of clergymen, lawyers, physicians, teachers, governmental officials, farmers, military men, and other groups. Several works which list many of these histories are:
_M. J. Kaminkow, US LOCAL HISTORIES IN THE LIBRARY OF CONGRESS, Magna Carta, Baltimore, MD, 1975, 4 volumes.
_P. W. Filby, BIBLIOGRAPHY OF COUNTY HISTORIES IN AMERICA, Genealogical Publishing Co., Baltimore, MD, 1985.
_BIBLIOGRAPHIES OF ARTICLES AND BOOKS ON MD (annually since 1975) and BOOK REVIEWS (most issues) in MD Historical Magazine, MD Historical Society, Baltimore, MD, 1906–.
_NY Public Library, US LOCAL HISTORY CATALOG, Hall, Boston, MA, 1974, 2 volumes, with BIBLIOGRAPHIC GUIDE TO NORTH AMERICAN HISTORY, Hall, Boston, MA, annual supplements, 1977–.

_National Society of the DAR, DAR LIBRARY CATALOG, VOLUME 2, STATE AND LOCAL HISTORIES AND RECORDS, The Society, Washington, DC, 1988.
_M.-J. Whittaker, GENEALOGY AND LOCAL HISTORY, A UMBC BIBLIOG-RAPHY, University of MD, Baltimore Campus, Baltimore, MD, 1979.
_B. S. Giles, SELECTED MD BIBLIOGRAPHY AND RESOURCES, The Au-thor, Seattle, WA, 1988, 2 volumes.

Most of the MD city, county, and community history volumes in these bibliographies can be found in MHS, MSLL, the DAR Library in Washington, DC, the Library of Congress in Washington, DC, and some are available in FHL (FHC). RL and LL are likely to have those relating to their particular areas. In Chapter 4, you will find listed under the counties recommended county (and some city) histories. In libraries, the easiest way to find local histories is to look in their catalogs under the names of the county, city, town, and community.

10. Colonial records

The colonial period of MD extended from 1634 to 1775. The period can be conve-niently divided into these subperiods: The Early Proprietorship (1634–89), The Roy-al Colony (1689–1715), and The Restored Proprietorship (1715–75). Many other sections of this chapter describe types of records relating to colonial MD, particularly the sections on census records (early census–like lists), church records, court records, DAR records, emigration and immigration records, land records, manu-scripts, colonial and Revolutionary military records, newspaper records, will and probate records, and vital records (birth, marriage, death). This section presents the most important published colonial records, and is made up of two subsections: one dealing with general reference materials to all the colonies (including MD), and a second which sets out published items on MD only.

Among the most important genealogical materials relating to all the colonies are the following. However, some of the volumes must be used with care since some of the information in them is not from original sources and is therefore often inaccurate.
_C. E. Banks, PLANTERS OF THE COMMONWEALTH, Genealogical Pub-lishing Co., Baltimore, MD, 1972.
_BURKE'S DISTINGUISHED FAMILIES OF AMERICA, Burke's Peerage, London, England, 1948.
_M. L. Call, INDEX TO THE COLONIAL AMERICAN GENEALOGY LIBRARY, Call, Salt Lake City, UT, 1982. Index to over 10,000 lineage charts in the NEHGS.

_W. M. Clemens, AMERICAN MARRIAGE RECORDS BEFORE 1699, Genealogical Publishing Co., Baltimore, MD, 1926(1979). [10,000 entries]

_P. W. Coldham, BONDED PASSENGERS TO AMERICA, 1663-75, Genealogical Publishing Co., Baltimore, MD, 1983.

_P. W. Coldham, CHILD APPRENTICES IN AMERICA, FROM CHRIST'S HOSPITAL, LONDON, 1617-1778, Genealogical Publishing Co., Baltimore, MD, 1990.

_P. W. Coldham, ENGLISH ADVENTURERS AND EMIGRANTS, 1609-1773, Genealogical Publishing Co., Baltimore, MD, 1984/5.

_P. W. Coldham, ENGLISH CONVICTS IN COLONIAL AMERICA, Genealogical Publishing Co., Baltimore, MD, 1982, 3 volumes.

_P. W. Coldham, ENGLISH ESTATES OF AMERICAN COLONISTS, Genealogical Publishing Co., Baltimore, MD, 1980-1, 3 volumes.

_P. W. Coldham, THE BRISTOL REGISTERS OF SERVANTS SENT TO FOREIGN PLANTATIONS, 1654-86, Genealogical Publishing Co., Baltimore, MD, 1988.

_P. W. Coldham, THE COMPLETE BOOK OF EMIGRANTS, 1607-60, Genealogical Publishing Co., Baltimore, MD, 1987.

_P. W. Coldham, THE COMPLETE BOOK OF EMIGRANTS IN BONDAGE, 1614-1775, Genealogical Publishing Co., Baltimore, MD, 1988.

_M. B. Colket, Jr., FOUNDERS OF EARLY AMERICAN FAMILIES, Order of Founders and Patriots of America, Cleveland, OH, 1985.

_THE COLONIAL GENEALOGIST, incorporated later in THE AUGUSTAN, OMNIBUS VOLUMES, The Augustan Society, Harbor City, CA, 1970-.

_G. R. Crowther, III, SURNAME INDEX TO 65 VOLUMES OF COLONIAL AND REVOLUTIONARY PEDIGREES, National Genealogical Society, Washington, DC, 1975.

_N. Currer-Briggs, COLONIAL SETTLERS AND ENGLISH ADVENTURERS, Genealogical Publishing Co., Baltimore, MD, 1971. [5000 names]

_Daughters of American Colonists, BICENTENNIAL ANCESTOR INDEX, The Daughters, Washington, DC, 1976-84.

_Daughters of the American Revolution, DAR PATRIOT INDEX, The Daughters, Washington, DC, 1966, 1979, 2 volumes.

_Daughters of Colonial Wars, BICENTENNIAL ANCESTOR INDEX, The Daughters, Washington, DC, 1976.

_Daughters of Founders and Patriots of America, INDEX TO LINEAGE BOOKS, The Daughters, Somerville, MA, 1943, with recent SUPPLEMENTS.

_H. K. Eilers, NSDAC BICENTENNIAL ANCESTOR INDEX, National Society Daughters of American Colonists, Ft. Worth, TX, 1976.

_P. W. Filby and M. K. Meyer, PASSENGER AND IMMIGRATION LISTS INDEX, Gale Research, Detroit, MI, 1981, 3 volumes, plus annual SUPPLEMENTS. [Over 1.6 million names]

_G. Fothergill, EMIGRANTS FROM ENGLAND, 1773-6, Genealogical Publishing Co., Baltimore, MD, 1964.

_E. French, LIST OF EMIGRANTS TO AMERICA FROM LIVERPOOL, 1697–1707, Genealogical Publishing Co., Baltimore, MD, 1962.

_M. Ghirelli, A LIST OF EMIGRANTS FROM ENGLAND TO AMERICA, 1682–92, Magna Carta, Baltimore, MD, 1968.

_T. P. Hughes and others, AMERICAN ANCESTRY, Genealogical Publishing Co., Baltimore, MD, 1968(1887–9), 12 volumes.

_J. and M. Kaminkow, A LIST OF EMIGRANTS FROM ENGLAND TO AMERICA, 1718–59, Magna Carta, Baltimore, MD, 1981.

_G. M. MacKenzie and N. O. Rhoades, COLONIAL FAMILIES OF THE USA, Genealogical Publishing Co., Baltimore, MD, 1966(1907–20), 7 volumes. [125,000 names]

_National Genealogical Society, INDEX OF REVOLUTIONARY WAR PENSION APPLICATIONS IN THE NATIONAL ARCHIVES, The Society, Washington, DC, 1976.

_National Society Colonial Dames 17th Century, 17TH CENTURY COLONIAL ANCESTORS, Genealogical Publishing Co., Baltimore, MD, 1976 (1984).

_National Society of Colonial Dames of America, REGISTERS OF ANCESTORS, The Society, Richmond, VA, 1905/17/27/44/79.

_National Society of Colonial Daughters 17th Century, NEW LINEAGE BOOK, D. Baird, Rotan, TX, 1980.

_National Society Daughters of Colonial Wars, BICENTENNIAL ANCESTOR INDEX, R. Moncure, Clifton, VA, 1984.

_Order of Founders and Patriots of America, REGISTER, The Order, New York, NY, 1927, with SUPPLEMENTS, 1940, 1960, 1981.

_H. D. Pittman, AMERICANS OF GENTLE BIRTH AND THEIR ANCESTORS, A GENEALOGICAL ENCYCLOPEDIA, Genealogical Publishing Co., Baltimore, MD, 1970.

_F. Rider, THE AMERICAN GENEALOGICAL BIOGRAPHICAL INDEX, Godfrey Memorial Library, Middletown, CT, 1942–52, 48 volumes; THE AMERICAN GENEALOGICAL BIOGRAPHICAL INDEX, NEW SERIES, Godfrey Memorial Library, Middletown, CT, 1952–, in progress, over 170 volumes published.

_G. F. T. Sherwood, AMERICAN COLONISTS IN ENGLISH RECORDS, Sherwood, London, England, 1932, 2 volumes.

_Society of Colonial Wars, INDEX TO ANCESTORS AND ROLL OF MEMBERS, The Society, New York, NY, 1921, with SUPPLEMENTS, 1941 and 1971.

_W. W. Spooner, HISTORIC FAMILIES OF AMERICA, The Author, New York, NY, 1907–8, 3 volumes. Be careful.

_M. Tepper, PASSENGERS TO AMERICA, A CONSOLIDATION OF SHIP PASSENGER LISTS FROM THE NEW ENGLAND HISTORICAL AND GENEALOGICAL REGISTER, Genealogical Publishing Co., Baltimore, MD, 1977.

_R. G. Thurtle and L. S. King, PEDIGREES OF DESCENDANTS OF THE COLONIAL CLERGY, Society of the Descendants of the Colonial Clergy,

Lancaster, MA, 1976, with SUPPLEMENT, Mayo, Manchester, CT, 1978.

_F. A. Virkus, THE ABRIDGED COMPENDIUM OF AMERICAN GENEALOGY, Genealogical Publishing Co., Baltimore, MD, 1968(1925-42), 7 volumes. [425,000 names of colonial people]

_J. Wareing, EMIGRANTS TO AMERICA, INDENTURED SERVANTS RECRUITED IN LONDON, 1718-33, Genealogical Publishing Co., Baltimore, MD, 1985.

_H. Whittemore, GENEALOGICAL GUIDE TO THE EARLY SETTLERS OF AMERICA, Genealogical Publishing Co., Baltimore, MD, 1967 (1898-1906).

Now Let us turn to published reference materials for colonial MD. Among the most valuable of these are as follows. Considerable care must be exercised with some of these volumes since data may be unreliable. In all cases, all data must be checked against the original records.

_J. H. Alexander and E. Allen, INDEX TO THE CALENDAR OF MD STATE PAPERS, MD Archives, Baltimore, MD, 1861.

_ARCHIVES OF MD, MHS, Baltimore, MD, 1883-1972, 72 volumes. Transcripts of many colonial records. Includes Proceedings of the Provincial Council, 1636-1770 (Volumes 3, 5, 8, 15, 17, 20, 23, 25, 28, 31, 32), Proceedings of the Provincial Court, 1637-83 (Volumes 4, 10, 41, 49, 57, 65-70), Proceedings and Acts of the General Assembly, 1637-1774 (Volumes 1-2, 7, 13, 19, 22, 24, 26-27, 29-30, 33-40, 42, 44, 46, 50, 52, 55-56, 58-59, 61-64), Proceedings of the Court of Chancery, 1669-79 (Volume 51). Volumes are indexed.

_R. W. Barnes, MD MARRIAGES, 1634-1899, Genealogical Publishing Co., Baltimore, MD, 1975/8, 2 volumes.

_J. L. Bozman, HISTORY OF MD FROM 1633 TO 1660, Lucas and Deaver, Baltimore, MD, 1837, 2 volumes.

_G. M. Brumbaugh, MD RECORDS, COLONIAL, REVOLUTIONARY, COUNTY, AND CHURCH, FROM ORIGINAL SOURCES, Genealogical Publishing Co., Baltimore, MD, 1975, 2 volumes.

_A. W. Burns, INDEX TO MD COLONIAL JUDGMENTS, The Author, Annapolis, MD, 1938 ff., 7 volumes. Use with care.

_A. W. Burns, MD ACCOUNT BOOKS, NOS. 1-74, The Author, Annapolis, MD, 1936-9. Use with care.

_A. W. Burns, MD BALANCES OF FINAL DISTRICT BOOK, The Author, Annapolis, MD, 1939, 4 volumes. Use with care.

_A. W. Burns, MD INDEX TO INVENTORIES, 1745-62, The Author, Annapolis, MD, about 1937. Use with care.

_A. W. Burns, MD INDICES TO TESTAMENTARY PROCEEDINGS, PROBATES OF WILLS, AND ADMINISTRATIONS OF ESTATES, The Author, Annapolis, MD, 1938, 26 volumes. Use with care.

_A. W. Burns, MD INVENTORIES AND ACCOUNTS, The Author, Annapolis, MD, 1938, 5 volumes. Use with care.

_A. W. Burns, MD MARRIAGE RECORDS, 1659-1807, The Author, Washington, DC, 1937 ff., 39 volumes. Marriages inferred in other records. Use with care.

_A. W. Burns, MD RECORD OF DEATHS, 1718-77, The Author, Annapolis, MD, 1936. Use with care.

_A. W. Burns, MD RENT ROLLS, The Author, Annapolis, MD, 1939, 2 volumes. Use with care.

_A. W. Burns, MD WILL BOOKS, 1686-1744, The Author, Annapolis, MD, 1938-45, many volumes. Use with care.

_CALENDARS OF MD STATE PAPERS, Publications Nos. 1, 5-8, 10-11, Hall of Records, MSA, Annapolis, MD, 1943-58. Refer to state papers in the Red, Brown, Blue, and Black Books. See later under MD STATE PAPERS.

_CHANCERY (EQUITY) COURT DEPOSITIONS, 1668-1789, MD Historical Magazine, Volume 23, 1928, pages 101-54, 197-242, 293-343.

_Colonial Dames of America, Baltimore Chapter, ANCESTRAL RECORDS AND PORTRAITS, Genealogical Publishing Co., Baltimore, MD, 1969.

_J. B. Cotton and R. B. Henry, THE MD CALENDAR OF WILLS, 1635-1743, Genealogical Publishing Co., Baltimore, MD, 1968. Abstracts of wills.

_R. J. Cox, A PRELIMINARY LIST OF EARLY BALTIMOREANS, 1729-66, MD Genealogical Society Bulletin, Volume 21, Nos. 2-3, 1980.

_M. Crowe, DESCENDANTS FROM FIRST FAMILIES OF VA AND MD, The Author, Washington, DC, 1980.

_DAR Chapters of MD, DAR TYPESCRIPT RECORDS COLLECTION, many volumes of transcribed records, various DAR Chapters, various places, various dates. Arranged by county. Most indexed. See section entitled DAR Records in this chapter for details and list of volumes.

_E. G. Greene and V. D. Harrington, AMERICAN POPULATION BEFORE 1790, The Authors, New York, NY, 1932. Colonial censuses of MD.

_E. Hartsook and G. Skordas, LAND OFFICE AND PREROGATIVE COURT RECORDS OF COLONIAL MD, Genealogical Publishing Co., Baltimore, MD, 1968.

_R. V. Jackson and others, EARLY MD, 1700-09, 1740-49, Accelerated Indexing Systems, Bountiful, UT, 1980. Over 25,000 names.

_A. F. Johnson, KINFOLK IN GERMAN KINFOLK IN MD, The Author, Columbus, OH, 1983. German settlements in the early 1700s.

_LAND NOTES OF MD, 1634-55, in MD Historical Magazine, Volumes 5-9, 1910-14. Taken from Libers (Books) F, A, B. Many early settlers.

_J. M. Magruder, Jr., INDEX OF MD COLONIAL WILLS, 1635-1777, Genealogical Publishing Co., Baltimore, MD, 1967. Name index.

_J. M. Magruder, Jr., MD COLONIAL ABSTRACTS: WILLS, ACCOUNTS, INVENTORIES, Genealogical Publishing Co., Baltimore, MD, 1968. Abstracts for 1772-7.

_L. B. Marks, DR. WIESENTHAL'S PATIENTS, 1733-89, in MD Genealogical Society Bulletin, Volume 21, No. 3, 1980. About 2000 listings.

_MD STATE PAPERS: RED, BROWN, BLUE, AND BLACK BOOKS, in MSA, Annapolis, MD. See CALENDARS OF MD STATE PAPERS, Publication Nos. 1, 5-8, 10-11, Hall of Records, MSA, Annapolis, MD, 1943-58. Colonial correspondence, petitions, military returns, muster rolls, resolutions.

_M. K. Meyer, DIVORCES AND NAMES CHANGED IN MD BY ACT OF THE LEGISLATURE, 1634-1854, The Author, Pasadena, MD, 1970.

_E. D. Neil, THE FOUNDERS OF MD, Munsell, Albany, NY, 1876.

_H. W. Newman, THE FLOWERING OF THE MD PALATINATE, 1634-54, The author, Annapolis, MD, 1961. Genealogies of passengers on the Ark and the Dove.

_H. W. Newman, SEIGNIORY IN EARLY MD, Society of Descendants of Lords of the MD Manors, Washington, DC, 1949. Lists of manors and manor lords.

_D. M. Owings, HIS LORDSHIP'S PATRONAGE, OFFICES FOR PROFIT ON COLONIAL MD, MHS, Baltimore, MD, 1953. Early office holders.

_H. S. Richardson, SIDE LIGHTS ON MD HISTORY, WITH SKETCHES OF EARLY MD FAMILIES, Genealogical Publishing Co., Baltimore, MD, 1967. Over 5000 names.

_G. Skordas, THE EARLY SETTLERS IN MD, AN INDEX TO NAMES OF IMMIGRANTS COMPILED FROM LAND GRANTS, 1633-80, Genealogical Publishing Co., Baltimore, MD, 1979.

_D. O. Virdin and R. B. Clark, Jr., MD FAMILY GENEALOGIES AND HISTORIES, Clark, St. Michaels, MD, 1984. A bibliography of about 470 MD family histories.

_A. M. Warfield, FOUNDERS OF ANNE ARUNDEL AND HOWARD COUNTIES, Kohn, Pollock Publishers, Baltimore, MD, 1909.

_J. A. and F. L. Wyand, COLONIAL MD NATURALIZATIONS, Genealogical Publishing Co., Baltimore, MD, 1975.

Most of the published works mentioned in the previous paragraphs are available in MHS, many in MSLL, FHL (FHC), and LGL, and some in RL and larger LL. As was mentioned at the beginning of this section, numerous other sections of this chapter give references to other colonial records. These should not be overlooked. Please remember that the above listings are for published colonial records, and that there are many, many unpublished ones. Some of the above works will be listed again in sections to which they are very important so that you will not run any chance of overlooking them. The possibility of finding your colonial ancestor in the above volumes is fairly high, provided you take the time and pains to carefully examine them all.

11. Court records

Down through the many years of the existence of the colony and the state of MD, its laws have been administered by a wide variety of courts. These courts may be seen during all these years as operating at three levels: the upper level (courts operating at the colony or state level), the intermediate level (courts operating at the county level), and the lower level (courts operating at the local or sub-county level). Each MD court, with some exceptions at the lower level, had a clerk or register or recorder who kept the records. Among the most important records generally kept by the most of the courts were: (1) docket books listing cases in chronological order, (2) minute books briefly describing actions taken by the court, (3) orders given by judges, (4) judgments or final decisions made by the court, (4) case files containing original papers generated by the trial or other court action, (5) record books with case summaries and/or special types of records, and often with indexes, and (6) loose and miscellaneous papers, indexes, and record types. As you read in Chapter 1, MD courts have undergone a number of changes in name, jurisdiction, and geographical coverage. These changes sometimes accompanied alterations in the overall gover-nance of the colony or state. The histories of the government and the courts of MD were discussed in detail in Chapter 1. Please turn back and review those materials.

At the upper level of MD courts were Governor/Council and the Gen-eral Assembly (1635-50), the Governor/Council (1650-1776), the East-ern and Western General Courts (1776-1806), and the Court of Appeals (1776-). All of these courts were (are) basically appeals courts. Their records are as follows:
_Proceedings of the Provincial Council (1636-1770), ARCHIVES OF MD, MHS, Baltimore, MD, 1883 ff., Volumes 3, 5, 8, 15, 17, 20, 23, 25, 28, 31-32.
_Proceedings and Acts of the General Assembly (1637-1774), ARCHIVES OF MD, MHS, Baltimore, MD, 1883 ff., Volumes 1-2, 7, 13, 19, 22, 24, 26-27, 29-30, 33-40, 42, 44, 46, 50, 52, 55-56, 58-59, 61-64.
_RECORDS OF EASTERN AND WESTERN GENERAL COURTS, Judgments (1776-1806), Appeals Cases, MSA, Annapolis, MD. With indexes. Also on microfilm at FHL (FHC).
_MD COURT OF APPEALS RECORDS, Judgments and Decrees (1788-1891), MSA, Annapolis, MD. Indexes in most volumes. Also on micro-film at FHL (FHC).
_MD REPORTS, 1658-, various authors and compilers, various publishers, 1809-. Summaries of appeal cases.

At the intermediate level of MD courts were some state-wide courts and some local (county or city) courts. Among the state-wide intermediate courts were the Provincial Court (1635-1776) and its successor court the General Court (1776-1806, with Eastern and Western branches), the Chancery Court (1669-1851), the Admiralty Court (1694-1789), and the Prerogative Court (1670-1776). Local courts included the County or Circuit Courts (1637-), the County Orphan's Courts (1777-), and the various Baltimore City Courts (1851-). The state-wide records are as follows:

_Proceedings of the Provincial Court (1637-83), ARCHIVES OF MD, MHS, Baltimore, MD, 1883 ff., Volumes 4, 10, 41, 49, 57, 65-70.

_RECORDS OF THE PROVINCIAL COURT, Judgments (1679-1776), MSA, Annapolis, MD, with indexes. Also on microfilm at FHL (FHC).

_RECORDS OF THE EASTERN AND WESTERN GENERAL COURTS (1776-1806), MSA, Annapolis, MD, with indexes. Also on microfilm at FHL (FHC).

_Proceedings of the Court of Chancery (1669-79), ARCHIVES OF MD, MHS, Baltimore, MD, 1883 ff., Volume 51.

_MD LAND OFFICE INDEX TO SUITS BROUGHT TO THE MD CHANCERY COURTS, Annapolis, MD.

_CHANCERY (EQUITY) COURT DEPOSITIONS, 1668-1789, WITH INDEX, MD Historical Magazine, Volume 23, 1928, pages 101-54, 197-242, 293-343.

_RECORDS OF THE COURT OF CHANCERY (1669-1851), MSA, Annapolis, MD, with indexes for 1669-1806 and 1817-51. Often have vital record data.

_RECORDS OF THE PREROGATIVE COURT (1670-1776), MSA, Annapolis, MD, with indexes. To be treated in detail in the section entitled Wills and probate. Please see that section later in this chapter.

_RECORDS OF THE ADMIRALTY COURT (1694-1789), MSA, Annapolis, MD, with indexes.

_MD COLONY COURT AND PROBATE RECORDS, COUNCIL PROCEEDINGS, 1634-1774, Hall of Records Commission, Annapolis, MD, 1963.

The intermediate courts, operating at the local level (county or city) include the following: County or Circuit Courts (1637-), County Orphan's Courts (1777-), St. Mary's City Mayor's Court, Annapolis City Mayor's Court (1708-1818), and Baltimore City Courts (1851-). The records of these courts are to be found in MSA, the court houses in the counties (CH), and/or the Baltimore City Archives. Many of them are also on microfilm at MSA. The records are listed in detail in the following publication and the exact locations are given as of 1991. Up-to-date listings of the holdings of MSA, Baltimore City Archives, and FHL are to be found in those repositories.

_E. C. Papenfuse and others, A GUIDE TO GOVERNMENT RECORDS AT THE MSA, The Archives, Annapolis, MD, 1991.

The Baltimore city courts were constituted in 1851 when Baltimore City was made a separate governmental unit and after. As indicated in Chapter 1, they were the court of common pleas (1851–), superior court (1851–), criminal court (1851–), circuit court (1851–), city court (1867–), and 2nd circuit court (1888–). Their records are in the Baltimore City Archives, the Baltimore CH, and the MSA. The FHL (FHC) also has microfilms of many of them. The Annapolis Mayor's Court records and corporation proceedings (1720-2, 1753-1869) are in the MSA. Not to be overlooked is the following set of miscellaneous data:

_MISCELLANEOUS COURT RECORDS, 1729-1904, MSA, Annapolis, MD, with index. Many assorted records including county court data, bonds, depositions, manumissions, mortgages, naturalizations, and some others.

Also do not overlook:

_A. W. Burns, INDEX TO MD COLONIAL JUDGMENTS, The Author, Annapolis, MD, 1938 ff., 7 volumes. Use with care.

_G. E. Russell, COURT DEPOSITIONS AND AFFIDAVITS AS EVIDENCE OF AGE IN MD, 1637-57, in MD Magazine of Genealogy, Volume 2, No. 2, Fall, 1979.

The intermediate court records for MD counties and Baltimore City will be listed in detail in Chapter 4. The dates for which they are available and their locations will be given. It is always well to seek the case files when you are searching court records. These are folders, or envelopes, or packets which contain the many papers generated by a lawsuit or other court action. For early times, these have often been preserved, but after 1817 the laws regarding record keeping were relaxed, and fewer data were retained. Most of what is available is often described as original papers and will be located in the CH, although some are now in the MSA.

The lower courts of MD were justices of the peace courts (1635–), magistrates' courts, police magistrates' courts (1882–), city peoples' court (1912–), city traffic court (1918–), and trial magistrates' courts (1939–). The dockets of a number of Justices of the Peace are available at MSA: Allegany (1871-2), Anne Arundel (1833-1939), Baltimore City (1821-52), Baltimore (1815-1935), Calvert (1868-1933), Caroline (1813-1939), Dorchester (1859-64), Frederick (1814-20), Garrett (1872-73), Howard (1840-51, 1854-1938), Kent (1823-1922), Prince George's (1815-1939), Queen Anne's (1811-1939), St. Mary's (1816-1939), Talbot (1813-1915), Washington (1848-92), Worcester (1888-1900). Magistrates' records in the MSA include: Anne Arundel (1862-1962), Baltimore City (1867-1939), Baltimore (1873-1981), Calvert (1882-1931), Caroline (1837-38, 1819-1916), Frederick (1837-1948), Garrett (1872-1950), Howard (1859-1972), Kent (1836-38), Montgomery (1868-1966), Prince George's (1851-1977), Queen Anne's (1862-1908), Somerset (1838-1971), St. Mary's (1837-42, 1869-1952).

In considering court records pertaining to MD, the federal circuit and district courts should not be overlooked. They contain civil (law, equity, admiralty), criminal, bankruptcy, and naturalization materials. The records of the two courts are:

_National Archives, MINUTES OF THE US CIRCUIT COURT FOR MD, 1790–1911, Microfilm M931, The Archives, Washington, DC, 7 rolls.

_National Archives, CRIMINAL CASE FILES OF THE US CIRCUIT COURT FOR MD, 1795–1860, Microfilm M1010, The Archives, Washington, DC, 4 rolls.

_National Archives Philadelphia Branch RECORDS OF THE US CIRCUIT COURT OF MD, 1790–1911, The Branch, Philadelphia, PA.

_National Archives, ACT OF 1800 BANKRUPTCY CASE FILES OF THE US DISTRICT COURT OF MD, 1800–03, Microfilm M1031, The Archives, Washington, DC, 2 rolls.

_National Archives, INDEX TO NATURALIZATION PETITIONS FROM THE US CIRCUIT AND DISTRICT COURTS FOR MD, 1797–1956, Microfilm M1168, The Archives, Washington, DC, 25 rolls.

_National Archives, Philadelphia Branch, RECORDS OF THE US DISTRICT COURT OF MD, 1790–1966, The Branch, Philadelphia, PA.

There is an exceptionally useful set of volumes which indexes plaintiffs (those bringing suit) in MD appeal cases and in some other cases of notable legal interest, including cases in several of the above-listed courts. No MD researcher should fail to consult this resource in an ancestor quest:

_1906 DECENNIAL EDITION OF THE AMERICAN DIGEST: A COMPLETE TABLE OF AMERICAN CASES FROM 1658 TO 1906, West Publishing Co., St. Paul, MN, 1911, Volumes 21–25. Alphabetical by surname. Subsequent volumes cover decade periods up to the present.

Included in this massive index are MD Appeals cases from the Provincial Court (1658–74), the General Court (1780–1806), and the Court of Appeals (1788–).

Another volume which indexes MD cases from state and federal courts, the indexing being both by plaintiff and defendant, is:

_MD DIGEST TABLE OF CASES, INDEX TO CASES FROM STATE AND FEDERAL COURTS, 1658–, Volume 16, Supplement 16, West Publishing Co., St. Paul, MN, 1960/91.

Courts covered are US District and Circuit Courts, MD Provincial Court, MD General Court, MD Court of Appeals, and MD Chancery Court.

You must be sure to look up all your MD progenitors in these two very large indexes (1908 Decennial and MD Digest). They, along with the hundreds of volumes to which they refer, will be found in large law libraries. These can be most readily located in Colleges of Law at universities.

12. DAR records

The MD chapters of the Daughters of the American Revolution have done genealogists a helpful service by compiling and indexing a number of volumes (mostly typescript) of MD family history records. Included in these books are records of the following types: Bible, birth, cemetery, church, court, deed, land, marriage, obituary, newspaper, probate, death, tax, will/probate. These works will be found in the MHS, the DAR Library in Washington, DC, the FHL (FHC), and pertinent RL and LL. Many of the volumes are arranged by county.

_DAR Chapters of MD and DC, DAR COLLECTION FOR MD, numerous volumes, by different chapters, at several places in MD.

They are listed in detail in:

_National Society, DAR, DAR LIBRARY CATALOG, VOLUME TWO, STATE AND LOCAL HISTORIES AND RECORDS, The Society, Washington, DC, 1986.

They may also be located in the catalog at the MHS and in the FHL catalog. Every MD county is represented in the numerous volumes making up this collection. They can save you much time and effort, because they often contain otherwise unpublished indexes.

In addition to the above typescripts, there are some large compilations put together by the National DAR listing Revolutionary War ancestors and detailing lineages from present-day DAR members back to them. These may be accessed by looking in the following volumes, the references of which will lead you to the pertinent ancestors and/or lineages.

_DAR PATRIOT INDEX, The Society, Washington, DC, 1969-79, 2 volumes.

_DAR, INDEX TO THE ROLLS OF HONOR (ANCESTOR INDEX) IN THE LINEAGE BOOKS OF THE NATIONAL SOCIETY OF THE DAR, Genealogical Publishing Co., Baltimore, MD, 1980. Indexes 166 volumes of lineages published 1890-1921.

The DAR does not vouch for the accuracy of the materials in the above volumes (both MD and national), but they can be exceedingly valuable in leading you to original records.

13. Death records

In 1640, just 6 years after the initial settlement, the MD Assembly mandated the keeping of burial records. Because of non-compliance, erratic record keeping, and losses, very few early records survived. Those which are known to exist are all in the MSA: Charles County (1666-94), Kent County (1655-82, 1694-5), Somerset County (1663-95), and Talbot County (1669-70). In 1692, the Anglican (Episcopalian) Church was made the established church of MD, and the parishes were ordered to keep death records. The establishment remained in place until 1776. A number of these parish records have been preserved, and they were discussed in a previous section entitled Church records. During 1776-1865, very few governmental death records were kept, except for some that appear in land and other types of records (especially will and probate).

In 1865, MD passed a law mandating death recording by the counties, but only slightly more than half the counties complied, and even these kept erratic, incomplete, and/or discontinuous records. During this record period, 1865-98, the counties and dates of the records are as follows: Anne Arundel (1865-80), Caroline (1865-84), Carroll (1865-1902), Charles (1865-6), Dorchester (1864-7), Frederick (1865-81), Harford (1865-7), Kent (1865-71), Montgomery (1865-78), Prince George's (1865-6), Somerset (1865-77), Talbot (1865-71), Washington (1865-7), and Wicomico (1869). Most of these are in MSA; a few are in the county CH. These are indexed.

Baltimore City began recording deaths in 1875 and a state law required all deaths in the counties to be registered with the state from 1898 forward. The MD Division of Vital Records (PO Box 13146, Baltimore, MD 21203-3146) holds these records, and issues certified copies. However, genealogical researchers should request information from these death records from the MSA, which has microfilm copies and indexes.

There are several indexes and published death record compilations which are important to MD genealogical searchers:
_INDEX 31, DEATH RECORD INDEX, 1655-95, 1898-1930, incomplete, MSA, Annapolis, MD.
_INDEX TO ANNE ARUNDEL DEATHS, 1865-80, MSA, Annapolis, MD.
_MD DAR, MD DAUGHTERS OF THE AMERICAN REVOLUTION COLLECTION OF TYPESCRIPT VOLUMES, MD Chapters of the DAR, Baltimore, MD, various dates, numerous volumes. Arranged by county, most of them with a surname index, contain Bible, birth, cemetery, church, death, marriage, and will records.
_FHL CATALOG, LOCALITY SECTION, on microfiche and CD disk, FHL, Salt Lake City, UT, look under MD-Vital records, MD-[County]-Vital records, and MD-Baltimore (Independent City)-Vital records. Also available at every FHC.
_E. P. Passano, INDEX TO THE SOURCE RECORDS OF MD, Genealogical Publishing Co., Baltimore, MD, 1974, reprint of a 1940 volume. An older bibliography which lists many death records.
_A. W. Burns, MD RECORD OF DEATHS, 1718-77, The Author, Annapolis, MD, 1936. Use with care.
_R. F. Haynes, BALTIMORE CITY'S DEAD PRIOR TO 1806, in MD Historical and Genealogical Bulletin.

_H. Chance, WESTERN MD PIONEERS, LISTS OF MARRIAGES, BIRTHS, AND DEATHS OF 8000 EARLY SETTLERS, Library of the PA Historical Society, Philadelphia, PA, 1968.
_F. W. Wright, MD EASTERN SHORE RECORDS, 1648-1825, Family Line Publications, Silver Spring, MD, 1982-6, 5 volumes.
_C. Torrence, OLD SOMERSET ON THE EASTERN SHORE, Regional Publishing Co., Baltimore, MD, 1966.
Since MD is so short on death records before 1865, other types of records often have to be consulted. Among the better sources of death data are Bible, biography, cemetery, census, church, estate, genealogical periodicals, manuscripts, marriage, military, mortuary, newspaper, published genealogy, and will. All of these are treated in other sections of this chapter. When you are seeking death date and place information in archives and libraries, be certain to explore all the above-mentioned sources, and do not fail to look under the county listings and the following heading in library catalogs: Registers of births, etc. (Etc. includes deaths.)

14. Divorce records

Prior to the Revolutionary War, there were no divorces in MD. However, the Governor and his Council did grant some separations. From the end of the Revolution to 1842 divorce could be granted only by a special act of the Assembly. In 1842, the Chancery Court and the County (Circuit) Courts were given concurrent jurisdiction. Then, in 1851, the jurisdiction went completely to the County (Circuit) Courts. From 1851-1908, the counties kept the divorce records in with the equity records, but in 1908, it was ordered that separate divorce records be maintained. State-wide recording of divorces did not begin until 1961.

The divorces granted by the Assembly are given in the following indexed volume:
_M. K. Meyer, DIVORCES AND NAME CHANGES IN MD BY ACTS OF THE LEGISLATURE, 1634-1954, The Author, Pasadena, MD, 1970.
Divorces from 1842 to 1851-3 should be sought in records of both the County (Circuit) Courts and the Chancery Court, and from 1853 forward in the County (Circuit) Court records. The reason that 1851-3 is given instead of 1851 is that the Chancery Court went out slowly over these years. Beginning in 1908, the divorce data can be found in separate county record books. Many of the divorce records 1842-1961 remain in the counties, although some may be found at MSA.

15. Emigration and immigration records

The earliest settlers of MD were predominantly English, with a few Scots. Many came as indentured servants or convicts or refugees. They settled on land bordering the Chesapeake Bay and the Potomac River and rivers that fed them. About 1700, black slaves began being brought in from the Barbados, and soon thereafter Africa became the source of the rapidly increasing numbers. In the 1730s and 1740s English, Scots–Irish, and Scottish people began moving into western MD. They were joined by Rhineland Germans who came from PA and immigrated through Philadelphia and Baltimore. In 1755, French Acadians came to Baltimore when they were driven out of Nova Scotia. More French arrived in 1793 when they left Santo Domingo because of race riots. The 1790 census, according to some estimates, showed these percentages in MD: 52% English, 32% black, 7% Scottish, 6% German, 2% Irish, and 1% other. During the period 1820–50 sizable numbers of Germans and Irish came to MD, many of them remaining in urban areas, especially Baltimore. Irish immigration increased during 1846–50 because of the many fleeing from the great famine in Ireland. German immigration was increased in the 1850s as refugees from the failed German democratic revolution arrived. Numerous Germans kept coming through the early 1900s. In the 1890s, people from Eastern and Southern Europe began to arrive: Poles, Bohemians, Lithuanians, Greeks, Jews (Russia), Czechs, and Italians.

Migration out of MD followed two major routes. The first opened up about 1730 and led from western MD southwestwardly along the Shenandoah Valley of VA. Early on, the migrants settled in the Valley and turned back eastward into the back country of VA, NC, and SC. Later, during and after the Revolution, migrants began moving westward out of the Valley into KY and TN. The second route also opened up during and after the Revolution. It was the route from western MD westward on Braddock's Road to the Pittsburgh area, then down the OH River to KY and the southern sections of OH, IN, and IL.

There are a number of good volumes available which list immigrants to the areas that became the US. You should consult these volumes because they include both people who came directly to MD and people who came to some other colony or state and then to MD. The first set of volumes is an index to thousands of ship passenger lists in over 1400 sources and contains well over 1.7 million listings. These references have been abstracted from many published lists. Each listing gives the full known name of the immigrant, the names of accompanying relatives, ages, the date and port of arrival, and the source of the information. The books in this set are:

_P. W. Filby and M. K. Meyer, PASSENGER AND IMMIGRATION LISTS INDEX, Gale Research Co., Detroit, MI, 1981, with ANNUAL SUPPLEMENTS thereafter.

Do not fail to look for every possible immigrant ancestor of yours in this very large index, which is especially valuable for the period of time up to 1820. Also of importance for locating passengers or passenger lists are:

_P. W. Filby, PASSENGER AND IMMIGRATIONS LISTS BIBLIOGRAPHY, 1538-1900, Gale Research Company, Detroit, MI, 1981-4.

There are several other valuable passenger lists and finding aids for locating passenger lists which include some or many MD immigrants. These must not be overlooked. They include:

_US National Archives and Records Service, GUIDE TO GENEALOGICAL RESEARCH IN THE NATIONAL ARCHIVES, The Service, Washington, DC, 1982, pages 41-57.

_A. Eakle and J. Cerny, THE SOURCE, Ancestry Publishing Co., Salt Lake City, UT, 1984, pages 453-516.

_M. Tepper, AMERICAN PASSENGER ARRIVAL RECORDS, Genealogical Publishing Co., Baltimore, MD, 1988.

_US National Archives, IMMIGRANT AND PASSENGER ARRIVALS, A SELECT CATALOG OF NA MICROFILM PUBLICATIONS, National Archives, Washington, DC, 1983.

_C. W. Baird, HISTORY OF THE HUGUENOT EMIGRATION TO AMERICA, Genealogical Publishing Co., Baltimore, MD, 1973.

_V. R. Cameron, EMIGRANTS FROM SCOTLAND TO AMERICA, 1774-5, Genealogical Publishing Co., Baltimore, MD, 1959.

_P. W. Coldham, BONDED PASSENGERS TO AMERICA, 1663-75, Genealogical Publishing Co., Baltimore, MD, 1983.

_P. W. Coldham, CHILD APPRENTICES IN AMERICA FROM CHRIST'S HOSPITAL, LONDON, 1617-1778, Genealogical Publishing Co., Baltimore, MD, 1990.

_P. W. Coldham, ENGLISH ADVENTURERS AND EMIGRANTS, ABSTRACTS OF EXAMINATIONS IN THE HIGH COURT OF ADMIRALTY WITH REFERENCE TO COLONIAL AMERICA, 1609-1773, Genealogical Publishing Co., Baltimore, MD, 1984-5.

_P. W. Coldham, ENGLISH CONVICTS IN COLONIAL AMERICA, Genealogical Publishing Co., Baltimore, MD, 1982, 3 volumes.

_P. W. Coldham, ENGLISH ESTATES OF AMERICAN COLONISTS, AMERICAN WILLS AND ADMINISTRATIONS IN THE PREROGATIVE COURT OF CANTERBURY, 1610-1858, Genealogical Publishing Co., Baltimore, MD, 1980-1.

_P. W. Coldham, THE BRISTOL REGISTERS OF SERVANTS SENT TO FOREIGN PLANTATIONS, 1654-86, Genealogical Publishing Co., Baltimore, MD, 1983.

_P. W. Coldham, THE COMPLETE BOOK OF EMIGRANTS IN BONDAGE, 1614-1775, Genealogical Publishing Co., Baltimore, MD, 1988.

_P. W. Coldham, THE COMPLETE BOOK OF IMMIGRANTS, 1607-60, COMPILED FROM ENGLISH PUBLIC RECORDS, THOSE WHO TOOK SHIP FOR AMERICA, THOSE WHO WERE DEPORTED, AND THOSE WHO WERE SOLD TO LABOR, Genealogical Publishing Co., Baltimore, MD, 1987.

_R. J. Dickson, ULSTER IMMIGRATION TO COLONIAL AMERICA, 1718–75, Ulster-Scot Historical Foundation, Belfast, Ireland, 1976.

_D. Dobson, DIRECTORY OF SCOTTISH SETTLERS IN NORTH AMERICA, Genealogical Publishing Co., Baltimore, MD, 1984–6, 6 volumes.

_A. B. Faust, G. M. Brumbaugh, and L. Schelbert, LISTS OF SWISS EMIGRANTS IN THE EIGHTEENTH CENTURY TO THE AMERICAN COLONIES, 1706–95, Genealogical Publishing Co., Baltimore, MD, 1976.

_G. Fothergill, EMIGRANTS FROM ENGLAND, 1773–6, Genealogical Publishing Co., Baltimore, MD, 1964.

_E. French, LIST OF EMIGRANTS TO AMERICA FROM LIVERPOOL, 1697–1707, Genealogical Publishing Co., Baltimore, MD, 1962.

_M. Ghirelli, A LIST OF EMIGRANTS FROM ENGLAND TO AMERICA, 1682–92, Magna Carta Book Co., Baltimore, MD, 1968.

_M. S. Giuseppi, NATURALIZATIONS OF FOREIGN PROTESTANTS IN THE AMERICAN AND WEST INDIAN COLONIES, Genealogical Publishing Co., Baltimore, MD, 1964.

_I. A. Glazier and P. W. Filby, GERMANS TO AMERICA, LISTS OF PASSENGERS ARRIVING AT US PORTS, 1850–93, Scholarly Resources, Wilmington, DE, 1988, further volumes to follow.

_M. Hargreaves-Mawdsley, BRISTOL AND AMERICA, A RECORD OF THE FIRST SETTLERS IN THE COLONIES OF NORTH AMERICA, Genealogical Publishing Co., Baltimore, MD, 1970.

_D. A. Haury, INDEX TO MENNONITE IMMIGRANTS ON US PASSENGER LISTS, 1872–1904, Mennonite Library and Archives, North Newton, KS, 1986.

_J. and M. Kaminkow, A LIST OF EMIGRANTS FROM ENGLAND TO AMERICA, 1718–59, Magna Carta Book Co., Baltimore, MD, 1981.

_M. Kaminkow, PASSENGERS WHO ARRIVED IN THE US, September 1821–December 1823, Magna Carta Book Co., Baltimore, MD, 1969.

_D. L. Kent, BARBADOS AND AMERICA, The Author, Arlington, VA, 1980.

_B. Mitchell, IRISH PASSENGER LISTS, 1847–71, LISTS OF PASSENGERS SAILING FROM LONDONDERRY TO AMERICA ON SHIPS OF THE J. AND J. COOKE LINE AND THE McCORKELL LINE, Genealogical Publishing Co., Baltimore, MD, 1988.

_G. O. P. Nicholson and F. Sharpe, SOME EARLY EMIGRANTS TO AMERICA, Genealogical Publishing Co., Baltimore, MD, 1965. About 1000 MD indentured servants.

_N. W. Olsson, SWEDISH PASSENGER ARRIVALS IN US PORTS 1820–50 EXCEPT NY, North Central Publishing Co., St. Paul, MN, 1979.

_G. E. Reaman, THE TRAIL OF THE HUGUENOTS IN EUROPE, THE US, SOUTH AFRICA, AND CANADA, Genealogical Publishing Co., Baltimore, MD, 1972.

_T. Schenk, R. Froelke, and I. Bork, THE WUERTTEMBERG EMIGRATION INDEX, Ancestry, Salt Lake City, UT, 1986–, in progress, 8 volumes so far.

_D. M. Schlegel, PASSENGERS FROM IRELAND ARRIVING AT AMERICAN PORTS, 1811-7, Genealogical Publishing Co., Baltimore, MD, 1980.

_R. P. Swierenga, DUTCH IMMIGRANTS IN US SHIP PASSENGER MANIFESTS, 1820-80, Scholarly Resources, Wilmington, DE, 1983.

_US Department of State, PASSENGER ARRIVALS, 1819-20, IN THE US, Genealogical Publishing Co., Baltimore, MD, 1967.

_F. A. Virkus, IMMIGRANTS TO THE COLONIES BEFORE 1750, Genealogical Publishing Co., Baltimore, MD, 1965.

_J. Wareing, EMIGRANTS TO AMERICA, INDENTURED SERVANTS RECRUITED IN LONDON, 1718-33, Genealogical Publishing Co., Baltimore, MD, 1985.

_H. F. Waters, GENEALOGICAL GLEANINGS IN ENGLAND, Genealogical Publishing Co., Baltimore, MD, 1969.

Having explored the above records, especially the books by Filby and Meyer (PASSENGER AND IMMIGRATION LISTS INDEX), you can then look into some published materials dealing particularly with immigration to MD:

_E. P. Bentley, PASSENGER ARRIVALS AT THE PORT OF BALTIMORE, 1820-34, Genealogical Publishing Co., Baltimore, MD, 1982. About 50,000 names.

_P. W. Coldham, BONDED PASSENGERS TO AMERICA, 1663-1775, Genealogical Publishing Co., Baltimore, MD, 1983. Many MD indentured servants.

_COMMISSION BOOK 82, in MD Historical Magazine, Volumes 26-27, 1931-2. Many entries 1733-50, 1762-73.

_R. J. Cox, MD RUNAWAY CONVICT SERVANTS, 1745-80, National Genealogical Society Bulletin, Volume 68, No. 2, June 1980, and Volume 69, No. 4, December 1981.

_G. N. Mackenzie, IMMIGRANTS TO MD AND MA, Genealogical Publishing Co., Baltimore, MD, 1966.

_C. Mares, SHIP PASSENGER LISTS, PORT OF BALTIMORE, 1874, Eastern NE Genealogical Society, Fremont, NE, 1984. 7500 entries.

_D. W. Nead, THE PA GERMANS IN THE SETTLEMENT OF MD, Genealogical Publishing Co., Baltimore, MD, 1975.

_H. W. Newman, TO MD FROM OVERSEAS, JACOBITE LOYALISTS SOLD INTO WHITE SLAVERY IN MD, Genealogical Publishing Co., Baltimore, MD, 1985. About 1400 persons, 1634-1790.

_M. H. Pritchett and K. Wust, GERMAN IMMIGRANTS TO BALTIMORE, THE PASSENGER LIST OF 1854, The Report: A Journal of German-American History, Number 38, 1982. 5400 names, most from Bremen.

_G. E. Russell, NEW ENGLANDERS IN MD, in The Genealogist, Volume 2, No. 2, Fall 1981.

The above books (both general and specific for MD) are of a wide variety. Some give direct information on immigrants, others simply locate early settlers and thus indirectly indicate that immigration has taken place, still others make references to sources of immigration data. Many of the volumes have been indexed in Filby and Meyer's large compiled index, so you should use this index before going into the numerous volumes. Be sure that you examine all the supplements. Many of the works in the section on colonial records also carry direct or indirect immigration information, so they need to be carefully considered also. The books indicated above will be found in MHS, many of them in MSLL, FHL (FHC), and LGL, and some in RL and LL, especially the ones pertaining to their particular areas.

For the period of time after 1820, federal and city passenger lists are quite good. The most important of these are indexed, and both the indexes and the records have been microfilmed. The indexes are:

_National Archives, INDEX TO PASSENGER LISTS OF VESSELS ARRIVING AT BALTIMORE, 1820-97 (FEDERAL PASSENGER LISTS), Microfilm M327, The Archives, Washington, DC, 171 rolls.

_National Archives, INDEX TO PASSENGER LISTS OF VESSELS ARRIVING AT BALTIMORE, 1833-66 (CITY PASSENGER LISTS), Microfilm M326, The Archives, Washington, DC, 22 rolls.

_National Archives, A SUPPLEMENTAL INDEX TO PASSENGER LISTS OF VESSELS ARRIVING AT ATLANTIC AND GULF COAST PORTS (EXCLUDING NY), 1820-74, Microfilm M334, The Archives, Washington, DC, 188 rolls. Includes further Baltimore records, Annapolis (1849), and Havre de Grace (1820).

_National Archives, INDEX (SOUNDEX) TO PASSENGER LISTS OF VESSELS ARRIVING AT BALTIMORE, 1897-1952, Microfilm T520, The Archives, Washington, DC, 43 rolls.

The microfilmed lists to which these indexes refer are:

_National Archives, PASSENGER LISTS OF VESSELS ARIVING AT BALTIMORE, 1820-91, Microfilm M255, The Archives, Washington, DC, 50 rolls.

_National Archives, QUARTERLY ABSTRACTS OF PASSENGER LISTS OF VESSELS ARRIVING AT BALTIMORE, 1820-69, Microfilm M596, The Archives, Washington, DC, 6 rolls.

_National Archives, COPIES OF LISTS OF PASSENGERS ARRIVING AT MISCELLANEOUS PORTS ON THE ATLANTIC AND GULF COASTS AND AT PORTS ON THE GREAT LAKES, 1820-73, Microfilm M575, The Archives, Washington, DC, 16 rolls. Includes Baltimore, Annapolis (1849) and Havre de Grace (1820).

_National Archives, PASSENGER LISTS OF VESSELS ARRIVING AT BALTIMORE, 1891-1909, Microfilm T844, The Archives, Washington, DC, 77 rolls.

These microfilms (indexes and records) are available at the NA, NARB, MHS, MSA, and FHC, and they may be borrowed through FHC and from the AGLL. Your attention needs to be drawn also to two non-microfilm sources of MD immigration materials:

_Baltimore City Archives, CARD INDEX TO CITY LISTS OF PASSENGERS ARRIVING AT BALTIMORE, 1833-66, The Archives, Baltimore, MD.

_National Archives, TRANSCRIPTS OF PASSENGER LISTS OF VESSELS ARRIVING AT BALTIMORE, 1820, 1822-7, 1829, Record Group 36, 8 volumes, The Archives, Washington, DC. Not microfilmed, but partly indexed in M334.

Not only did people immigrate to MD, they, of course, emigrated from it, many going south, southwest, and west into neighboring states, and many going farther west and southwest. There are some published materials on this. It is possible that they might help you in your search for a migratory MD progenitor.

_R. W. Barnes, MD PIONEERS TO THE FRONTIERS, MD and DE Genealogist, Volume 18, 1977-9.

_T. J. O'Rourke, MD CATHOLICS ON THE FRONTIER, THE MO AND TX SETTLEMENTS, Brefney Press, Parsons, KS, 1980.

_J. B. C. Nicklin, LIST OF IMMIGRANTS BETWEEN VA AND MD IN THE 17TH CENTURY, in The William and Mary Quarterly, 2nd Series, Volume 18, page 440.

_EMIGRATION FROM MD TO WI, in WI Magazine of History, Volume 3, page 432.

_D. A. Avant, FL PIONEERS AND THEIR AL, GA, CAROLINA, MD, AND VA ANCESTORS, L'Avant Studios, Tallahassee, FL, 1974.

_MD MEN WHO SERVED IN THE OR VOLUNTEERS, MD Genealogical Society Bulletin, Volume 16, No. 2, page 107.

_EARLY SETTLERS OF WHATCOM, WA, FROM MD, The Bulletin of the Whatcom Genealogical Society, Volume 6, No. 3, March 1976, page 97.

_US Bureau of the Census, A CENTURY OF POPULATION GROWTH, 1790-1900, The Bureau, Washington, DC, 1909. Tables showing numbers of people in each state who were born in MD.

_J. D. B. DeBow, compiler, THE 7TH CENSUS OF THE US, 1850, EMBRACING A STATISTICAL VIEW OF EACH OF THE STATES AND TERRITORIES, US Bureau of the Census, Washington, DC, 1853. Information on MD natives who have moved to other states.

The last two references illustrate the value of census records, particularly those of 1850 and after, in tracing emigration patterns out of MD to other states. The same census records are equally valuable in discerning population movements into MD from other states and from overseas countries.

In your immigrant ancestor quest, do not forget to look into the catalogs of MHS, MSA, FHL (FHC), and LGL under the heading MA-Emigration and Immigration. Also be sure and seek emigration and immigration materials at the county and city levels. In addition, sometimes naturalization records carry passenger arrival data, so do not overlook this possibility.

16. Ethnic records

The early settlement and colonial history of MD were dominated by one ethnic group, namely the English. The next largest ethnic group was the black, then the Scottish, the German, and the Irish. Less than half a percent contribution was made by each of the French, the Dutch, and the Jewish. After the War of 1812, German and Irish immigration picked up considerably and remained sizable for the entire century. Appreciable numbers of people from eastern and southern Europe began arriving in MD after the Civil War, and the numbers rose at the turn and after the 20th century came in. These people were chiefly Polish, Italian, Czech, Jewish, and Lithuanian.

Two blacks were among the 1634 settlers of MD. By 1700, black slaves were quite numerous, most of them being laborers on the plantations. At the time of the Revolution, almost 32% of the population of MD was black. However, by 1860, the percentage had dropped, due to the depletion of the soil by tobacco farming. MD slaveowners began to free slaves long before the Civil War. And by 1860 13% of the people in MD were free blacks. However, there was strong discrimination practiced against them, and they were not afforded much actual freedom. After the Civil War, their lot did not improve greatly, with most of them working as common laborers, menial servants, or poor farmers. Segregation in practically every arena of societal and commercial life was practiced. This remained so until the civil rights changes in the post–World–War–II period.

The various ethnic groups of MD tended to each be largely affiliated with a particular religious persuasion. The English tended to be Episcopalian, with some Catholics in the early years. A goodly number were also Quaker. Many of these people turned Methodist later. Blacks tended to be Methodist and Baptist. Early Germans were Lutheran, Brethren, Dunkard, Moravian, and Reformed. Later Germans included numerous Catholics. The Scots-Irish and the Scots were mainly Presbyterian, and the Irish were usually Catholic.

Among the historical, reference, and source materials for blacks are the following volumes which will get you started if you have interest in this ethnic group:
_J. Brackett, THE NEGRO IN MD, Johns Hopkins Press, Baltimore, MD, 1889.
_A. K. Callum, FLOWER OF THE FOREST BLACK GENEALOGICAL JOURNAL, Baltimore, MD, Volume 2-, 1982-. Excellent on MD black genealogical research.
_P. Campbell, THE MD STATE COLONIZATION SOCIETY, 1831-57, University of IL Press, Urbana, IL, 1971. Blacks from MD who colonized Liberia and other African countries.

_B. S. Carothers, MD SLAVE OWNERS AND SUPERINTENDENTS, 1798, The Author, Lutherville, MD, 1974-5, 2 volumes.
_R. Cassimere, Jr., THE ORIGINS AND EARLY DEVELOPMENT OF SLAVERY IN MD, 1633-1715, PhD Thesis, Lehigh University, University Microfilms, Anne Arbor, MI, 1975.
_N. H. Clark, HISTORY OF THE 19TH CENTURY BLACK CHURCHES IN MD AND DC, Vantage Press, New York, NY, 1983.
_R. Clayton, SLAVEHOLDERS OF BALTIMORE, 1860, in MD Genealogical Society Bulletin, Volume 25, No. 1, Winter, 1984. About 1400 names.
_R. P. Fuke, THE BALTIMORE ASSOCIATION FOR THE MORAL AND EDUCATIONAL IMPROVEMENT OF THE COLORED PEOPLE, in MD Historical Magazine, Volume 66 (1971).
_L. Graham, BALTIMORE, THE 19TH CENTURY BLACK CAPITAL, University Press of America, Washington, DC, 1982.
_W. D. Hoyt, Jr., THE PAPERS OF THE MD STATE COLONIZATION SOCIETY, MD Historical Magazine, Volume 32 (1937), pages 247-71.
_P. R. Jacobsen, RESEARCHING BLACK FAMILIES AT THE HALL OF RECORDS, MSA, Annapolis, MD, 1984.
_C. Wagandt, THE MIGHTY REVOLUTION, NEGRO EMANCIPATION IN MD, 1862-4, Johns Hopkins Press, Baltimore, MD, 1964.
_J. M. Wright, THE FREE NEGRO IN MD, 1634-1860, Columbia University Press, New York, NY, 1921.

In a quest for a black ancestor, it is well to recognize that free blacks bought and sold and mortgaged land; were involved in civil, criminal, and equity court cases; were taxed, took out marriage licenses; and wrote wills and had estates probated. Slaves were personal property of their owners. As such, they were bought, sold, mortgaged, taxed, and distributed to heirs in estate settlements. In 1752, a manumission law was passed, and the action was increasingly taken after that. In 1805, a law providing for the issuance of certificates of freedom was passed. Later, owners who brought slaves into MD were required to declare them, and free blacks needed to obtain a permit to leave MD temporarily. All of these records will be found among the county records (originals at CH or MSA, copies of many at MSA and FHL).

A number of helpful works relating to the German ethnic communities of MD are:

_D. Cunz, THE MD GERMANS, A HISTORY, Kennikat Press, Port Washington, NY, 1972.
_L. P. Henninghausen, HISTORY OF THE GERMAN SOCIETY OF MD, The Society, Baltimore, MD, 1909.
_A. F. Johnson, KINFOLK IN GERMAN-KINFOLK IN MD, The Author, Columbus, OH, 1983. Early settlements.
_D. W. Nead, THE PA GERMAN IN THE SETTLEMENT OF MD, Genealogical Publishing Co., Baltimore, MD, 1980. War and tax lists.

_E. T. Schultz, FIRST SETTLEMENT OF GERMANS IN MD, Ephra, Miami, FL, 1976. Many names.
_Society for the History of Germans in MD, ANNUAL REPORT, The Society, Baltimore, MD, 1887–1966, 32 volumes.
_Society for the Preservation of the History of Germans in MD,THE REPORT, A JOURNAL OF GERMAN-AMERICAN HISTORY, Continuation of the Annual Reports, The Society, Baltimore, MD, 1968, Volumes 33–.
_J. A. Weishaar, THE GERMAN ELEMENT IN MD UP TO 1700, Society for History of Germans in MD, Baltimore, MD, 1901.

Other ethnic groups are represented in the following very useful reference works:
_(Czech) E. Slezak, CZECHS IN MD BEFORE 1900, in MD Genealogical Society Bulletin, Volume 21, No. 1, Winter, 1980.
_(French) G. A. Wood, THE FRENCH PRESENCE IN MD, 1524–1800, Gateway Press, Baltimore, MD, 1978.
_(Jews) J. M. Fein, THE MAKING OF AN AMERICAN JEWISH COMMUNITY, THE HISTORY OF BALTIMORE JEWRY FROM 1773 TO 1920, Jewish Publication Society of America, Philadelphia, PA, 1971.
_(Jews) GENERATIONS, Jewish Historical Society of MD, Baltimore, MD, a journal published 1978–.
_(Jews) JEWS OF BALTIMORE TO 1830, American Jewish Historical Quarterly, Volumes 64 and 67.
_(Jews) I. Rosenwaike, THE JEWS OF BALTIMORE, in American Jewish Quarterly, Volume 64, No. 4, June 1975; Volume 67, No. 2, December 1977; Volume 67, No. 3, March 1978.
_(Native Americans) H. R. Manakee, INDIANS OF EARLY MD, MD Historical Society, Baltimore, MD, 1959.
_(Native Americans) J. A. McAllister, INDIAN LANDS IN DORCHESTER COUNTY, MD, SELECTED SOURCES, 1669–1870, The Author, Cambridge, MA, 1962.
_(Native Americans) F. W. Porter, III, MD INDIANS, YESTERDAY AND TODAY, MD Historical Society, Baltimore, MD, 1983.

The best places to find MD ethnic materials are in the MSA and the MHS. The FHL (FHC) has some. However, in no case should the holdings of RL and LL be overlooked since some ethnic groups tended to concentrate in certain areas of the state. The sources listed in the sections on church records and manuscripts are often closely related to ethnic records. So do not forget them.

---

17. Gazetteers, atlases, and maps

Detailed information regarding MD geography is exceptionally useful to the genealogical searcher, especially with regard to land records, migration routes, and settlement patterns. Land records usually mention locations in terms requiring an understanding of local geographical features. And migration routes and settlement patterns are largely governed by the lay and type of the land. Several sorts of geographical aids are valuable in this regard: gazetteers, atlases, and maps. Gazetteers are volumes which list geographical features (towns, villages, crossroads, settlements, districts, rivers, streams, creeks, hills, mountains, valleys, ridges, coves, lakes, ponds), locate them, and sometimes give a few details concerning them. An atlas is a collection of maps in book form. Among the better gazetteer-type materials for MD are:

_R. S. Fisher, GAZETTEER OF THE STATE OF MD, Colton, New York, NY, 1852.

_MD State Planning Commission, GAZETTEER OF MD, Johns Hopkins Univ. Press, Baltimore, MD, 1941.

_US Board on Geographic Names, GEOGRAPHIC NAMES ALPHABETICAL FINDING LIST, US Geological Survey, Washington, DC, 1982.

_H. Kenny, PLACE NAMES OF MD, THEIR ORIGINS AND MEANING, MD Historical Society, Baltimore, MD, 1984.

_M. J. Kaminkow, MD FROM A TO Z, A TOPOGRAPHICAL DICTIONARY, Magna Carta Book Co., Baltimore, MD, 1985.

The above gazetteers may be found in MHS, MSA, MSLL, Enoch Pratt Free Library (Baltimore), Johns Hopkins University Library (Baltimore), University of MD Library (College Park), some RL, and some LL.

Atlases (collections of maps) published before 1906 (the time in which most researchers are interested) are available for the state of MD, for its counties, and for Baltimore. Some of the atlases have maps which give names of landowners and some give various businesses. Listings of the numerous available atlases for MD are in:

_C. E. LeGear, US ATLASES, Library of Congress, Washington, DC, 1950/3, 2 volumes.

Among the more important state atlases and other geographical works carrying MD maps are these volumes:

_W. H. Bayliff, MD-PA AND MD-DE BOUNDARIES, MD Board of Natural Resources, Annapolis, MD, 1939.

_M. R. Brown, AN ILLUSTRATED GENEALOGY OF THE COUNTIES OF MD AND THE DC, French-Bray, Baltimore, MD, 1967. Maps of county changes and 1850/60/70/80 Baltimore ward maps.

_S. J. Martinet, MARTINET'S MAPS OF MD, The Compiler, Baltimore, MD, 1866.

_S. J. Martinet, NEW TOPOGRAPHICAL ATLAS OF THE STATE OF MD AND THE DC, The Author, Baltimore, MD, 1872.

_E. B. Mathews, MAPS AND MAP-MAKERS OF MD, In MD Genealogical Survey, Baltimore, MD, Volume 2, 1898.

_R. Morrison and others, ON THE MAP, Washington College, Chestertown, MD, 1983. Early MD maps.

_E. C. Papenfuse and J. M. Coale, III, THE HAMMOND-HARWOOD HOUSE ATLAS OF HISTORICAL MAPS OF MD, 1608-1908, Johns Hopkins Press, Baltimore, MD, 1982.

_Wicomico Bicentennial Commission, THE 1877 ATLASES AND OTHER EARLY MAPS OF THE EASTERN SHORE OF MD, The Commission, Salisbury, MD, 1976. Shows property owners.

_W. Thorndale and W. Dollarhide, MAP GUIDE TO THE US FEDERAL CEN-SUSES, 1790-1920, American Genealogical Lending Library, Bounti-ful, UT, 1986.

Atlases (with dates in parentheses) exist for MD counties as follows: Alle-gany (1900), Anne Arundel (1878), Baltimore (1877/98), Carroll (1877), Cecil (1877), Dorchester (1877), Frederick (1873), Howard (1878), Kent (1877), Montgomery (1879), Prince George's (1878), Queen Anne's (1877), Somerset (1877), Talbot (1877), Washington (1877), Wicomico (1877), and Worcester (1877). Pre-1900 atlases for Baltimore City are available for 1876-7, 1885-6, 1889, 1896, and 1897. The atlases mentioned here and most of the others listed in the book by LeGear may be found in the same repositories referred to at the end of the previous para-graph.

Many maps are available for MD, its counties, its cities, and its towns. There are several books which either list MD maps and give sources of them or give descriptions of good map collections:

_National Archives and Records Service, GUIDE TO CARTOGRAPHIC RE-CORDS IN THE NATIONAL ARCHIVES, The Service, Washington, DC, 1971.

_D. A. Cobb, GUIDE TO US MAP RESOURCES, American Library Associa-tion, Chicago, IL, 1986.

_US Geological Survey, INDEX TO MAPS OF MD, DE, AND DC, Government Printing Office, Washington, DC, 1963.

_National Archives and Records Service, GUIDE TO GENEALOGICAL RE-SEARCH IN THE NATIONAL ARCHIVES, The Service, Washington, DC, 1982, pages 255-62.

_American Geographic Society, INDEX TO MAPS IN BOOKS AND PERI-ODICALS, G. K. Hall, Boston, MA, 1968, 10 volumes, with SUPPLE-MENTS.

_D. K. Carrington and R. W. Stephenson, MAP COLLECTIONS IN THE US AND CANADA, A DIRECTORY, Special Libraries Assn., New York, NY, 1978.

_J. C. Wheat, MAPS AND CHARTS PUBLISHED IN AMERICA BEFORE 1800, Yale Univ. Press, New Haven, CT, 1969.

_J. R. Hebert, PANORAMIC MAPS OF ANGLO-AMERICAN CITIES IN THE LIBRARY OF CONGRESS, The Library, Washington, DC, 1984. Beauti-ful pre-1900 maps available for MD cities and towns.

_R. W. Stephenson, LAND OWNERSHIP MAPS IN THE LIBRARY OF CON-GRESS, The Library, Washington, DC, 1967. Maps which show landowners for these MD counties: Anne Arundel (1650, 1649–65, 1860), Baltimore (1639–1705, 1850, 1857, 1863), Caroline (1875), Carroll (1862, 1863), Cecil (1858), Frederick and Washington (1808), Frederick (1858, 1860), Harford (1858, 1878), Howard (1860), Kent (1860), Montgomery (1863, 1865), Prince George's (about 1696, 1860, 1861), Talbot (1858), Washington (1859), Worcester (about 1800).

_Library of Congress, FIRE INSURANCE MAPS IN THE LIBRARY OF CONGRESS, The Library, Washington, DC, 1981. Maps of cities and towns 1884–, much detail.

_M. H. Shelley, WARD MAPS OF US CITIES, Library of Congress, Washington, DC, 1975. Ward maps also appear in many city directories.

Your attention needs to be drawn to several specialized types of maps which can assist you as you attempt to locate your progenitor's land holdings and as you look for streams, roads, bridges, churches, cemeteries, and villages in the vicinity. The first of these are highly detailed maps issued by the US Geological Survey which has mapped the entire state of MD, and has produced a series of numerous maps, each covering a very small area. These maps are available at very reasonable cost. Write the following address and ask for the Catalog of and Index to Topographic Maps of MD, DE, and DC and a MO–DE–DC Map Order Form.

_Distribution Branch, US Geological Survey, PO Box 25286, Denver Federal Center, Denver, CO 80225.

These maps have been issued in several editions since about 1884. Older ones often show things which are not in more recent ones. The older maps can be located in the repositories mentioned at the end of the first paragraph. A second type of map which is very useful are the landowner maps which show the names of the persons who own each piece of property. These are available as separate maps and some of them are also often in atlases (see the book by Stephenson above). A third type of map is represented by the city panorama maps which are careful depictions of cities as they would be viewed from a balloon flying overhead (see book by Hebert above). The fourth special type of maps are detailed city maps which were drawn for fire insurance purposes (see book by Library of Congress above). A fifth category of map is made up of those which have marked the ward boundaries of larger cities. Such maps are useful when you want to search unindexed census records for city dwellers, especially when they are employed with city directories (which give street addresses, and also sometimes contain ward maps or give ward boundaries). A sixth category consists of county maps which can be obtained from the MD Geological Survey. (2300 St. Paul Street, Baltimore, MD 21218), or which have been published as collections:

_C. D. Hevenor, THE HEVENOR BOOK OF COUNTY MAPS OF MD, Hevenor Co., Buffalo, NY, 1931.

_MD State Roads Commission, COUNTY MAPS SHOWING IMPROVED ROADS, The Commission, Baltimore, MD, 1933.

Finally, a <u>seventh</u> group of excellent recent county atlases is available from:
_ADC, 6440 General Green Way, Alexandria, VA 22312.

The best collections of genealogically-related maps and atlases of MD are in MSA, MHS, Enoch Pratt Free Library (Baltimore), Johns Hopkins University Library (Baltimore), and the University of MD Library (College Park). Other good collections are found in NA and the Library of Congress, as well as RL and LL in the areas where you are interested. When you seek gazetteers, atlases, and maps in these repositories, please be sure to look both in the main catalogs and the special map catalogs, indexes, listings, inventories, and collections. Most of the volumes mentioned in this section are available in MHS, Enoch Pratt Free Library, Johns Hopkins University Library, and University of MD Library, and some will be found in MSLL, FHL (FHC), LGL, RL, and LL.

18. Genealogical indexes and compilations

There are a number of indexes and compilations for the thirteen colonies and for all the states which list large numbers of MD names. These are of considerably utility because they may save you going through many small volumes and detailed records, especially in the early stages of your search for MD ancestors. The nation-wide indexes and compilations of this sort include:
_SURNAME CATALOG, INTERNATIONAL GENEALOGICAL INDEX, FAMILY REGISTRY, and ANCESTRAL FILE at FHL, Salt Lake City, UT, also available at every FHC. [See section on FHL and FHC in Chapter 3.] Over 160 million entries.
_FAMILY GROUP RECORDS COLLECTION, FHL, Salt Lake City, UT, access through FHC. [Be sure to search both the Patron and the Archives Sections of the Family Group Records Collection.] Over 9 million entries.
_National Archives, GENERAL INDEX TO COMPILED MILITARY SERVICE RECORDS OF REVOLUTIONARY WAR SOLDIERS, SAILORS, AND MEMBERS OF ARMY STAFF DEPARTMENTS, The Archives, Washington, DC, Microfilm M860, 58 rolls.
_F. Rider, AMERICAN GENEALOGICAL-BIOGRAPHICAL INDEX, Godfrey Memorial Library, Middletown, CT, 1942-, over 180 volumes. Over 12 million entries. Be sure to check both series.
_P. W. Filby and M. K. Meyer, PASSENGER AND IMMIGRATION LISTS INDEX, Gale Research Co., Detroit, MI, 1981-, 3 basic volumes plus annual supplements. Over a million entries.
_M. J. Kaminkow, GENEALOGIES IN THE LIBRARY OF CONGRESS, Magna Carta, Baltimore, MD, 1972-7, 3 volumes, plus A COMPLEMENT TO GENEALOGIES IN THE LIBRARY OF CONGRESS, Magna Carta, Baltimore, MD, 1981. Over 50,000 names.

_New York Public Library, DICTIONARY CATALOG OF THE LOCAL HISTO-
RY AND GENEALOGY DIVISION, New York Public Library, G. K. Hall,
Boston, MA, 1974.
_Library of Congress, NATIONAL UNION CATALOG OF MANUSCRIPT
COLLECTIONS, The Library, Washington, DC, annual volumes since
1959, index in each volume.
_National Society of the DAR, LIBRARY CATALOG, VOLUME 1: FAMILY
HISTORIES AND GENEALOGIES, The Society, Washington, DC, 1982.
_Newberry Library, GENEALOGICAL INDEX OF THE NEWBERRY LIBRARY,
G. K. Hall, Boston, MA, 1960, 4 volumes.
_Everton Publishers, COMPUTERIZED ROOTS CELLAR and COMPUTER-
IZED FAMILY FILE, The Publishers, Logan, UT.
_J. Munsell's Sons, INDEX TO AMERICAN GENEALOGIES, 1711-1908,
Genealogical Publishing Co., Baltimore, MD, 1967. 60,000 referenc-
es.

In addition to the above nation-wide indexes and compilations, there
are a sizable number of large indexes and compilations dealing exclusively
with MD. Among the most notable of these are:
_INDEXES TO THE FEDERAL MD CENSUS SCHEDULES OF 1790, 1800/
10/20/30/40/50/60, 1880, 1900. See census section in this chap-
ter.
_CARD, COMPUTER, AND PRINTED CATALOGS, SPECIAL INDEXES, AND
LISTS IN MHS, MSA, RL, and LL. See details in Chapter 3.
_National Archives, MICROFILM INDEXES OF COMPILED SERVICE RE-
CORDS FOR MD SOLDIERS: (1) IN THE REVOLUTIONARY WAR, Micro-
film Publication M860, 58 rolls, (2) IN THE WAR OF 1812, Microfilm
Publication M602, 238 rolls, (3) ON THE UNION SIDE IN THE CIVIL
WAR, Microfilm Publication M388, 13 rolls, (4) ON THE CONFEDERATE
SIDE IN THE CIVIL WAR, Microfilm Publication M253, 535 rolls, all Na-
tional Archives, Washington, DC.
_LARGE GENEALOGICAL COMPILATIONS AND INDEXES: DAR Collection
of Transcribed records (100s of thousands of names), Holdcraft Col-
lection available at FHL (FHC) (over 230,000 items), Dielman-Hayward
File at MHS (over 240,000 items), Genealogical File Folders at MHS,
WPA-HRS Index of Baltimore 1756-1938 (over 220,000 names) at
BCA AND MSA, Land Patent Index 1634- in MSA, Harris Church Regis-
ter Index at MHS, Wilkins File Index to histories in MHS.
_E. P. Passano, AN INDEX TO THE SOURCE RECORDS OF MD, GENEA-
LOGICAL, BIOGRAPHICAL, HISTORICAL, The Author, Baltimore, MD,
1940.
_MD GENEALOGIES, A CONSOLIDATION OF ARTICLES FROM THE MD
HISTORICAL MAGAZINE, Genealogical Publishing Co., Baltimore, MD,
1980, 3 volumes.

_G. M. Brumbaugh, MD RECORDS, COLONIAL, REVOLUTIONARY, COUNTY, AND CHURCH, FROM ORIGINAL SOURCES, Lancaster, Press, Lancaster, PA, 1928.

_D. O. Virdin and R. B. Clark, Jr., MD FAMILY GENEALOGIES AND HISTORIES, Clark, St. Michaels, MD, 1984.

_National Archives, INDEXES TO PASSENGER LISTS OF VESSELS ARRIVING AT BALTIMORE, FEDERAL PASSENGER LISTS 1820-97, Microfilm M327, 171 rolls, CITY PASSENGER LISTS 1833-66, Microfilm M326, 22 rolls, The Archives, Washington, DC.

_National Archives, INDEX (SOUNDEX) TO PASSENGER LISTS OF VESSELS ARRIVING AT BALTIMORE, 1897-1952, Microfilm T520, The Archives, Washington, DC, 43 rolls.

_R. W. Barnes, MD MARRIAGES, 1634-1800, Genealogical Publishing Co., Baltimore, MD, 1975/8, 2 volumes.

_BALTIMORE CITY DIRECTORIES, 1752-1901, Research Publications, New Haven, CT.

_P. W. Coldham, BONDED PASSENGERS TO AMERICA, 1663-1775, Genealogical Publishing Co., Baltimore, MD, 1983, 3 volumes. MD indentured servants.

_G. Skordas, EARLY SETTLERS OF MD: AN INDEX TO NAMES OF IMMIGRANTS COMPILED FROM RECORDS OF LAND PATENTS, 1633-80, Genealogical Publishing Co., Baltimore, MD, 1968.

_J. M. Magruder, Jr., INDEX OF MD COLONIAL WILLS, 1635-1777, Genealogical Publishing Co., Baltimore, MD, 1967.

_INDEXES to ARCHIVES OF MD, MHS, Baltimore, MD, 1883-1972, 72 volumes.

_A. W. Burns, MD MARRIAGE RECORDS, The Compiler, Baltimore, MD, 1937 ff., 39 volumes. Use with care.

_F. E. Wright, MD EASTERN SHORE VITAL RECORDS, 1648-1825, Family Line Publications, Silver Spring, MD, 1982-9, 5 volumes.

_REGISTER OF PROVINCIAL FAMILIES, George Peabody Library, Baltimore, MD. A registry of colonial families.

_A. N. Parran, REGISTER OF MD'S HERALDIC FAMILIES, 1634-1935, Roebuch and Sons, Baltimore, MD, 1935.

_PIONEER INDEX, MD Genealogical Society, Baltimore, MD. Card index of early inhabitants of MD.

_H. W. Newman, HERALDIC MARYLANDIA, MD FAMILIES WHICH USED COATS OF ARMS IN THE COLONIAL AND EARLY POST-REVOLUTIONARY RECORDS, The Author, Annapolis, MD, 1968.

_MD Genealogical Society, INDEX FOR THE MD GENEALOGICAL SOCIETY BULLETIN, VOLS. 1-10, 12-13, The Society, Baltimore, MD.

_LOCATOR FILE, MHS, Baltimore, MD. Card index to families being researched.

_M. Ljungstedt, THE COUNTY COURT NOTEBOOK AND ANCESTRAL PROOFS AND PROBABILITIES, Genealogical Publishing Co., Baltimore, MD, 1972.

_E. K. Kirkham, AN INDEX TO SOME OF THE FAMILY RECORDS OF THE SOUTHERN STATES, Everton Publishers, Logan, UT, 1979.

_E. A. Kanely, BALTIMORE AND OHIO RAILROAD EMPLOYEES, 1842/ 52/55/57, The Author, Baltimore, MD, 1982. About 9700 listings.

_GENEALOGICAL MATERIALS FILING CASES, alphabetical, MSA, Baltimore, MD. Manuscript data on many families.

_M. Crowe, DESCENDANTS FROM FIRST FAMILIES OF VA AND MD, The Author, Washington, DC, 1980.

_R. J. Cox, EARLY (18TH CENTURY) RESIDENTS OF BALTIMORE, National Genealogical Society Quarterly, Volume 67, Nos. 3-4, 1979; MD Genealogical Society Bulletin, Volume 22, No. 3, 1981.

_J. B. Cotton and R. B. Henry, MD CALENDAR OF WILLS, 1635-1743, Genealogical Publishing Co., Baltimore, MD, 1968, 8 volumes.

_R. B. Clark, Jr., and D. O. Pinder, MD GENEALOGIES, The Authors, St. Michaels, MD, 1984.

_A. W. Burns, MD GENEALOGIES AND HISTORICAL RECORDER, The Author, Washington, DC, 1941-2, 3 volumes. Use with care.

_H. C. Bromwell, OLD MD FAMILIES, Genealogical Publishing Co., Baltimore, MD, 1962.

_R. W. Barnes, BALTIMORE COUNTY FAMILIES, 1659-1759, Genealogical Publishing Co., Baltimore, MD, 1989.

Most of the published works mentioned above are available in MHS, with many being found in FHL (FHC), MSLL, LGL, and RL, and some in LL. The microfilms should be sought in MSA, MHS, FHL (FHC), NA, and NARB. The above references are by no means all of the large indexes and compilations of genealogical materials for MD. They represent only a selection of some of the major ones. Numerous others are listed in other sections of this chapter.

19. Genealogical periodicals

Several genealogical periodicals and some historical periodicals carrying genealogical data and/or aids have been or are being published for MD. These journals, serial publications, and newsletters contain genealogies, local history information, genealogical records, family queries and answers, book reviews, research aids and methodology, and other pertinent information. If you have a MD progenitor, you will find it of great value to subscribe to one or more of the state-wide periodicals, as well as any periodicals published in the region, county, or city where he/she lived. Periodicals pertinent to MD research may be divided into two classes: (1) those that have state-wide coverage, and (2) those that have regional or local coverage.

Chief among the periodicals which have a state-wide coverage of MD are the following:

_MD HISTORICAL MAGAZINE, published by the MD Historical Society, 201 West Monument St., Baltimore, MD 21201, 1906–, Volume 1–. Genealogical data published chiefly in earlier issues. MSA has card index for 1906–60. Much of the genealogical material is abstracted and reprinted in MD GENEALOGIES, A CONSOLIDATION OF ARTICLES FROM THE MD HISTORICAL MAGAZINE, Genealogical Publishing Co., Baltimore, MD, 1980. The MHS also publishes NEWS AND NOTES OF MHS.

_MD MAGAZINE OF GENEALOGY, published by the MD Historical Society, 201 West Monument St., Baltimore, MD 21201, 1978–, Volume 1–.

_MD GENEALOGICAL SOCIETY BULLETIN, published by the Society, 201 West Monument St., Baltimore, MD 21201, 1961–. Also publishes MGS NEWSLETTER.

_THE MD AND DE GENEALOGIST, published by R. B. Clark, Jr., PO Box 352, St. Michaels, MD 21663, 1959–, Volume 1–.

_MD HISTORICAL AND GENEALOGICAL BULLETIN, published by R. F. Hayes, Jr., Baltimore, MD, 1930–50, Volumes 1–21.

_MD ORIGINAL RESEARCH SOCIETY OF BALTIMORE BULLETINS, 1906–13, Genealogical Publishing Co., Baltimore, MD, 1979. Especially good for the Eastern Shore.

_MARYLAND QUERIES, published by Sims Publishing, PO Box 9576, Sacramento, CA 95823.

_GENERATIONS, Published by Jewish Historical Society of MD, 15 Lloyd St., Baltimore, MD 21202, 1978–, Volumes 1–.

_ROOTBOUND, published by Family Historians, Box 25 CWF, 9800 Savage Rd., Fort George G. Mead, MD 20755.

Among the very useful regional and local periodicals of MD are these listed below:

_(Allegany County) OLD PIKE POST, quarterly, published by Allegany County Genealogical Society, PO Box 3103, La Vale, MD 21504.

_(Anne Arundel County) ANNE ARUNDEL SPEAKS, quarterly published by Anne Arundel Genealogical Society, PO box 221, Pasadena, MD 21122.

_(Baltimore County) THE NOTEBOOK, quarterly, published by the Baltimore County Genealogical Society, PO Box 10085, Towson, MD 21204.

_(Calvert County) CALVERT COUNTY GENEALOGICAL NEWSLETTER, edited by J. and M. O'Brien, PO Box 9, Sunderland, MD 20689.

_(Carroll County) THE CARROLLTONIAN, quarterly, published by the Carroll County Genealogical Society, 50 East Main St., Westminster, MD 21157.

_(Cecil County) NEWSLETTER OF THE CECIL COUNTY GENEALOGICAL SOCIETY, quarterly, published by the Society, PO Box 11, Charlestown, MD 21814.

_(Dorchester County) DORCHESTER COUNTY GENEALOGICAL MAGAZINE, six issues per year, published by the Dorchester County Historical Society, 1058 Taylorsville Island Road, Cambridge, MD 21613.

_(Harford County) NEWSLETTER, six issues per year, published by the Harford County Genealogical Society, PO Box 15, Aberdeen, MD 21001.

_Heritage Genealogical Society, TAPROOTS, quarterly, published by the Society, PO Box 113, Lineboro, MD 21088.

_(Howard County) THE FAMILY TREE, ten issues per year, published by the Howard County Genealogical Society, PO Box 274, Columbia, MD 21045.

_Lower Delmarva Genealogical Society, MORE FROM THE SHORE, two issues per year, published by the Society, PO Box 3602, Salisbury, MD 21801. Interested in all Eastern Shore counties.

_(Montgomery County) LINE UPON LINE, ten issues per year, published by the Genealogical Club of the Montgomery County Genealogical Society, 103 West Montgomery Avenue, Rockville, MD 20850.

_(Prince George's County) PRINCE GEORGE'S COUNTY GENEALOGICAL SOCIETY BULLETIN, ten issues per year, published by the Society, PO Box 819, Bowie, MD, 20715.

_(St. Mary's County) THE GENERATOR, ten issues per year, published by the St. Mary's County Genealogical Society, General Delivery, Callaway, MD 20620.

_(Somerset County) OLD SOMERSET, edited and published by R. C. Pollitt, PO Box 308, Prince George, VA 23875. Somerset and counties derived from it.

_Upper Shore Genealogical Society of MD, CHESAPEAKE COUSINS, two issues per year, published by the Society, PO Box 275, Easton, MD 21601.

_WESTERN MD GENEALOGY, quarterly, edited by D. V. Russell, published by Catoctin Press, 709 East Main Street, Middletown, MD 21769. Covers Allegany, Carroll, Frederick, Garrett, Montgomery, and Washington Counties.

A useful reference source to periodicals which are held in fifty major MD libraries is:

_J. South, TITLE HOLDINGS OF PERIODICALS IN MD PUBLIC AND ACADEMIC LIBRARIES, MD Interlibrary Organization, Baltimore, MD, 1977.

Good collections of MD genealogical periodicals will be found in MHS and MSLL, some of the above periodicals are in FHL (FHC) and LGL, and those relating to specific localities can be found in appropriate RL and LL.

Not only do articles pertaining to MD genealogy appear in the above publications, they are also printed in other genealogical journals. Fortunately, indexes to articles in major genealogical periodicals are available. However, most of these indexes do not include all names, so it is generally necessary to consult the more-detailed indexes usually carried in each volume of each periodical. Further, the locality (county, city) should be looked up in all indexes, and every article mentioned under the listing should be checked.

_For periodicals published 1858–1953, consult D. L. Jacobus and C. Boyer, 3rd, INDEX TO GENEALOGICAL PERIODICALS, 1858–1953, Boyer, Newhall, CA, 1983. Lists only major names.

_For periodicals published 1962–9 and 1974–present, consult the annual volumes by various editors (E. S. Rogers, G. E. Russell, L. C. Towle, C. M. Mayhew), GENEALOGICAL PERIODICAL ANNUAL INDEX, various publishers, most recently Heritage Books, Bowie, MD, 1962–9, 1974–present.

_For periodicals published 1847–present, see M. B. Clegg and C. B. Witcher, PERIODICAL SOURCE INDEX, ACPL Foundation, PERSI Project, Ft. Wayne, IN. First 16 volumes cover 1947–1985, then annual volumes covering 1986–present. Volumes contain five sections: US places, Canadian places, foreign places, methodology articles, family names alphabetically arranged.

These index volumes should be sought in MHS, MSLL, and FHL (FHC). Most LGL, some RL, and a few LL also have them. In these indexes, you ought to consult all general MD listings, then all listings under the counties, cities, and towns which concern you, as well as listings under family names, if such are included. It is well also to remember that the surname listings are not complete; the surname indexes are not every–name indexes. In most instances, only the major surnames in various articles have been included.

20. Genealogical and historical societies

In the state of MD various societies for the study of genealogy, the discovery of hereditary lineages, the accumulation of ancestral data, and the publication of the materials have been organized. In addition to these genealogical societies, there are some historical societies which devote at least some time and effort to collection and publication of data which are useful to genealogists. Of course, there are some historical societies which have little or no genealogical interest. You should further recognize that some societies which once made notable genealogical and historical contributions no longer exist, and that smaller societies tend to come and go. The MD societies which have a genealogical focus are largely of two types: (1) state–wide or even wider, (2) local societies (regional, county, city).

The major societies in MD which have a state–wide or wider coverage are as follows:

_Family Historians, PO Box 215 CWF, 9800 Savage Road, Fort George E. Meade, MD 20755.

_Genealogical Council of MD, PO Box 274, Columbia, MD 21045.

_Heritage Genealogical Society, PO Box 113, Lineboro, MD 21088.

_Jewish Historical Society of MD, 15 Lloyd Street, Baltimore, MD 21202.

_MD Genealogical Society, 201 W. Monument St., Baltimore, MD 21201.
_MD Historical Society, Genealogy Committee, 201 W. Monument St., Baltimore, MD 21201.
_Mid-Atlantic Germanic Society, 347 Scott Dr., Silver Spring, MD 20904.
_North American Society of Genealogists, PO Box 29, Linthicum Heights, MD 21090.
_Unitarian-Universalist Genealogical Society, 10605 Lakespring Way, Hunt Valley, MD 21030.

In addition to the above genealogical organizations which have state-wide (or wider) coverage, there are some important local societies. Among them are these:
_Allegany County, Genealogical Society of, PO Box 3103, La Vale, MD 21504.
_Anne Arundel Genealogical Society, PO Box 221, Pasadena, MD 21122.
_Baltimore County Genealogical Society, PO Box 10085, Towson, MD 21204.
_Calvert County Historical Society, Genealogy Section, PO Box 300, Prince Frederick, MD 20678.
_Carroll County Genealogical Society, 50 E. Main St., Westminster, MD 21157.
_Catonsville Historical Society, Genealogical Section, 1824 Frederick Road, PO Box 9311, Catonsville, MD 21228.
_Cecil County Genealogical Society, PO Box 11, Charlestown, MD 21814.
_Dorchester County Historical Society, 1058 Taylors Island Road, Cambridge, MD 21613.
_Frederick County Genealogical Society, 1133 Apple Tree Court, Frederick, MD 21701.
_Harford County Genealogical Society, PO Box 15, Aberdeen, MD 21001.
_Howard County Genealogical Society, PO Box 74, Columbia, MD 21045.
_Lower Delmarva Genealogical Society, PO Box 3602, Salisbury, MD 21801.
_Lower Shore Genealogical Society, 1133 Somerset Avenue, Princess Anne, MD 21853.
_Montgomery County Historical Society, Genealogical Club of, 103 West Montgomery Avenue, Rockville, MD 20850.
_Prince George's County Genealogical Society, 12207 Tulip Grove Drive, PO Box 819, Bowie, MD 20715.
_Saint Mary's County Genealogical Society, General Delivery, Callaway, MD 20620.
_Upper Shore Genealogical Society of MD, PO Box 275, Easton, MD 21601.
It may be that the addresses of some of the above local societies will be in error since their addresses sometimes change when new officers are elected. If you fail to contact a society using the addresses above, inquire at the county library. They usually know of the organizations and can often

give you the current address. County libraries are named with their addresses in Chapter 4. It may also be that some of the above societies have become inactive. Again, the county libraries usually know. They also can tell you if new societies have been started up in their areas. Resident members of genealogical societies, particularly local ones, can often be of immense help to you. They are ordinarily very knowledgeable about the background, the early families, and the available records of their local areas. By consulting them, you can often save valuable time as they guide you in your work. The local societies also can often tell you if anyone else is working on or has worked on your family line.

In addition to the genealogical societies in MD, there are also many MD historical societies which may often be of help to you in your progenitor hunt. However, you must recognize, as was stated before, that not all these societies are interested in genealogy. Nonetheless, it often pays to contact them. These numerous societies are listed in:
_American Association of State and Local History, DIRECTORY OF HIS-
    TORICAL AGENCIES IN THE US AND CANADA, The Association, Nash-
    ville, TN, latest edition.
_E. P. Bentley, THE GENEALOGIST'S ADDRESS BOOK, Genealogical
    Publishing Co., Baltimore, MD, 1991.

---

21. Land records

One of the most important types of MD genealogical records is the type which deals with land. This is because throughout much of its history, especially early, MD was heavily involved in agriculture. As with all the original colonies, MD had an abundance of land which it distributed to those who would develop it. There are basically four kinds of land records in MD. (1) The first kind involves transactions in which the proprietor (the Calverts, the Lords Baltimore) or later the state government originally transferred land to private groups or individuals. These transactions made use of documents of several sorts and generated several types of records. Among them were patents, surveys, grants, warrants, survey certificates, plats and assignments. (2) The second kind of land records involves the transfer of western MD land as military land grants to MD Revolutionary War veterans. These records involve documents similar to those previously mentioned. (3) The third kind of land records consists of quit rent rolls, debt books, alienation fees, proprietary manor leases, and taxes. After the proprietor of MD granted land to an individual or private group, an annual quit rent (essentially a tax) had to be paid the proprietor. These were recorded in rent rolls and debt books. When an individual or private group subsequently sold or transferred the land to another individual or group, an alienation fee (essentially a transfer tax) had to be paid the proprietor. Taxes were assessed and collected by the state government after MD became a state. (4) The fourth kind of land records involves land transferred from one private individual or company owner to another private individual or company. The documents and records in these transactions include deeds, mortgages, leases, land commissions, plats, estate divisions, and tax sales.

The first category of land records (transfers from the colonial propri-etors or the state government to the first private owners) dates from the earliest years of MD. All the land of MD originally belonged to Lord Balti-more (Calvert), the proprietor, and remained under the jurisdiction of the Calverts until the Revolution. Even though the Calverts lost political control of MD during 1654-60 and 1692-1715, they retained control of the land. The proprietor, with the proprietary governor acting for him, during 1633-83 granted land to persons who would transport people to MD (the head-right system). Such a person would receive land for himself and additional land for each further individual he brought in. The names of these people (both transporters and transportees) have been published, and they are also available in records in MSA:
_G. Skordas, THE EARLY SETTLERS IN MD, AN INDEX TO NAMES OF IM-MIGRANTS COMPILED FROM LAND PATENTS, 1633-80, Genealogical Publishing Co., Baltimore, MD, 1979. Original records in MSA.
_A. W. Burns, MD EARLY SETTLERS (LAND RECORDS), The Author, An-napolis, MD, 1936-40, 38 volumes. Use with care.
_B. W. Gahn, ORIGINAL PATENTEES OF LAND AT WASHINGTON PRIOR TO 1700, Genealogical Publishing Co., Baltimore, MD, 1969.
_LAND NOTES OF MD, 1634-55, in MD Historical Magazine, Volumes 5-9, 1910-14. Many early settlers.
_J. B. RIGGS, CERTAIN EARLY MD LANDOWNERS IN THE VICINITY OF WASHINGTON, DC Historical Society, Washington, DC, 1949.

Beginning in 1684, the headright system was abandoned, and all land thereafter was sold. The MSA has the original records from 1634 forward, these records including both the headright grants (1633-83) and the cash sales (1684-present). An excellent detailed guide to these re-cords is:
_E. S. Hartsook and G. Skordas, LAND OFFICE AND PREROGATIVE COURT RECORDS OF COLONIAL MD, Genealogical Publishing Co., Baltimore, MD, 1968. History of land grants with inventory and descrip-tion of documents.
The records are well indexed:
_RECORDS OF EARLY SETTLERS, 1633-80, with INDEX, MSA, Annapolis, MD. See volumes by Skordas listed above.
_LAND PATENTS, 1634-present, with INDEXES (both by patentees and by tract name), MSA, Annapolis, MD. Copy of earlier ones at FHL (FHC).
_LAND WARRANTS AND ASSIGNMENTS, 1661-63, 1679-present, with INDEX, 1634-1842, MSA, Annapolis, MD. Copy of earlier ones at FHL (FHC).

_LAND CERTIFICATES, 1705–present, with INDEX, MSA, Annapolis, MD.
Copies of earlier ones at FHC.
The granted lands referred to above were surveyed by the metes and bounds method. This means that the descriptions of the lands were given by measuring along and with reference to natural boundary features (streams, ridges, trees). The measurements usually involved compass angles and distances in poles, perches, or rods (all 16.5 feet)

The second kind of MD land records are those which refer to the granting of bounty land by MD in 1781 to her Revolutionary War veterans. MD surveyed 50–acre lots west of Fort Cumberland (now in Allegany and Garrett Counties), and these were given to men who qualified. Officers received 200 acres and enlisted men 50 acres. The recipients of these bounty lands are listed in:
_J. T. Scharf, HISTORY OF WESTERN MD, Regional Publishing Co., Baltimore, MD, 1968.
_B. S. Carothers, MD SOLDIERS ENTITLED TO LANDS WEST OF FORT CUMBERLAND, The Author, Lutherville, MD, 1973. 2000 names.
_J. M. Brewer and L. Meyer, THE LAWS AND RULES OF THE LAND OFFICES OF MD, Baltimore, MD, 1871.
The original records are in the MSA, which also has indexes to them:
_RECORDS OF SOLDIERS ENTITLED TO LANDS WESTWARD OF FORT CUMBERLAND, alphabetically arranged, MSA, Annapolis, MD.
The materials in the above book by Scharf are partially indexed in:
_H. R. Long, INDEXES FOR THE FREDERICK AND WASHINGTON COUNTY SECTIONS OF SCHARF'S HISTORY OF WESTERN MD, ADR, Inc., Wichita, KS, 1984/6, 2 volumes.

The third kind of MD land record consists of those which relate to payments landowners were obligated for after they had been granted (or leased) land. When the proprietor granted land, the recipient was required to pay an annual quit rent (essentially a tax) to the proprietor. This was in force 1633–71, but in 1671 a tax on exported tobacco replaced it. The quit rent was restored in 1733 and continued until the Revolution. The quit rents were recorded in rent rolls and debt books. The rent rolls show the name of the tract of land, the name of the original grantee, the name of the current owner, the acreage of the land, and the date of the survey. The debt books give the name of the landowner, the acreage of land, the name of the tract, and the rent due. Some rent rolls and debt books are available for most counties, but a fair number are missing. The largest collection is in the MSA:
_MD RENT ROLLS, 1632–1775, 1782–90, with INDEXES, MSA, Annapolis, MD.
_MD DEBT BOOKS, 1733–74, with INDEX, MSA, Annapolis, MD.
There are also some rent rolls and debt books in the Calvert papers in the MHS. Copies of them are in the MSA. They are described in:

_MD Historical Magazine, Volume 19 (December, 1924) 341-369.
_D. M. Ellis and K. A. Stuart, THE CALVERT PAPERS, CALENDAR AND GUIDE TO THE MICROFILM EDITION, MHS, Baltimore, MD, 1989.

And many of them are printed in:
_MD Historical Magazine, Volumes 19-26.
Not only did the proprietor grant land, but he also leased it on his 30 (approximate) manors, which were large plantations he cultivated. The records of these proprietary manor leases are in the MSA:
_PROPRIETARY LEASES SERIES, 1707-77, MSA, Annapolis, MD. For Anne Arundel, Baltimore, Cecil, Charles, Dorchester, Kent, Prince George's, Queen Anne's, St. Mary's, Somerset, and Worcester Counties.
When a landowner decided to transfer land to another owner, he was charged an alienation fee (or fine) which went to the proprietor. Large grants of land of over 1000 acres (called manors) were made by the proprietor to over 60 individuals. They leased or rented land out to tenants. The records of these rents were kept by the private individuals and some may be located in manuscripts at MHS and MSA.

The fourth kind of land record has to do with the transfer of land from one private landowner to another. The records include deeds, mortgages, leases, land commissions, plats, estate divisions, and tax sales. These were recorded chiefly at the county level, and they are to be found in the offices of the County Circuit Court clerks. The one exception is that since 1851, these records have been kept in Baltimore City by the clerk of the Supreme Court. These records are either in the respective counties (and city) or at the MSA. The MSA has copies or originals of the following along with indexes to them. FHL has many of them, particularly early ones.
_MD COUNTY LAND RECORDS, Allegany (1791-1962), Anne Arundel (1653-1953, records before 1699 incomplete), Baltimore City (1659-1950), Baltimore (1659-1950), Calvert (1787-1817, 1840-1967, records before 1882 incomplete), Caroline (1774-1966), Carroll (1837-1967), Cecil (1674-1969), Charles (1655-1967), Dorchester (1669-1966), Frederick (1748-1967), Garrett (1872-1969), Harford (1773-1960), Howard (1840-1967), Kent (1648-1967), Montgomery (1777-1970), Prince George's (1696-1970), Queen Anne's (1706-1967), St. Mary's (1781-1964, records before 1827 incomplete), Somerset (1665-1967), Talbot (1662-1967), Washington (1777-1970), Wicomico (1867-1965), Worcester (1742-1965), with INDEXES, MSA Annapolis, MD. FHL (FHC) has copies of earlier ones (to about 1850).
These records are inventoried and considerable detail on them is given in
_M. L. Radoff, G. Skordas, and P. R. Jacobsen, THE COUNTY COURTHOUSES AND RECORDS OF MD, PART TWO, THE RECORDS, The Hall

of Records Commission, Annapolis, MD, 1963. For detail on the records, but use the next volume for inventory.
_E. C. Papenfuse and others, A GUIDE TO GOVERNMENT RECORDS AT THE MSA, Annapolis, MD, 1991.

---

22. Manuscripts

One of the most useful and yet one of the most unused sources of genealogical data are the various manuscript collections relating to MD. These collections will be found in state, regional, county, town, and private libraries, archives, museums, societies, and repositories in numerous places in MD, including universities, colleges, and church agencies. Manuscript collections consist of all sorts of records of religious, educational, patriotic, business, social, civil, professional, governmental, and political organizations; documents, letters, memoirs, notes, and papers of early settlers, ministers, politicians, business men, educators, physicians, dentists, lawyers, judges, land speculators, and farmers; records of churches, cemeteries, mortuaries, schools, corporations, and industries; works of artists, musicians, writers, sculptors, photographers, architects, and historians; and records, papers, letters, and reminiscences of participants in various wars, as well as records of military organizations and campaigns.

The holdings of many manuscript depositories in MD have been briefly or broadly described in special publications. Among the more valuable of these are:
_(DAMR) US National Historical Publications and Records Commission, DIRECTORY OF ARCHIVES AND MANUSCRIPT REPOSITORIES IN THE US, The Commission, Oryx Press, New York, NY, 1988.
_(NUCMC) US Library of Congress, THE NATIONAL UNION CATALOG OF MANUSCRIPT COLLECTIONS, The Library, Washington, DC, issued annually 1959-. Cumulative indexes 1959-62, 1963-6, 1967-9, 1970-4, 1975-9, 1980-4. Volumes indexed separately thereafter.
_(HAMER) P. M. Hamer, A GUIDE TO ARCHIVES AND MANUSCRIPTS IN THE US, Yale University Press, New Haven, CT, 1961.
_J. T. Guertler, THE RECORDS OF BALTIMORE'S PRIVATE ORGANIZATIONS, A GUIDE TO ARCHIVAL RESOURCES, Garland Publishing, New York, NY, 1981.

The major MD repositories for manuscripts of genealogical importance are listed below. Following each listing are references to books containing descriptions of the holdings. These books are those listed in the preceding paragraph and they are referred to with the abbreviations given there.
_In Annapolis, MD State Archives (MSA), St. John's Street and College Avenue, Annapolis, MD 21404. Archives for original records and copies of the colony and state of MD, and its counties, cities, and towns. Also

personal, church, and business records, and maps. 60,000 cubic feet of records, 1635–present. See MD Hall of records, A GUIDE TO THE INDEXED HOLDINGS AT THE HALL OF RECORDS, MSA, Annapolis, MD, 1972; E. C. Papenfuse and others, LOCAL JUDICIAL, AND ADMINISTRATIVE RECORDS ON MICROFORM, Hall of Records Commission, Annapolis, MD, 1978. See DAMR, NUCMC (1968), HAMER.

_In Annapolis, Nimitz Library, US Naval Academy, Special Collections Division, Annapolis, MD 21402. Ship records, naval personnel. See DAMR.

_In Baltimore, ANCIENT FREE AND ACCEPTED MASONS OF MD, GRAND LODGE MUSEUM, 225 North Charles Street, Baltimore, MD 21201. Masonic records. See DAMR.

_In Baltimore, ARCHIVES, (ROMAN CATHOLIC) ARCHDIOCESE OF BALTIMORE, 320 Cathedral Street, Baltimore, MD 21201. Records of archbishops, diocesan missions. See DAMR, NUCMC (1971).

_In Baltimore, DIVISION OF CITY ARCHIVES AND RECORDS MANAGEMENT, Room 201, 211 East Pleasant Street, Baltimore, MD 21202. Baltimore City administrative records (mayor, council), commissioner records, county superior court records, poll books (voter registries), tax records, municipal agencies records, election records, maps, WPA Index, ship passenger lists, naturalization records. See W. G. LeFurgy, THE RECORDS OF A CITY, A GUIDE TO THE BALTIMORE CITY ARCHIVES, The Archives, Baltimore, MD, 1984. See DAMR.

_In Baltimore, ARCHIVES OF CARMELITE MONASTERY OF BALTIMORE, 1318 Delaney Valley Road, Baltimore, MD 21204. Records 1790–present. See DAMR.

_In Baltimore, ENOCH PRATT FREE LIBRARY, 400 Cathedral Street, Baltimore, MD 21215. Biographical file, newspapers. See NUCMC (1959–61).

_In Baltimore, JEWISH HISTORICAL SOCIETY OF MD, 3809 Clark's Lane, Baltimore, MD 21215. Jewish family records. See DAMR.

_In Baltimore, GEORGE PEABODY LIBRARY, THE JOHNS HOPKINS UNIVERSITY, 17 E. Mount Vernon Place, Baltimore, MD 21202. See NUCMC (1969).

_In Baltimore, LUTHERAN CHURCH IN AMERICA, MD SYNOD, 7604 York road, Baltimore, MD 21204. Proceedings of synod, brief church histories. See DAMR.

_In Baltimore, MANUSCRIPTS DIVISION, MD HISTORICAL SOCIETY (MHS), 201 West Monument Street, Baltimore, MD 21201. More than 2200 manuscript collections, over 2,500,000 items, Calvert papers, business records, diaries, organization records, historical materials, family data, maps. See R. J. Cox and L. E. Sullivan, GUIDE TO RESEARCH COLLECTIONS OF THE MHS, The Society, Baltimore, MD, 1981; A. J. M. Pedley, THE MANUSCRIPT COLLECTIONS OF THE MHS, The Society, Baltimore, MD, 1968, with annual updates in the MD Historical Magazine; D. M. Ellis and K. A. Stuart, THE CALVERT

PAPERS, CALENDAR AND GUIDE TO THE MICROFILM EDITION, MHS, Baltimore, MD, 1989. See DAMR, NUCMC (1967, 1969-71, 1973, 1975-6, 1978, 1981), HAMER.

_In Baltimore, MEDICAL AND CHIRURGICAL FACULTY OF MD LIBRARY, 1211 Cathedral Street, Baltimore, MD 21201. Medical and physician histories. See DAMR.

_In Baltimore, THE PEALE MUSEUM, 225 Holliday Street, Baltimore, MD 21202. Baltimore visual materials as contained in drawings, maps, histories, and records of institutions and organizations. See DAMR.

_In Baltimore, SOCIETY OF FRIENDS, BALTIMORE YEARLY MEETING, 3107 North Charles Street, Baltimore, MD 21218. Friends records.

_In Baltimore, UNITED METHODIST HISTORICAL SOCIETY, 2200 St. Paul Street, Baltimore, MD 21218. Methodist conference and church records of the Baltimore Conference, genealogical lists. See DAMR.

_In Baltimore, BALTIMORE REGION INSTITUTIONAL STUDIES CENTER, UNIVERSITY OF BALTIMORE, Charles and Mount Royal Streets, Baltimore, MD 21201. Records of public and private agencies and organizations. See DAMR, NUCMC (1977).

_In Baltimore, STEAMSHIP HISTORICAL SOCIETY COLLECTION, UNIVERSITY OF BALTIMORE, 1420 Maryland Avenue, Baltimore, MD 21201. Inland, coastal, and oceanic steam-powered ship materials. See DAMR.

_In Bel Air, HISTORICAL SOCIETY OF HARFORD COUNTY, 324 South Kenmore Avenue, Bel Air, MD 21014. Historical and genealogical manuscripts. See DAMR.

_In Cockeysville, BALTIMORE COUNTY HISTORICAL SOCIETY, 9811 Van Buren Lane, Cockeysville, MD 21030. Historical and genealogical manuscripts. See DAMR.

_In Cockeysville, UNITARIAN AND UNIVERSALIST GENEALOGICAL SOCIETY, 10605 Lakespring Way, Cockeysville, MD 21030. Genealogical data. See DAMR, NUCMC (1978).

_In Cumberland, ALLEGANY COUNTY HISTORICAL SOCIETY, 218 Washington Street, Cumberland, MD 21502. Genealogical information. See DAMR.

_In Easton, TALBOT COUNTY FREE LIBRARY, 100 West Dover Street, Easton, MD 21601. Genealogical data. See DAMR.

_In Ellicott City, HOWARD COUNTY HISTORICAL SOCIETY, 8328 Court Avenue, Ellicott City, MD 21043. Genealogical materials. See DAMR.

_In Frederick, FREDERICK COUNTY PUBLIC LIBRARIES, C. BURR ARTZ LIBRARY, 110 East Patrick Street, Frederick, MD 21701. County history. See DAMR, HAMER.

_In Hagerstown, WASHINGTON COUNTY HISTORICAL SOCIETY, SIMMS A. JAMIESON MEMORIAL LIBRARY, 135 West Washington Street, Hagerstown, MD 21740. See DAMR.

_In Hyattsville, PRINCE GEORGE'S COUNTY MEMORIAL LIBRARY, HYATTSVILLE BRANCH, 6530 Adelphi Road, Hyattsville, MD 20782. County history. See DAMR.

_In La Plata, CHARLES COUNTY COMMUNITY COLLEGE LEARNING RE- SOURCE CENTER, Mitchell Road, La Plata, MD 20646. Genealogical data. See DAMR.

_In Leonardtown, SAINT MARY'S COUNTY HISTORICAL SOCIETY, 11 Court House Drive, Leonardtown, MD 20650. Genealogical sources. See DAMR.

_In Rockville, MONTGOMERY COUNTY HISTORICAL SOCIETY, 103 West Montgomery Avenue, Rockville, MD 20850. Genealogical sources. See DAMR.

_In Westminster, HISTORICAL SOCIETY OF CARROLL COUNTY, 210 East Main Street, Westminster, MD 21157. County and genealogical histo- ries. See DAMR.

_In Washington, DC, ARCHDIOCESE OF WASHINGTON CHANCERY OF- FICE, 5001 Eastern Avenue, Washington, DC 20017. Parish records. See DAMR.

_In Westminster, HISTORICAL SOCIETY OF CARROLL COUNTY, 210 East Main Street, Westminster, MD 21157. County and genealogical histo- ries. See DAMR.

_In Washington, DC, ARCHDIOCESE OF WASHINGTON CHANCERY OF- FICE, 5001 Eastern Avenue, Washington, DC 20017. Parish records. See DAMR.

_In Washington, DC, COLUMBIA HISTORICAL SOCIETY LIBRARY, 1307 New Hampshire Avenue, NW, Washington, DC, 20036. History of the area. Business and organization records. See HAMER, NUCMC (1973), DAMR.

_In Washington, DC, EPISCOPAL DIOCESE OF WASHINGTON ARCHIVES, Washington Cathedral, Mount Saint Albans, Washington, DC 20016. Defunct church records. See HAMER, NUCMC (1966), DAMR.

_In Washington, DC, JEWISH HISTORICAL SOCIETY OF GREATER WASH- INGTON, 701 Third Street, NW, Washington, DC 20001. Synagogue records. See DAMR.

_In Washington, DC, LIBRARY OF CONGRESS, First Street and Indepen- dence Avenue, SE, Washington, DC 20540. Published genealogical material, maps, colonial manuscripts, historical manuscripts. See HAMER, DAMR. See J. Neagles, THE LIBRARY OF CONGRESS, An- cestry Publishing, Salt Lake City, UT, 1990.

_In Washington, DC, LUTHERAN CHURCH MO SYNOD, SOUTHEASTERN DISTRICT, 5121 Colorado Avenue, NW, Washington, DC 20011. Lu- theran congregation histories. See DAMR.

_In Washington, DC, NATIONAL ARCHIVES, Eighth Street and Pennsylvania Avenue, NW, Washington, DC 20408. See National Archives and Re- cords Administration, GENEALOGICAL RESEARCH IN THE NATIONAL ARCHIVES, The Administration, Washington, DC, 1982.

_In Washington, DC, NATIONAL SOCIETY OF THE DAUGHTERS OF THE
  AMERICAN REVOLUTION, GENEALOGICAL LIBRARY, 1776 D Street,
  NW, Washington, DE 20006. See HAMER, NUCMC (1966). See Na-
  tional Society of the DAR, DAR LIBRARY CATALOG, The Society, Wash-
  ington, DC, 2 volumes.
_In Washington, DC, SCOTTISH RITE OF FREE MASONRY ARCHIVES,
  1733 Sixteenth Street, NW, Washington, DC 20009. Masonic records.
  See HAMER, NUCMC (1959-61), DAMR.
_In Washington, DC, SEVENTH-DAY ADVENTIST ARCHIVES, 6840 Eastern
  Avenue, NW, Washington, DC 20012. Administrative records. See
  DAMR.
_In Washington, DC, SOCIETY OF THE CINCINNATI, 2118 Massachusetts
  Avenue, NW, Washington, DC 20008. Revolutionary War manuscripts.
  See DAMR.

     Now, we need to call to your attention the use of NUCMC, which is an
indispensable set of volumes which you must not fail to employ. These
books were published by the Library of Congress in order to put into print
summaries of the holdings of archives and repositories all over the US.
There is an annual volume from 1959 to the present. And best of all, this
tremendous finding aid is thoroughly indexed:
_US Library of Congress, THE NATIONAL UNION CATALOG OF MANU-
  SCRIPT COLLECTIONS (NUCMC), The Library, Washington, DC, issued
  annually 1959-. Cumulative indexes 1959-62, 1963-6, 1967-9,
  1970-4, 1975-9, 1980-4. Volumes indexed separately thereafter.
There is also an overall index covering the 1959-84 volumes:
_E. Altham and others, INDEX TO PERSONAL NAMES IN THE NATIONAL
  UNION CATALOG OF MANUSCRIPT COLLECTIONS, 1959-84,
  Chadwyck-Healey, Arlington, VA, 1988, 2 volumes.
Be certain to look in all of these indexes for your family surnames, then
under counties of interest to you, then under pertinent cities and towns,
then under MD, then under various subjects (for example, cavalry,
churches, Civil War, Colonial period, coroners, courts, customs, estates,
family papers, French and Indian War, genealogy, history, immigration,
Indian Wars, infantry, Jews, juries, justices of the peace, land, leases,
licenses, local history, magistrates, maps, military affairs, militia, mortgages, newspapers, pardon, parole, personal accounts, pioneer life, ports
of entry, prisons, Revolutionary War, slavery, surveys, tax records, travel,
trials, vital records, War of 1812, wills). Do not overlook the many listings
under the general heading GENEALOGY, and don't forget to look under
Baltimore, Annapolis, and other cities. These efforts will introduce you
quickly and easily to the large world of MD manuscript materials. Most of
the reference books mentioned above are available in MHS, MSLL, and in
MD university and college libraries. Many of them may be found at FHL
(FHC), LGL, and RL. If you find in these reference volumes materials which
you suspect relate to your progenitor, write to the appropriate repository

asking for details. Don't forget to send a long SASE and to request names of researchers if you cannot go in person. In MSA, MHS, and other MD manuscript repositories, there are special indexes, catalogs, inventories, and other finding aids to facilitate your search. In some cases, there are several of these, so you need to be careful to examine all.

23. Marriage records

Six years after its first settlement (in 1640), the MD Assembly mandated the recording of marriages by the clerk of every court and required that banns be posted by clergy three Sundays before the marriage. Very few of these early records exist, it being likely that they were not very well kept. Those which are known are all in the MSA: Charles County (1655-94), Kent County (1654-96), and Somerset (1650-1720), and they are indexed. In 1695, the Anglican (Episcopal) Church was established, and the parishes were instructed to register marriages. A number of these parish records have been preserved, and they were treated in a previous section entitled Church records. Until 1777, not many governmental marriage records were kept.

In 1777, the clerks of the MD county courts were given the task of issuing marriage licenses and retaining a list of them. The list was to record the date, the names of the man and woman, and sometimes the intended minister. There was no record as to whether the marriage actually took place. In 1865, a law was passed requiring the clerks of the county (circuit) courts and the clerk of the Court of Common Pleas of Baltimore City to record all marriages. The record was to consist of the date and place of the marriage; name, residence, and official position of the minister; name, age, color, residence, marital status, and occupation of the man; the same for the woman; and the date of the record.

The marriage licenses (1777-1865) and the marriage records (1865-1914) were kept by the counties. The originals will be found in the counties and Baltimore City or in the MSA, and microfilm copies of most are in MSA. In 1914, statewide registration of marriages went into effect. MSA has indexes to almost all of these records up to 1930. Many of the licenses up to 1851 and the indexes are also at FHL. Transcriptions of some of them have been published and are available at MHS, MSLL, and at some LGL and LL. Several sizable state or regional indexes of marriages are available, and compilations of marriages have been published:

_R. W. Barnes, MD MARRIAGES, 1634-1800, Genealogical Publishing Co., Baltimore, MD, 1975/8, 2 volumes. About 40,000 names.
_MD SURNAME INDEX: COMPUTER INDEXES TO MARRIAGE RECORDS, Hunting for Bears, North Salt Lake City, UT, 1984.
_F. E. Wright, MD EASTERN SHORE VITAL RECORDS, 1648-1825, Family Line Publications, Silver Spring, MD, 1982-9, 5 volumes.

_H. Chance, WESTERN MD PIONEERS, LISTS OF MARRIAGES, BIRTHS, AND DEATHS OF 8000 EARLY SETTLERS, Library of the PA Historical Society, Philadelphia, PA, 1968.

_INTERNATIONAL GENEALOGICAL INDEX (IGI), on microfiche and CD disk, FHL, Salt Lake City, UT, look under MD. Also available at every FHC.

_FHL CATALOG, LOCALITY SECTION, on microfiche and CD disk, FHL, Salt Lake City, UT, look under MD-Vital records, MD-[County]-Vital records, and MD-Baltimore (Independent City)-Vital records. Also available at every FHC.

_MD DAR, MD DAUGHTERS OF THE AMERICAN REVOLUTION COLLECTION OF TYPESCRIPT VOLUMES, MD Chapters of the DAR, Baltimore, MD, various dates, numerous volumes. Arranged by county, most of them with a surname index, contain Bible, birth, cemetery, church, death, marriage, and will records.

_R. T. Obert, BALTIMORE CITY AND COUNTY MARRIAGE LICENSES, 1777-99, Genealogy Shoppe, Salt Lake City, UT, 1975. Over 12,000 names.

_R. B. Clark, Jr., MD EASTERN SHORE MARRIAGE LICENSES, 17TH-19TH CENTURIES, The Author, St. Michaels, MD, 1963-82, several volumes.

_R. B. Clark, and S. C. Clark, MARRIAGE LICENSES OF MD COUNTIES, The Authors, St. Michaels, MD, 1963 ff, several volumes. Caroline, Kent, Queen Anne's, and Talbot Counties.

_CONSOLIDATED CARD INDEX OF SOME EARLY MARRIAGES, MSA, Annapolis, MD. Colonial marriages from Charles, Kent, and Somerset Counties; marriages 1777-1850s from Anne Arundel, Caroline, Cecil, Dorchester, and Prince George's Counties; marriages 1778-98 from Frederick County.

Since MD is so short on marriage records before 1777, other types of records need to be consulted. Among the better ones are Bible, cemetery, census, church, manuscript, military, pension, mortuary, newspaper, published genealogies, tax lists, and will and probate records. The most fruitful of these are usually church and newspaper records. All of them are treated in other sections of this chapter. There are several indexes and published compilations of records which imply marriages or indirectly indicate them:

_HODGES MARRIAGE REFERENCE INDEX, 1674-1851, MSA, Annapolis, MD, incomplete. Card index to indirect indications of marriages in land, probate, will, and other records.

_A. W. Burns (Bell), MD MARRIAGE RECORDS, 1659-1807, The Author, Washington, DC, 1937 ff, 39 volumes. Marriage implications in court, deed, and will records.

_H. W. Newman, MD REVOLUTIONARY RECORDS, Genealogical Publishing Co., Baltimore, MD, 1967. Includes 1000 marriages of MD soldiers.

_DIELMAN-HAYWARD FILE, MHS, Baltimore, MD. Over 250,000 bio-graphical, death, and marriage items from MD newspapers, 1780 to the present.
_I. S. Harper, MD MARRIAGE CLUES, The Author, St. Michaels, MD, 1980-4, 3 volumes. Mostly Eastern Shore data, 1600-1820s.
_W. P. Passano, INDEX TO THE SOURCE RECORDS OF MD, Genealogical Publishing Co., Baltimore, MD, 1974, a reprint of a 1940 volume. An older bibliography with references to many indirect and some direct marriage records.

When you are seeking marriage date and place information in archives and libraries, be certain to explore all the above mentioned publications, and don't fail to look under the county listings and the following heading in library catalogs: Register of births, etc. (Etc. includes marriages.)

24. Military records: colonial

Before going into detail on sources of military records (sections 24-27), you need to understand the types of records which are available and what they contain. There are five basic types which are of value to genealogists: (a) service, (b) pension, (c) bounty land, (d) claims, and (e) military unit history. Service records contain a number of the following: name, rank, military unit, personal description, plus dates and places of enlistment, mustering in, payrolls, wounding, capture, death, imprisonment, hospital stay, release, oath of allegiance, desertion, promotion, battles, heroic action, re-enlistment, leave of absence, mustering out, and discharge. Pension records (applications and payment documents) contain a number of the following: name, age, rank, military unit, personal description, name of wife, names and ages of children, residences during pension period, plus dates and places of enlistment, service, wartime experiences, birth, marriage, pension payments, and death. Bounty land records (applications and awards of land) contain a number of the following: name, age, rank, military unit, plus dates and places of enlistment, service, wartime experience, and birth. Claims of military participants for back pay and of civilians for supplies or service contain some of the following: name, details of the claim, date of the claim, witnesses to the claim, documents supporting the claim, action on the claim, amount awarded. Military unit history records trace the detailed events of the experiences of a given military unit throughout a war, often referring to officers, enlisted men, battles, campaigns, and deaths, plus dates and places of organization, mustering in, reorganization, mustering out, and other pertinent events. Now with this background, you are ready to learn where these records may be found.

Essentially from the beginning, colonial MD maintained a militia for defense and other emergencies. Unlike many other colonies, MD did not have an extensive series of Indian conflicts in the pre-1756 period,

although there were a few. The major wars (or armed engagements) in which MD participated in this period were struggles with groups who challenged the Calverts' authority and either temporarily took over the colony or tried to do so. These encounters included the Claiborne clashes (1635/7), the Ingle takeover (1645-7), and the Puritan-Loyalist engagements (1655). Other colonies fought in the wars between Great Britain and France for control of North America [King William's War 1689-97, Queen Anne's War 1701-13, the War of Jenkins' Ear 1739, and King George's War 1744-8], but MD contributed little or none to them. However, MD was sizably involved in the final British-French conflict, the French and Indian War (1755-63). The early defeat of British forces just beyond western MD (1755) exposed the MD frontier to Indian attack. Most settlers on the frontier retreated to eastern MD. Eventually the British triumphed (1763), and France and her Spanish allies ceded to Britain all of Canada and essentially all lands resting east of the MS River including FL. An excellent treatment of the history of MD's military involvements (both colonial and after) is:
_J. H. F. Brewer, MILITARY MD, in M. L. Radoff, THE OLD LINE STATE, A HISTORY OF MD, Hall of Records Commission, Annapolis, MD, 1971, pages 247-266.

MD military men participated in the wars mentioned above, and a fair number of records exist, but they are seldom very detailed. The records related to these wars and transcripts of the records which contain names of participants and describe the MD activities include:
_M. J. Clark, COLONIAL SOLDIERS OF THE SOUTH, 1732-74, Genealogical Publishing Co., Baltimore MD, 1983. MD militia (1732-63) on pages 1-123.
_E. F. Stormont and B. D. Aul, MD COLONIAL MILITARY SERVICE INDEX, National Society, Daughters of Colonial Wars in FL, Tallahassee, FL, 1988.
_COLONIAL MUSTER AND PAYROLLS, 1732-72, original records with INDEX, MSA, Annapolis, MD.
_C. Johnston and F. B. Culver, SOCIETY OF COLONIAL WARS, MD, Friedenwald Co., Baltimore, MD, 1905 and 1940, 2 volumes.
_COLONIAL MILITIA FOR 1740 AND 1748, MD Historical Magazine, Volume 6 (1911).
_FRENCH AND INDIAN WAR TROOPS, 1757-9, MD Historical Magazine, Volumes 5 and 11 (1910 and 1914).
_FRENCH AND INDIAN WAR ACCOUNT BOOK, Manuscript 375, MHS, Baltimore, MD. Ledger with detailed listings of soldiers, 1762.
_FRENCH AND INDIAN WAR RECORDS AND CLAIMS, Manuscript 375.1, MHS, Baltimore, MD. Muster and payrolls, provisions for troops, soldiers' claims.
_E. P. Passano, AN INDEX OF THE SOURCE RECORDS OF MD, The Author, Baltimore, MD, 1940, page 451. Bibliography of many MD colonial military records.

The published volumes will be found in MHS, MSLL, LGL, and FHL (FHC). The manuscript materials are located in the places indicated (MSA, MHS).

---

25. Military records: Revolutionary War

No military action of the Revolutionary War took place on MD soil. Even so, MD personnel fought in almost every major battle of the conflict, and they distinguished themselves on many occasions as the best of the Continental Army. MD sent about 13,900 to the Continental Army and also contributed about 3900 militiamen. In 1781, MD passed laws granting bounty land to her Revolutionary veterans. These bounty land grants were discussed in the section on Land records. There were numerous Loyalists (faithful to England) in MD, especially in the Eastern Shore counties of Caroline, Dorchester, Somerset, and Worcester. They rebelled several times against MD's revolutionary government and were forcefully subdued. The properties of many Loyalists were seized by the state officials and sold to raise funds for support of the war.

The first step you should take in searching for your MD ancestor who may have served in this war or supported it is to employ the following large indexes and compilations and look for him in them:
_MD Historical Society, MUSTER ROLLS AND OTHER RECORDS OF SERVICE OF MD TROOPS IN THE AMERICAN REVOLUTION, Genealogical Publishing Co., Baltimore, MD, 1972. About 20,000 entries. Same as Volume 18 of THE ARCHIVES OF MD, MHS, Baltimore, MD, 1883 ff.
_S. E. Clements and F. E. Wright, MD MILITIA IN THE REVOLUTIONARY WAR, Family Line Publications, Westminster, MD, 1987.
_The National Archives, GENERAL INDEX TO COMPILED SERVICE RECORDS OF REVOLUTIONARY WAR SOLDIERS, SAILORS, ARMY STAFF, The Archives, Washington, DC, Microfilm Publication M860, 58 rolls. [Mostly Continental forces plus militia who supported them. Copies in NA, NARB, FHL (FHC), may be borrowed through your LL or directly from AGLL, PO Box 244, Bountiful, UT 84010.]
_The National Archives, INDEX TO COMPILED SERVICE RECORDS OF NAVAL PERSONNEL DURING THE REVOLUTIONARY WAR, The Archives, Washington, DC, Microfilm Publication M879, 1 roll. [Includes Marines. Sources same as above.]
_The National Genealogical Society, INDEX TO REVOLUTIONARY WAR PENSION [AND SOME BOUNTY LAND] APPLICATIONS IN THE NATIONAL ARCHIVES, The Society, Washington, DC, 1976.
_F. Rider, AMERICAN GENEALOGICAL INDEX, Godfrey Memorial Library, Middletown, CT, 1942-52, 48 volumes, and F. Rider, AMERICAN GENEALOGICAL-BIOGRAPHICAL INDEX, Godfrey Memorial Library, Middletown, CT, 1952-, over 180 volumes, more to come. [Continental, state, and militia service.]

_US Pay Department, War Department, REGISTERS OF CERTIFICATES ISSUED BY JOHN PIERCE TO OFFICERS AND SOLDIERS OF THE CONTINENTAL ARMY, Genealogical Publishing Co., Baltimore, MD, 1983.

_National Society of the DAR, DAR PATRIOT INDEX, The Society, Washington, DC, 1966/79, 2 volumes. [Continental, state, militia, public service, military aid.] DAR no longer accepts this index as authoritative. New applications must be based on original source material.

_National Society of the DAR, INDEX TO THE ROLLS OF HONOR [Ancestor Index], Genealogical Publishing Co., Baltimore, MD, 1972, and LINEAGE BOOKS, The Society, Washington, DC, 1890-1921, 166 volumes.

The seven printed reference works just mentioned (not the microfilms) will be found in MHS, MSLL, FHL (FHC), and in many LGL. Some of them are available at MSA and some RL and LL. Locations of the microfilms are given above along with the listings.

If you discover from these sources that your ancestor served in the Continental forces or militia units which aided them, you may proceed to obtain his service records from the NA or to read them from these microfilms:

_The National Archives, COMPILED SERVICE RECORDS OF SOLDIERS WHO SERVED IN THE AMERICAN ARMY DURING THE REVOLUTIONARY WAR, The Archives, Washington, DC, Microfilm Publication M881, 1097 rolls.

_The National Archives, COMPILED SERVICE RECORDS OF AMERICAN NAVAL, QUARTERMASTER, AND COMMISSARY PERSONNEL WHO SERVED DURING THE REVOLUTIONARY WAR, The Archives, Washington, DC, Microfilm Publication M880, 4 rolls.

_The National Archives, REVOLUTIONARY WAR ROLLS, 1775-83, The Archives, Washington, DC, Microfilm Publication M246, 138 rolls.

Your veteran progenitor's federal pension and/or bounty land records can be obtained from the NA or read from:

_The National Archives, REVOLUTIONARY WAR PENSION AND BOUNTY LAND WARRANT APPLICATION FILES, The Archives, Washington, DC, Microfilm Publication M804, 2670 rolls.

These microfilm sets are available at NA, NARB, FHL (FHC), and some can be borrowed from your LL, or AGLL, PO Box 244, Bountiful, UT 84010, or CMRF, PO Box 2940, Hyattsville, MD 20784. Alternately, you can write the NA (8th and PA Ave., Washington, DC 20408) for 3 copies of NATF-80 which you can use to request service, pension, and bounty land records by mail. A third alternative is to hire a searcher in Washington, DC to go to the NA for you. Lists of such searchers will be found in:

_J. N. Chambers, editor, THE GENEALOGICAL HELPER, Everton Publishers, Logan, UT, latest September/October issue.

Another very rewarding type of record to ask for from the NA are the pension payment records. The records are useful for following your forebear from the time he obtained a pension until he died. And, then, ofttimes his widow applied for and received a pension, and there will be pension payment records for her. Here are some of the sources of these records:

_National Archives, REVOLUTIONARY WAR AND ACTS OF MILITARY ESTABLISHMENT, INVALID PENSIONERS' PAYMENTS, March 1801 through September 1815, manuscript, Records of the Veterans Administration, Record Group 15, The Archives, Washington, DC. Show semi-annual payments. Arranged by state, then alphabetically by first letter of the surname.

_National Archives, PAYMENTS TO REVOLUTIONARY WAR PENSIONERS, UNDER ACTS APPROVED 1818-53, 14 unnumbered volumes, Records of the Veterans Administration, Record Group 15, The Archives, Washington, DC. Arranged by state, see volume containing PA, MD, and IL. Look under date of act, then alphabetically by first letter of surname.

_National Archives, US PENSIONERS UNDER ACTS OF 1818 THROUGH 1858, LEDGERS OF PAYMENTS 1818-72, Microfilm T718, 23 rolls, The Archives, Washington, DC. Arranged by act of Congress, then name of pension agency, then by first letter of surname. Obtain act of Congress from pension application.

_National Archives, FINAL PAYMENT VOUCHERS, REVOLUTIONARY WAR PENSIONERS, Records of the US General Accounting Office, record Group 217, The Archives, Washington, DC. Arranged by state, then alphabetically by surname.

The third item above is on microfilm. It is available at NA and some NARB. The other three items are available only at NA.

The second step you should take is to look into further state sources. These are of many types: bounty land lists, pension lists, oaths of fidelity, veterans' burial places, pension abstracts, and pacifists.

_J. M. Brewer and L. Meyer, THE LAWS AND RULES OF THE LAND OFFICES OF MD, Baltimore, MD, 1871. Soldiers who were entitled to bounty land west of Fort Cumberland.

_G. M. Brumbaugh, MD RECORDS, COLONIAL, REVOLUTIONARY, COUNTY, AND CHURCH, FROM ORIGINAL SOURCES, Genealogical Publishing Co., Baltimore, MD, 1975, 2 volumes. Includes 1776/8 censuses, military records, pensions, and oaths of allegiance.

_G. M. Brumbaugh and M. R. Hodges, REVOLUTIONARY RECORDS OF MD, Genealogical Publishing Co., Baltimore, MD, 1967.

_G. R. Brunk, J. C. Lehman, and M. J. Kraybill, A GUIDE TO SELECT REVOLUTIONARY WAR RECORDS PERTAINING TO MENNONITES AND OTHER PACIFIST GROUPS IN SOUTHWESTERN PA AND MD, 1775-1800, Eastern Mennonite College, Harrisonburg, VA, 1974, 2 volumes.

_A. W. Burns, SOLDIERS OF THE REVOLUTIONARY WAR, WAR OF 1812, AND INDIAN WARS, WHO DREW PENSIONS WHILE RESIDING IN KY, The Author, Washington, DC, 1940. Use with care.

_B. S. Carothers, MD SOLDIERS ENTITLED TO LANDS WEST OF FORT CUMBERLAND, The Author, Lutherville, MD, 1973.

_B. S. Carothers, MD OATHS OF FIDELITY, 1778, The Author, Lutherville, MD, 1980, 2 volumes.

_R. B. Clark, Jr., MARYLANDERS IN THE INDEX OF REVOLUTIONARY WAR PENSION APPLICANTS, The Author, St. Michaels, MD, 1982.

_DAR Chapters of MD, DAR GENEALOGICAL RECORD VOLUMES, type-scripts, numerous volumes, various MD DAR Chapters, several MD cities and towns. Contain many Revolutionary War records.

_M. R. Hodges, UNPUBLISHED REVOLUTIONARY RECORDS OF MD, The Author, Baltimore, MD, 1939, 7 volumes.

_H. R. Long, INDEXES TO THE FREDERICK AND WASHINGTON COUNTY SECTIONS OF SCHARF'S HISTORY OF WESTERN PA, ADR, Wichita, KS, 1984; leads to listings of Revolutionary War bounty land recipients in J. T. Scharf, HISTORY OF WESTERN MD, Regional Publishing Co., Baltimore, MD, 1968.

_MD Hall of Records Commission, CALENDAR OF MD STATE PAPERS, The Commission, Annapolis, MD, 1943-58, 7 volumes. Guide to MD Colonial and Revolutionary records.

_MSA, MD CENSUS OF 1776, original records with card index, MSA, Annapolis, MD. Taken to determine the population of the new state.

_MSA, OATHS OF FIDELITY TO THE STATE OF MD, 1778, original records with card index, MSA, Annapolis, MD.

_MSA, MD CENSUS OF 1778, original records with card index, MSA, Annapolis, MD. Taken to ascertain males over the age of 18 who had failed to take the 1778 oath of fidelity.

_MSA, MD REVOLUTIONARY RECORDS, 1775-95, original records with card index, MSA, Annapolis, MD. Essential, be sure to use it. Includes enlistments, rolls, ledgers, day books, letter books, rosters.

_MSA, MD REVOLUTIONARY PAPERS, 1775-94, original records with card index, MSA, Annapolis, MD. Includes accounts, returns, rolls, discharges, ships' records, Loyalist records.

_MSA, REVOLUTIONARY WAR MD TAX ASSESSMENT OF 1783, original records with card index, MSA, Annapolis, MD.

_MSA, MD SOLDIERS ENTITLED TO LANDS WESTWARD OF FORT CUM-BERLAND, 1788, records alphabetically arranged, MSA, Annapolis, MD.

_MSA, MD REVOLUTIONARY WAR PENSION ROLL, original records with card index, MSA, Annapolis, MD. Index also refers to laws.

_MD Treasurer's Office, REPORT OF THE TREASURER OF THE WESTERN SHORE, ON THE PENSION LIST, The Office, Annapolis, MD, 1824. Revolutionary War pension list.

_L. K. McGhee, MD PENSION ABSTRACTS: REVOLUTIONARY WAR, WAR OF 1812, AND INDIAN WARS, The Author, Washington, DC, 1966. Use with care.

_L. K. McGhee, MD REVOLUTIONARY WAR PENSIONERS, WAR OF 1812, AND INDIAN WARS, The Author, Washington, DC, 1952. Use with care.

_M. Motsinger, DIRECTORY OF THE MD DAR SOCIETY AND THEIR REVOLUTIONARY ANCESTORS, 1892-1965, The Society, Bel Air, MD, 1966.

_D. W. Nead, THE PA GERMAN IN THE SETTLEMENT OF MD, Genealogical Publishing Co., Baltimore, MD, 1980. Revolutionary War and tax lists.

_H. W. Newman, MD REVOLUTIONARY RECORDS, Genealogical Publishing Co., Baltimore, MD, 1967. Data from over 3000 MD Revolutionary pension and bounty land applications.

_THE PATRIOTIC MARYLANDER, MD Society of the DAR, Baltimore, MD, 1914-7, 3 volumes. Information on MD men in the Revolution and the War of 1812.

_R. Stewart, THE MD LINE IN THE REVOLUTIONARY WAR, 1775-83, The Author, Baltimore, MD, 1969.

_E. P. Passano, AN INDEX TO THE SOURCE RECORDS OF MD, The Author, Baltimore, MD, 1940, pages 451-61. Bibliography of many MD Revolutionary War records.

The above volumes may be found in MHS, MSLL, and other LGL. The original records along with indexes are in the MSA, and copies of some of the indexes are in MHS. The FHL (FHC) has some of the above books and copies of some of the records.

The Loyalists in MD, their activities, and the actions against them gave rise to records, both within and outside the state. Many MD Loyalists went to the area around Fredericton, New Brunswick, Canada shortly after the War. They settled in a district called Maryland. Attention should be paid to the following:

_MSA, MD REVOLUTIONARY PAPERS, original records with card index, MSA, Annapolis, MD. Contain Loyalist papers.

_R. A. Overfield, THE LOYALISTS OF MD DURING THE AMERICAN REVOLUTION, Thesis at University of MD, University Microfilms, Ann Arbor, MI, 1968.

_P. L. Ford, ORDERLY BOOK OF THE MD LOYALIST REGIMENT KEPT BY CAPTAIN CALEB JONES, 1778, Brooklyn, NY, 1891.

_P. J. Bunnell, THE NEW LOYALIST INDEX, Heritage Books, Bowie, MD, 1989.

_MSA, RECORDS OF CONFISCATED BRITISH PROPERTY, 1781-1824, original volumes which are indexed, MSA, Annapolis, MD.

_P. W. Coldham, AMERICAN LOYALIST CLAIMS, National Genealogical Society, Washington, DC, 1980.

_C. S. Dwyer, AMERICAN LOYALIST CLAIMS, A.O.12, Series 1, and A.O.13, Series 2, index to records in British Public Record Office (Lon-

don), RAM Publishing, De Funiak Springs, FL, 1985. Microfilm of the
records in Library, University of FL, Gainesville, FL.
_MAPS OF LAND GRANTS IN NEW BRUNSWICK SHOWING LOYALISTS,
Lands Branch, Department of Natural Resources, PO Box 6000, Fred-
ericton, NB, E3B 5H1, Canada
_LAND GRANTS AND LAND SURVEY MAPS OF NEW BRUNSWICK 1785-
1986, on microfiche with indexes, The Provincial Archives of New
Brunswick, PO Box 6000, Fredericton, NB, E3B 5H1. Many other
Loyalist-related records in this repository.
_MD LOYALIST PAPERS, 1771-90, in FISHER TRANSCRIPTS, Manuscript
MS 360, MHS, Baltimore, MD. Also on microfilm (No. 434).
_MD LOYALIST MUSTER ROLLS, 1777-83, Manuscript MS 548, MHS,
Baltimore, MD. MD Loyalists who enlisted in the British Army in Canada.
Further Loyalist records can be located by consulting:
_G. Palmer, BIBLIOGRAPHY OF LOYALIST SOURCE MATERIAL IN THE US,
CANADA, AND GREAT BRITAIN, Meckler, Westport, CT, 1982.
_P. J. Bunnell, RESEARCH GUIDE TO LOYALIST ANCESTORS, Heritage
Books, Bowie, MD, 1990.
_R. M. Gephart, REVOLUTIONARY AMERICA, 1763-89, A BIBLIOGRA-
PHY, Library of Congress, Washington, DC, 1984, 2 volumes.

For considerably more detail about genealogical data which can be
gleaned from Revolutionary War records, you may consult a book especially
dedicated to this:
_Geo. K. Schweitzer, REVOLUTIONARY WAR GENEALOGY, available from
the author at the address shown on the title page of this volume.
This volume goes into detail on local, state, and national records, discusses
both militia and Continental Army service, deals in detail with service, pension, bounty land, and claims records, and treats the subject of regimental
histories, battle accounts, medical records, courts-martial, foreign participants, Loyalist data, maps, museums, historic sites, patriotic organizations,
and many other related topics. Three other very useful detailed source
books listing Revolutionary War records are:
_R. B. Clark, Jr., MD REVOLUTIONARY RECORDS, HOW TO FIND THEM
AND INTERPRET THEM, The Author, St. Michaels, MD, 1976.
_J. C. and L. L. Neagles, LOCATING YOUR REVOLUTIONARY WAR AN-
CESTOR, Everton Publishers, Logan, UT, 1983.
_M. Deputy and others, REGISTER OF FEDERAL US MILITARY RECORDS,
VOLUME 1, 1775-1860, Heritage Books, Bowie, MD, 1986, pages 1-
137.

26. Military records: War of 1812

During the period between the Revolutionary War and the Civil War (1784-1861), the US was involved in two major foreign wars: The War of 1812 (1812-5) and the Mexican war (1846-8).

Early in the War of 1812, action in MD consisted largely of the use of Chesapeake Bay ports by MD privateers who captured and looted British merchant ships. Baltimore was the home base for more privateeers than any other US port. However, by 1813, the British had blockaded Chesapeake Bay and were raiding and ravaging towns along its shores. When American forces were defeated at Bladensburg in 1814, and Washington, DC was occupied and burned, the British turned to attack Baltimore. Both the land and sea attacks were repelled by valiant efforts, and the British withdrew. MD contributed many regular soldiers to the conflict, plus numerous militia and many civilians who aided in the defense of Baltimore and in other defensive actions. The state of MD sent about 2000 men into service in the Mexican War, but only the Washington and Baltimore Battalion saw action.

A number of MD men were involved in the War of 1812. They served both in national and state organizations, and therefore several types of national records (service, bounty land, pension), as well as state records need to be sought. Only relatively few national pensions were given before 1871, by which time not too many veterans were still living. To obtain national records (only for men who served in national units) you may write the NA and request copies of NATF-80, which may be used to order military service, bounty land, and pension information. Or you may choose to visit the NA or to employ a searcher in Washington to do the work for you. Alternately, some of the indexes and records are available on loan from AGLL, PO Box 244, Bountiful, UT 84010, and also through your local library. Among the microfilm indexes and alphabetical files which you need to search or have searched for you are:
_The National Archives, INDEX TO COMPILED SERVICE RECORDS OF VOLUNTEER SOLDIERS WHO SERVED DURING THE WAR OF 1812, The Archives, Washington, DC, Microfilm Publication M602, 234 rolls. [Leads to service records, which are available at the NA.]
_The National Archives, INDEX TO WAR OF 1812 PENSION (AND SOME BOUNTY LAND) APPLICATIONS, The Archives, Washington, DC, Microfilm Publication M313, 102 rolls. [Leads to applications, which are available at the NA.]
_The National Archives, WAR OF 1812 MILITARY BOUNTY LAND WARRANTS, 1815-58, The Archives, Microfilm Publication M848, 14 rolls, 4 indexes in first roll. [Leads to bounty land warrant applications, which are alphabetically filed in NA.]
_The National Archives, POST-REVOLUTIONARY WAR BOUNTY LAND WARRANT APPLICATION FILE, The Archives, Washington, DC, arranged alphabetically.
Copies of the three microfilm publications mentioned above are available at NA, some NARB, some LGL, and at FHL (and through FHC). Microfilm

publications M602, M313, and M848 are available on interlibrary loan from
AGLL (address above). Among published national sources for War of 1812
data are:
_F. I. Ordway, Jr., REGISTER OF THE GENERAL SOCIETY OF THE WAR
OF 1812, The Society, Washington, DC, 1972.
_E. S. Galvin, 1812 ANCESTOR INDEX, National Society of the US Daugh-
ters of 1812, Washington, DC, 1970.
_C. S. Peterson, KNOWN MILITARY DEAD DURING THE WAR OF 1812,
The Author, Baltimore, MD, 1955.

Among the state source volumes, records, and reference works
which you should search for MD War of 1812 military service records are:
_MSA, MD MILITIA RECORDS, 1794–1824, original records with card
index, The Archives, Annapolis, MD.
_MSA, MD PENSION RECORDS, WAR OF 1812, 1867–89, original re-
cords with card index, The Archives, Annapolis, MD.
_W. H. Marine, THE BRITISH INVASION OF MD, 1812-5, Genealogical
Publishing Co., Baltimore, MD, 1977. Includes MD roster of over
11,000 participants.
_F. E. Wright, MD MILITIA, WAR OF 1812, Family Line Publications, Silver
Spring, MD, 1979-, 8 volumes. Over 40,000 names of men aged 18-
45.
_N. Hickman, CITIZEN SOLDIERS OF NORTH POINT AND FORT
McHENRY, MD, 1889. List of many participants.
_T. V. Huntsberry, WESTERN MD, PA, AND VA MILITIA IN THE DEFENSE
OF MD, 1805-15, The Author, Baltimore, MD, 1979.
_THE PATRIOTIC MARYLANDER, MD Society of the DAR, Baltimore, MD,
1914-7, 3 volumes. Includes men in War of 1812.
_M. P. Andrews, MD IN THE WAR OF 1812, in TERCENTENARY OF MD,
Clarke, Chicago, IL, 1925, Volume 1, pages 686-740.
_J. T. Scharf, HISTORY OF MD, Piet, Baltimore, MD, 1879, Volume 2,
pages 1-137.
_J. T. Scharf, HISTORY OF BALTIMORE CITY AND COUNTY, Piet, Balti-
more, MD, 1874.
_T. V. and J. M. Huntsberry, MD WAR OF 1812 PRIVATEERS, The Authors,
Baltimore, MD, 1975.
_MHS, BALTIMORE INDEPENDENT COMPANY RECORD BOOK, 1814,
manuscript MS79, MHS, Baltimore, MD.
_MHS, FORT McHENRY HISTORICAL RECORDS, 1814-1958, manu-
script MS 1549, MHS, Baltimore, MD.
_MHS, HARFORD COUNTY HISTORICAL SOCIETY PAPERS, manuscript
MS 2000, MHS, Baltimore, MD.
_MHS, BALTIMORE DEFENDERS' ASSOCIATION RECORDS, VETERANS
OF THE BATTLE OF BALTIMORE, manuscript MS 72, MHS, Baltimore,
MD.

_MHS, WAR OF 1812 COLLECTION, manuscript MS 1846, MHS, Balti-
more, MD.
_A. W. Burns, MD SOLDIERS OF THE REVOLUTIONARY WAR, WAR OF
1812, AND INDIAN WARS WHO DREW PENSIONS WHILE RESIDING IN
KY, The Author, Washington, DC, 1940. Use with care.
_L. K. McGhee, MD REVOLUTIONARY WAR PENSIONERS, WAR OF 1812,
AND INDIAN WARS, The Author, Washington, DC, 1952. Use with care.
_L. K. McGhee, MD PENSION ABSTRACTS, REVOLUTIONARY WAR, WAR
OF 1812, AND INDIAN WARS, The Author, Washington, DC, 1966. Use
with care.
_E. P. Passano, AN INDEX TO THE SOURCE RECORDS OF MD, The Au-
thor, Baltimore, MD, 1940, pages 461-2. Bibliography of many MD War
of 1812 records. Includes citizens in Battle of Baltimore, lists of sol-
diers in various battles, county militia lists, wounded and killed at Fort
McHenry, muster rolls, names of privateers, pay rolls.
For numerous other War of 1812 works relating to MD, see the following
excellent bibliography:
_J. C. Fredriksen, FREE TRADE AND SAILORS' RIGHTS, A BIBLIOGRAPHY
OF THE WAR OF 1812, Greenwood Press, Westport, CT, 1985.
And for a volume which goes into much detail about genealogical records of
the War of 1812, consult:
_Geo. K. Schweitzer, WAR OF 1812 GENEALOGY, available from the au-
thor at the address shown on the title page of this volume.
This work gives information on local, state, and national records, discusses
service, pension, bounty land, and claims records, and treats the subjects
of regimental histories, hospital records, courts-martial, prisoners, militia
activity, battle sites, museums, officer biographies, and many other related
topics. Published works mentioned above should be sought in MHS, MSLL,
LGL, and FHL (FHC). Some are available in RL and LL. The manuscripts
can be located in the places noted in the individual listings.

The Mexican War was fought 1846-8. As before, NATF-80 should
be obtained and used, or you should visit the NA, or you should hire a re-
searcher as indicated in previously-given instructions (see Revolutionary
War section). Again, military service, pension, and bounty land records
should all be asked for. The NA indexes which lead to the records and
some alphabetical national records include:
_The National Archives, INDEX TO THE COMPILED SERVICE RECORDS OF
VOLUNTEER SOLDIERS DURING THE MEXICAN WAR, The Archives,
Washington, DC, Microfilm Publication M616, 41 rolls.
_The National Archives, INDEX TO MEXICAN WAR PENSION FILES, The
Archives, Washington, DC, Microfilm Publication T317, 14 rolls.
_The National Archives, POST-REVOLUTIONARY WAR BOUNTY LAND
APPLICATION FILE, The Archives, Washington, DC, arranged alphabet-
ically.

Four useful publications, one a complete roster of officers in the Mexican War, another a list of the dead, and two indexes to pension applications, are:
_W. H. Roberts, MEXICAN WAR (OFFICER) VETERANS, 1846-8, Washington, DC, 1887.
_C. S. Peterson, KNOWN MILITARY DEAD DURING THE MEXICAN WAR, The Author, Baltimore, MD, 1957.
_B. S. Wolfe, INDEX TO MEXICAN WAR PENSION APPLICATIONS, Ye Olde Genealogie Shoppe, Indianapolis, IN.
_V. D. White, INDEX TO MEXICAN WAR PENSION FILES, National Historical Publc. Co., Waynesboro, TN, 1989.

27. Military records: Civil War

Over 83,000 MD men participated in the Civil War, about 63,000 for the Union, and about 20,000 for the Confederacy. Records which are available for these participants include national service records, national pension records, national claims records, and numerous state records. No bounty land awards were made for service in this war, and MD awarded no pensions.

First, we will discuss the Union (Federal, Yankee) records. A major index lists military service records of MD Union soldiers:
_National Archives, INDEX TO COMPILED SERVICE RECORDS OF VOLUNTEER UNION SOLDIERS WHO SERVED IN ORGANIZATIONS FROM THE STATE OF MD, The Archives, Washington, DC, Microfilm M388, 13 rolls.
This index leads to the following microfilmed compiled service records:
_National Archives, COMPILED SERVICE RECORDS OF VOLUNTEER UNION SOLDIERS WHO SERVED IN ORGANIZATIONS FROM THE STATE OF MD, The Archives, Microfilm M384, 238 rolls.
The index to Union veteran (and widow) national pension applications is:
_National Archives, GENERAL INDEX TO PENSION FILES, 1861-1934, The Archives, Washington, DC, Microfilm T288, 544 rolls.
This pension file index points to pension records which are filed in the NA. The above microfilms are available at NA, NARB, MHS, and FHL (FHC). They can also be borrowed by your local library or by you from AGLL. Or you may choose to have them examined by submitting NATF-80 to the NA. Alternately, you may visit NA or NARB yourself, or you may dispatch a researcher to do the work for you. Instructions for these three possibilities were given in the Revolutionary War section. The pension applications are not on microfilm. They exist only as the originals in the NA. Hence, you must send NATF-80 to the NA, visit the NA personally, or commission a researcher to get copies for you.

Second, we will discuss the <u>Confederate</u> (Rebel, Southern) records. The southern and eastern sections of MD were predominantly southern in their sympathies. Early in the conflict, Federal troops occupied MD and put it under martial law to safeguard Washington and to prevent MD from seceding. MD men who fought for the Confederacy left MD and enlisted in VA. A few also went into other states to enlist. These enlistees were handled in three ways. (1) Large groups of them were gathered together in regiments which were designated as MD regiments. (2) Medium-sized groups were constituted as companies (10 companies in a regiment); they bore a MD designation, but became part of a VA regiment. (3) Individuals and small groups joined VA or other state's regiments, and officially lost their MD identity. However, many of these could be discovered by using various MD records to identify them. A major index which lists many MD Confederates is:

_National Archives, INDEX TO COMPILED SERVICE RECORDS OF CON-
  FEDERATE SOLDIERS WHO SERVED IN ORGANIZATIONS FROM THE
  STATE OF MD, The Archives, Washington, DC, Microfilm M379, 2 rolls.

Also very useful is an overall Confederate index, which lists soldiers serving the Confederacy from all states. This can be of assistance in finding MD men serving in other states.

_National Archives, CONSOLIDATED INDEX TO COMPILED SERVICE RE-
  CORDS OF CONFEDERATE SOLDIERS, The Archives, Washington, DC,
  Microfilm M253, 535 rolls.

The MD index (M379) leads to the following microfilm of MD Confederate service records:

_National Archives, COMPILED SERVICE RECORDS OF CONFEDERATE
  SOLDIERS WHO SERVED IN ORGANIZATIONS FROM THE STATE OF
  MD, The Archives, Washington, DC, Microfilm M321, 22 rolls.

The overall Confederate index (M253) leads to similar microfilms for other states. The above microfilms are available at the same places and by the same procedures as the Union microfilms discussed two paragraphs back.

Among the notable <u>state</u> materials relating to the Confederate soldiers of MD are the following:

_W. W. Goldsborough, THE MD LINE IN THE CONFEDERATE ARMY, 1861-
  5, Kennikat Press, Port Washington, NY, 1972.

_D. P. Hartzler, MARYLANDERS IN THE CONFEDERACY, Family Line Pub-
  lishers, Silver Spring, MD, 1986. About 12,000 servicemen from MD in
  units throughout the south.

_L. Q. Lewis, RECORDS OF MARYLANDERS IN THE CONFEDERATE NA-
  VY, The Author, Baltimore, MD, 1944, typescript.

_G. W. Booth, MD LINE CONFEDERATE SOLDIERS' HOME, The Author,
  Pikesville, MD, 1894. Lists soldiers who lived in the home.

_S. L. Pompey, MUSTER LISTS OF RIFLES, ARTILLERY, AND ZOUAVES
OF MD IN THE CONFEDERACY, The Author, Baltimore, MD, 1965, typescript.
_S. H. Miller, CONFEDERATE HILL, LOUDON PARK CEMETERY, MD, The
Author, Baltimore, MD, 1962, typescript. List of Confederates buried in
the Baltimore National Cemetery.
_H. W. Newman, MD AND THE CONFEDERACY, Old Quenzal Store, Port
Tobacco, MD, 1976.
_A DESCRIPTIVE LIST OF BURIAL PLACES OF CONFEDERATE SOLDIERS
WHO FELL IN THE BATTLES OF SOUTH MOUNTAIN, MONOCACY, AND
OTHER POINTS IN WASHINGTON AND FREDERICK COUNTIES, MD,
State Government, Annapolis, MD, 1868. Burials in Antietam National
Cemetery.
_MHS, CONFEDERATE PAPERS AND RECORD BOOKS, The Society,
Baltimore, MD, Manuscripts MSS 255-59, 770, 1860.

Details of many other Civil War records which are in the NA will be
found in:
_National Archives Staff, GUIDE TO GENEALOGICAL RESEARCH IN THE
NA, The Archives, Washington, DC, 1982, Chapters 4-10, 16.
For an in-depth discussion of Civil War records as sources of genealogical
information, consult:
_Geo. K. Schweitzer, CIVIL WAR GENEALOGY, order from the author at the
address given on the title page of this book.
This book treats local, state, and national records, service and pension
records, regimental and naval histories, enlistment rosters, hospital records, court-martial reports, burial registers, national cemeteries, grave-
stone allotments, amnesties, pardons, state militias, discharge papers,
officer biographies, prisons, prisoners, battle sites, maps, relics, weapons,
museums, monuments, memorials, deserters, black soldiers, Indian soldiers, and many other topics. Also to be recommended for an excellent
coverage of Confederate history and records is:
_J. C. Neagles, CONFEDERATE RESEARCH SOURCES, Ancestry, Salt
Lake City, UT, 1986. For MD, see pages 193-7 and 260.

There is in the NA an index to service records of the Spanish-Ameri-
can War (1898-9) which has been microfilmed:
_The National Archives, GENERAL INDEX TO COMPILED SERVICE RE-
CORDS OF VOLUNTEER SOLDIERS WHO SERVED DURING THE WAR
WITH SPAIN, The Archives, Washington, DC, Microfilm Publication
M871, 126 rolls, leads to service records in the NA.
The pension records for this war are indexed in:
_The National Archives, GENERAL INDEX TO PENSION FILES, 1861-
1934, The Archives, Washington, DC, Microfilm Publication T288, 544
rolls, leads to pension records in the NA.
Both these indexes should be sought in NA, NAFB, FHL(FHC), and from
AGLL. Again properly submitted NATF-80s (see section 26 for instruc-

tions) will bring you both military service and pension records (there were no bounty land records). Or you may choose to hire a searcher or go to the NA yourself. The best MD reference volume for this war is:

_H. R. Riley and C. S. Carrington, ROSTER OF THE SOLDIERS AND SAIL-ORS WHO SERVED IN ORGANIZATIONS FROM MD DURING THE SPANISH-AMERICAN WAR, House of Delegates of MD, Baltimore, MD, 1901.

Some national records for World War I and subsequent wars may be obtained from the following address. However, many documents were destroyed by an extensive fire in 1972. Write for Form 160:

_National Personnel Records Center (MPR), 9700 Page Blvd., St. Louis, MO 63132.

Draft records for World War I are in Record Group 163 (Records of the Selective Service System of World War I) at:

_The National Archives, Atlanta Branch, 1557 St. Joseph Ave., East Point, GA 30344.

A useful source of data on MD's World War I soldiers is:

_MD War Records Commission, MD IN WORLD WAR I, 1917-9, MILITARY AND NAVAL SERVICE RECORDS, The Commission, Baltimore, MD, 1933, 2 volumes.

There is a similar compilation for World War II:

_MHS, MD IN WORLD WAR II, REGISTER OF SERVICE PERSONNEL, The Society, Baltimore, MD, 1965, 5 volumes.

28. Mortuary records

Very few MD mortuary records have been transcribed or microfilmed, even though a few are to be found in manuscript form in archives. This means that you must write directly to the mortuaries which you know or suspect were involved in burying your ancestor. Sometimes a death account will name the mortuary; sometimes it is the only one nearby; sometimes you will have to write several to ascertain which one might have done the funeral arrangements. And you need to realize that before there were mortuaries, the furniture or general merchandise store in some communities handled burials, especially in the supplying of coffins. You may discover that the mortuary that was involved is now out of business, and so you will have to try to discover which of the existing ones may have inherited the records. Mortuaries for MD with their addresses are listed in the following volumes:

_C. O. Kates, editor, THE AMERICAN BLUE BOOK OF FUNERAL DIREC-TORS, Kates-Boyleston Publications, New York, NY, latest issue.

_YELLOW BOOK OF FUNERAL DIRECTORS AND SERVICES, Nomis Publi-cations, Youngstown, OH, latest issue.

One or both of these reference books will usually be found in the offices of most mortuaries. In general, the older mortuaries should be the more likely sources of records on your progenitor. Please don't forget that contemporary mortuaries are listed in city directories. In all correspondence with mortuaries be sure to enclose an SASE and make your letters very brief and to the point.

29. Naturalization

In the colonial period, many of the immigrants to the territory that later became the US were from the British Isles, and since the colonies were British, they were citizens. When immigrants of other nationalities began to arrive, they found that British traditions, customs, governmental structures, and language generally prevailed. During the period 1607–1740, English law set forth that only the Crown and the Parliament could issue naturalization. However, because of the long distance to London, the critical need for settlers to work the new land, the general spirit of independence, and the British reluctance to alter the law, colonies often took it upon themselves to naturalize alien immigrants. The naturalizations, given by the colonial governor, proprietor, council, or legislature, were for the individual colony, not for total British citizenship. Some alien groups came through London to secure naturalization before coming to the colonies. The major tests for naturalization were an oath of allegiance, and a Protestant religious test, one which the Crown sometimes did not invoke. For three years, 1709–12, a law allowed for naturalization by (a) an oath of allegiance to the Crown, (b) the recent taking of the sacrament, and (c) the disavowal of transubstantiation. The law was repealed in 1712 and aliens once again had to petition the Crown or Parliament.

In 1740, a law providing for naturalization of foreigners in the colonies was enacted by Parliament. It required (a) residence in a colony for seven years, (b) an oath of allegiance to the Crown and the profession of Christian belief in a colonial court, and (c) evidence of the taking of the sacrament in a Protestant and Reformed Congregation. Exemptions were allowed for Quakers and Jews, but not for Catholics. Just after the beginning of the Revolution, each newly formed American state declared all patriotic inhabitants citizens, and passed naturalization laws. Most states required an oath of allegiance, a demonstration of good character, a specified period of residency, and a disavowal of allegiance to any foreign power. The Articles of Confederation (1778/81) required that all states honor citizenship in all other states. The Constitution (1789) provided for federal naturalization which replaced the individual states' control. The new national naturalization act required one year's state residence, two years' US residence, and a loyalty oath taken in court. In 1795, a five years' residence came to be required along with a declaration of intent three years before the oath. Then in 1798, these times became 14 and 5 years respectively. Revised statutes of 1802 reverted to the 5 and 3 years of 1795. The declaration and oath could be carried out in any court which kept records (US, MD, county, city). Wives and children of naturalized males became citizens automatically. And persons who gave military service to the US and received an honorable discharge also received citizenship.

In 1906, the Bureau of Immigration and Naturalization was set up, and this agency has kept records on all naturalizations since then. Thus, if you suspect your ancestor was naturalized after September 1906, write to the following address for a Form 6641 which you can use to request records:
_Immigration and Naturalization Service, 425 I Street, Washington, DC, 20536.
For naturalization records before October 1906, you need to realize that the process could have taken place in any of several courts, in fact, any court which kept records could have been used.

For the colonial period of MD (1634-1776), during which the governor, council, and legislature naturalized citizens, consult:
_MSA, PROVINCIAL MD NATURALIZATIONS INDEX, 1634-1776, The Archives, Annapolis, MD. Refers to original records, many in the published ARCHIVES OF MD.
_J. A. and F. L. Wyand, COLONIAL MD NATURALIZATIONS, 1660-1775. Genealogical Publishing Co., Baltimore, MD, 1975. About 2600 entries.
_M. S. Giuseppe, NATURALIZATIONS OF FOREIGN PROTESTANTS IN THE AMERICAN COLONIES PURSUANT TO STATURE 13, GEORGE II (1740), Huguenot Society of London, London, England, Volume 24. Naturalizations 1743-72. About 6500 names.
_MSA, BACON'S LAWS OF MD INDEX, 1637-1763, The Archives, Annapolis, MD.
_J. T. Scharf, HISTORY OF MD, Gale Research, Detroit, MI, 1967, Volume 2, page 11. 175 naturalizations by the Provincial Legislature 1669-1750.
_COMMISSION BOOK 82, in MD Historical Magazine, Volumes 26-7, 1931-2. Many entries 1733-50, 1762-73 of naturalizations, ship registries, designations.

In the early years of the Republic (1776-89), these indexes will lead you to naturalization records in the General Courts (1781-1805):
_MSA, MD NATURALIZATION Index, 1777-1917, The Archives, Annapolis, MD.
During the period (1789-1906), before the US took over most naturalization matters, naturalizations could be carried out in any court which kept records (US, MD, county, city). It is wise to look into several indexes before starting a court-by-court search. These indexes include:

_MSA, MD NATURALIZATION INDEX, 1777-1917, The Archives, Annapolis, MD. Contains records of General Courts (1781-1805) and some county courts (not all).

_MSA, BALTIMORE COUNTY (1795-1851) AND BALTIMORE CITY (1796-1933) NATURALIZATION INDEX, The Archives, Annapolis, MD. Includes all courts in the county (1796-1851) and city (1796-1933).

_MSA, BALTIMORE COUNTY NATURALIZATION INDEX, 1852-1923. The Archives, Annapolis, MD.

_National Archives, INDEX TO NATURALIZATION PETITIONS FROM THE US CIRCUIT AND DISTRICT COURTS FOR THE DISTRICT OF MD, 1797-1956, The Archives, Washington, DC, Microfilm M1168, 25 rolls. At NA, NAPB, and MSA.

_INDEX OF THE NATURALIZATIONS AND DECLARATIONS OF INTENT FROM THE LEDGERS OF THE US CIRCUIT COURT OF BALTIMORE CITY, MD, 1797-1853, in MD Genealogical Society Bulletin, Volume 20, No. 4, Fall 1979.

Should you not find your ancestor in the above indexes, then it will be necessary to consult the county records. County (circuit) court naturalization records date back to the early 1790s, in several counties to 1791, and in one (Frederick) to 1785. MSA has the originals or copies of most of these records, and they are usually indexed. In some counties, the naturalization records or indexes to them will be kept separately, in other counties, they will be in the regular records.

---

30. Newspapers

In 1727, William Parks began publishing the MD Gazette in Annapolis. The newspaper was issued irregularly starting in 1730, and in 1734 it was discontinued. Eleven years later, in 1745, James Green started another MD Gazette in Annapolis, and it lasted until 1839. The MD Journal and Baltimore Advertiser was inaugurated in Baltimore in 1773, and the Baltimore General Advertiser took its beginning in 1775. The first newspaper in western MD was the MD Chronicle and the Deutsche Zeitung, established in 1786 in Fredericktown. In 1790, the Washington Spy was started in Hagerstown (then called Elizabeth Town), and it was joined there by the Westliche Correspondent in 1795. The first Eastern Shore newspaper was initially published at Easton in 1790. Early newspapers were not intended to cover local news and much was disregarded, including the majority of detailed data which genealogists are interested in. At first, newspapers were weekly, or biweekly, or even monthly, with daily papers coming only after the Revolution. By the early 19th century (1800-20), there were a number of newspapers in MD. As time went on, they had better coverage of local events, and thereby became more valuable as genealogical sources. There is an increase in their treatment of marriages, anniversaries, deaths (obituaries), court actions, legal notices, and town and county governmental activities.

The best repositories for originals and microfilm copies of MD news-papers are the Enoch Pratt Free Library in Baltimore, the MHS, the MSLL, and the MSA. In addition, LL and historical societies, as well as some of the larger MD universities, have newspaper holdings. It is advisable also to check with newspaper offices. To locate these newspapers, consult first these three MD guides:

_E. O. Hofstetter and M. S. Eustis, NEWSPAPERS IN MD LIBRARIES, A UNION LIST, MD State Department of Education, Baltimore, MD, 1977.

_MSA, NEWSPAPERS OF MD, A GUIDE TO THE MICROFILM COLLECTION OF NEWSPAPERS IN THE MSA, The Archives, Annapolis, MD, 1989.

_MD NEWSPAPER PROJECT LISTINGS, The Project, McKeldin Library, University of MD, College Park, MD, 1991. Lists holdings of original and microfilmed MD newspapers in numerous repositories.

Then you can look into three national listings which are very valuable for locating newspapers:

_C. S. Brigham, HISTORY AND BIBLIOGRAPHY OF AMERICAN NEWSPA-PERS, 1690-1820, American Antiquarian Society, Worcester, MA, 1961, 2 volumes.

_W. Gregory, AMERICAN NEWSPAPERS, 1821-1936, H. W. Wilson, New York, NY, 1937.

_Library of Congress, NEWSPAPERS IN MICROFORM, The Library, Wash-ington, DC, 1973, plus SUPPLEMENTS, to date.

In the major MD newspaper repositories (MHS, Enoch Pratt Free Library, MSLL, MSA), you will discover finding aids and catalogs which will lead you to newspapers which they hold for MD and for your progenitor's county. Also be sure to inquire about newspaper holdings of RL and LL, local archives, local historical and genealogical societies, museums, and newspaper offices. Some older still-existing MD newspaper publishers have files of previous issues, and a few have indexed some of their hold-ings. However, most newspapers have never been indexed, so you will need to go through them one-by-one during the times pertinent for your ancestor. This means you can avoid arduous searching only if you have a good idea of the approximate dates of the events you are seeking (mar-riage, anniversary, death, court action, legal notice, newsworthy event).

Even though few newspapers have been indexed, there are a number of volumes of genealogical data which have been abstracted from MD newspapers and indexed. There are also some volumes outside of MD which carry MD information. In addition, some useful files of newspaper excerpts are available. Among these materials are:

_W. E. Arps, Jr., BEFORE THE FIRE, GENEALOGICAL GLEANINGS FROM THE CAMBRIDGE, MD, CHRONICLE, 1830-55, Carothers, Lutherville, MD, 1978.

_W. E. Arps, Jr., MD MORTALITIES, 1876-1915, ABSTRACTED FROM THE BALTIMORE SUN ALMANAC, Family Line Publications, Silver Spring, MD, 1983.

_R. W. Barnes, GLEANINGS FROM MD NEWSPAPERS, 1727-95, Carothers, Lutherville, MD, 1975-6, 4 volumes. Deaths, marriages, legal notices.

_R. W. Barnes, MARRIAGES AND DEATHS FROM BALTIMORE NEWSPAPERS, 1796-1816, Genealogical Publishing Co., Baltimore, MD, 1978. About 8000 listings.

_R. W. Barnes, MARRIAGES AND DEATHS FROM THE MD GAZETTE, 1727-1839, Genealogical Publishing Co., Baltimore, MD, 1979. About 3000 listings.

_DIELMAN-HAYWARD FILE, MHS, Baltimore, MD. Over 250,000 biographical, death, and marriage items from MD newspapers, 1780-present. Arranged alphabetically.

_K. M. Green, THE MD GAZETTE, 1727-61, GENEALOGICAL AND HISTORICAL ABSTRACTS, Frontier Press, Galveston, TX, 1990. Over 40,000 entries.

_T. L. Hollowak, INDEX TO MARRIAGES AND DEATHS IN THE BALTIMORE SUN, 1837-50, Genealogical Publishing Co., Baltimore, MD, 1978. About 60,000 persons.

_T. L. Hollowak, INDEX TO MARRIAGES IN THE BALTIMORE SUN, 1851-60, Genealogical Publishing Co., Baltimore, MD, 1978. About 35,000 names.

_T. L. Hollowak, INDEX TO OBITUARIES AND DEATH NOTICES APPEARING IN THE JEDNOSC-POLONIA, 1926-46, Polish Genealogical Society, Chicago, IL, 1983. The earliest Polish newspaper in Baltimore.

_G. C. Keidel, EARLIEST GERMAN NEWSPAPERS OF BALTIMORE, The Author, Baltimore, MD, 1927. Chiefly historical.

_G. C. Keidel, EARLY MD NEWSPAPERS, A LIST OF TITLES, MD Historical Magazine, Volumes 28-30, 1933-5. Bibliographical.

_E. E. Lantz, SERIES OF GENEALOGICAL AND HERALDIC ARTICLES ON VA AND MD FAMILIES IN THE BALTIMORE SUN, 1905-8, 2 volumes, with A. H. Keller, INDEX, both in MHS, Baltimore, MD.

_F. J. Metcalf and G. H. Martin, MARRIAGES AND DEATHS, 1800-20, FROM THE INTELLIGENCER, WASHINGTON, DC, National Genealogical Society, Washington, DC, 1968. Contains MD data.

_K. Scott, ABSTRACTS FROM FRANKLIN'S PA GAZETTE, 1728-48, Genealogical Publishing Co., Baltimore, MD, 1975. Includes some MD names.

_K. Scott, GENEALOGICAL DATA FROM COLONIAL NY NEWSPAPERS, Genealogical Publishing Co., Baltimore, MD, 1977. Contains MD data.

_K. Scott and J. R. Clarke, ABSTRACTS FROM THE PA GAZETTE, 1748-55, Genealogical Publishing Co., Baltimore, MD, 1977. Includes MD material.

_P. Winchester and F. D. Webb, NEWSPAPERS AND NEWSPAPER MEN OF
    MD, PAST AND PRESENT, Sibley and Co., Baltimore, MD, 1905.
    Chiefly historical.
_F. E. Wright, WESTERN MD NEWSPAPER ABSTRACTS, 1786-1810,
    Family Line Publications, Silver Spring, MD, 1981-3, 3 volumes.
_F. E. Wright and I. Harper, MD EASTERN SHORE NEWSPAPER AB-
    STRACTS, 1726-1834, Family Line Publications, Silver Spring, MD,
    1981-, Volumes 1-. Items from newspapers of Caroline, Dorchester,
    Kent, Queen Anne's, Talbot, and Somerset Counties.
These volumes should be sought in MHS, MSLL, and LGL. Some of them
are at FHL (FHC), and pertinent RL and LL.

---

31. Published indexes for the US

There are many published index-es, microfilm indexes, and card indexes which list exceptionally large numbers of published genealogies or lots of genealogical data at the national level. The most important indexes dealing exclusively with MD have been listed in a previous section, the one entitled genealogical indexes. This section sets out further indexes to genealogies all over the US (and overseas in some instances). These indexes contain many references to genealogies of MD people and therefore you must not fail to look into them. Among the larger ones are:

_INTERNATIONAL GENEALOGICAL INDEX, FHL and FHC, microfiche.
    [Over 147 million entries, largely birth and marriage records.] Search
    under MD for name(s).
_TEMPLE INDEX BUREAU, at FHL, applications to have it searched avail-
    able at FHC. [Over 32 million entries.]
_FAMILY SEARCH, a computer/compact disc search system available at
    FHL and FHC. Contains numerous large data files which are alphabeti-
    cally arranged or in the form of reference indexes.
_AIS INTEGRATED CENSUS INDEXES, 1790/1800/10, 1820, 1830,
    1840, 1850NE, 1850S, 1850MW&W, FHL and FHC. [19 million en-
    tries.]
_F. Rider, AMERICAN GENEALOGICAL (AND BIOGRAPHICAL) INDEX,
    Godfrey Memorial Library, Middletown, CT, Series 1(1942-52), 48
    volumes, Series 2(1952-), over 170 volumes, more to come. [13 million
    entries so far.]
_ANCESTRAL FILE, FHL and FHC, compact discs. [Over 8 million names.]
_FAMILY GROUP RECORDS COLLECTION, FHL and FHC, microfilms.
    [About 8 million records.]
_P. W. Filby and M. K. Meyer, PASSENGER AND IMMIGRATION LISTS
    INDEX, Gale Research Co., Detroit, MI, 1981-, 9 volumes, SUPPLE-
    MENT volumes being published. [1.8 million entries so far]

_COMPUTERIZED ROOTS CELLAR, COMPUTERIZED FAMILY FILE, AND COMPUTERIZED PEDIGREE LIBRARY, Genealogical Helper, PO Box 368, Logan, UT 84321. [Over 1.2 million names.]

_PERSI, PERIODICAL SOURCE INDEX, FHL and FHC, microfiche. [Over 600,000 articles.]

_The Newberry Library, THE GENEALOGICAL INDEX OF THE NEWBERRY LIBRARY, G. K. Hall, Boston, MA, 1960, 4 volumes. [512 thousand entries.]

_1906 DECENNIAL EDITION OF THE AMERICAN DIGEST: A COMPLETE TABLE OF AMERICAN CASES, 1658-1906, West Publishing Co., St. Paul, MN, 1911, volumes 21-25. [500 thousand entries.] Subsequent volumes bring the index up to date.

_COMPUTERIZED GENEALOGICAL LIBRARY, 1864 S. State, Salt Lake City, UT 84115. [400 thousand entries.]

_NY Public Library, DICTIONARY CARD CATALOG OF THE LOCAL HISTORY AND GENEALOGY DIVISION OF THE NY PUBLIC LIBRARY, G. K. Hall, Boston, MA, 1974, 20 volumes. [318 thousand entries.]

_FAMILY REGISTRY, FHL and FHC, microfiche. [About 300,000 listings.]

_Library of Congress, LIBRARY OF CONGRESS INDEX TO BIOGRAPHIES, The Library, Washington, DC, 40 rolls of microfilm. [170 thousand entries.]

_National Society of the DAR, DAR PATRIOT INDEX, The Society, Washington, DC, 1966/79, 2 volumes. [115 thousand entries.]

_FHL LIBRARY CATALOG, SURNAME SECTION, original at FHL, microfilm copies at each FHC. [About 85,000 entries.]

_J. Munsell's Sons, INDEX TO AMERICAN GENEALOGIES, 1711-1908, Genealogical Publishing Co., Baltimore, MD, 1967. [60 thousand entries.]

_M. J. Kaminkow, GENEALOGIES IN THE LIBRARY OF CONGRESS, Magna Carta, Baltimore, MD, 1981,and COMPLEMENT TO GENEALOGIES IN THE LIBRARY OF CONGRESS, Magna Carta, Baltimore, MD, 1981. [Over 50 thousand entries.]

The books listed above are generally available at MHS, MSLL, and FHL (FHC), as well as most LGL, some RL, and a few LL. The FHL materials are also at FHC or access to them can be had through FHC.

32. Regional publications

In addition to national, state, and local publications, there are also some regional publications which should not be overlooked by any MD researcher. For the most part, these are volumes which are basically historical in character, but carry much genealogical information. They vary greatly in accuracy and coverage, so it is well to treat the data cautiously. In general, they cover specific regions which are usually made up of a few MD counties. In deciding which ones of these books to search for your forebears, you will need to make good use of the state and county maps of Chapter 1.

The following works are ones which should prove useful to you if one or more deal with areas of concern to you:

_H. Chance, WESTERN MD PIONEERS, ALPHABETICAL LISTS OF MARRIAGES, BIRTHS, AND DEATHS OF 8000 EARLY SETTLERS, original at PA Historical Society, Philadelphia, PA, also on microfilm at FHL, Salt Lake City, UT

_C. B. Clark, THE EASTERN SHORE OF MD AND VA, The Author, New York, NY, 1950, 3 volumes. Volume 3 is family records.

_R. B. Clark, Jr., MD EASTERN SHORE MARRIAGE LICENSES, 17th–19th CENTURIES, The Author, St. Michaels, MD, 1963–82, several volumes.

_G. A. Hansen, OLD KENT, THE EASTERN SHORE OF MD, DesForges, Baltimore, MD, 1877.

_I. S. Harper, MD MARRIAGE CLUES, The Author, St. Michaels, MD, 1980-4, 3 volumes. Mostly Eastern Shore data, 1600s–1820s.

_HOLDCRAFT CARD FILE COLLECTION 1800–1977, Private collection, on microfilm at FHL. Over 250,000 alphabetical references to Bible, cemetery, church, county, and other genealogical records of Frederick County and surrounding counties.

_PORTRAIT AND BIOGRAPHICAL RECORD OF THE EASTERN SHORE (6TH CONGRESSIONAL DISTRICT) OF MD, New York, NY, 1898, 2 volumes.

_M. H. Pritchett and S. R. Woodcock, THE EASTERN SHORE OF MD, AN ANNOTATED BIBLIOGRAPHY, Queen Anne Press, Queenstown, MD, 1980. [About 1100 genealogical titles listed.]

_J. T. Scharf, HISTORY OF WESTERN MD, Regional Publishing Co., Baltimore, MD, 1968, with H. R. Long, INDEXES TO THE FREDERICK AND WASHINGTON COUNTY SECTIONS OF SCHARF'S HISTORY OF WESTERN MD, ADR, Wichita, KS, 1984–6. Biographical sketches, history, and Revolutionary records for Allegany, Carroll, Frederick, Garrett, Montgomery, and Washington Counties.

_G. L. Tracey and J. P. Dern, PIONEERS OF OLD MONOCACY, THE EARLY SETTLEMENT OF FREDERICK COUNTY, MD, 1721–43, Genealogical Publishing Co., Baltimore, MD, 1987.

_E. N. Vallandigham, DE AND THE EASTERN SHORE, A HISTORY, Lippincott, Philadelphia, PA, 1922.

_F. E. Wright, MD EASTERN SHORE VITAL RECORDS, 1648–1825, Family Line Publications, Silver Spring, MD, 1982-9, 5 volumes. More than 7000 listings of birth, marriage, death, court, and church records.

The listing of works dealing with colonial MD (Section 10) contains several volumes which are regional. Further, histories of counties and cities are important regional publications. These have been discussed in

Section 9 of this chapter, and are indicated in detail under the counties and Baltimore City in Chapter 4.

33. Tax and quitrent records

In the colonial period of MD (1634–1776), when land was granted by the proprietor (Lord Baltimore) or his agent, an annual rent (a quitrent) was to be paid to him thereafter. When land was sold to another person, an alienation (or transfer) fee was to be paid the proprietor. During the period of approximately 1671–1733, the quitrents were largely replaced by tobacco inspection fees. The records of quitrent payments were kept by the agents of the proprietor in volumes called rent rolls and debt books. The rent rolls list the property under a name assigned to the land (not the owner, but the land). The records are arranged by county, and give the name of the tract, acreage, date of survey, original grantee, location, and name of the present owner. The debt books record data under the name of the owner, the acreage, name of the tract, and the amount of rent due. Not all these records have survived, but a sizable number are extant. The best collection is in MSA, with MHS having the next largest holdings, particularly those in the Calvert Papers.

Records of colonial rents are as follows:
_MSA, MD COLONIAL DEBT BOOKS, with INDEXES, 1733–74, The Archives, Annapolis, MD.
_MSA, MD COLONIAL RENT ROLLS, with INDEXES, 1639–1775, The Archives, Annapolis, MD. Indexed by occupant and by tract name.
_MSA, MD PROPRIETARY PAPERS, 1636–1785, The Archives, Annapolis, MD. Contain many tax records. Also on microfilm at FHL (FHC).
_MHS, MD RENT ROLLS 1640–1762, in CALVERT PAPERS, MS 174, The Society, Baltimore, MD. Also available on Microfilms Nos. 307–12, 672–77. See D. M. Ellis and K. A. Sturart, THE CALVERT PAPERS, CALENDAR AND GUIDE TO THE MICROFILM EDITION, MHS, Baltimore, MD, 1989.
_MHS, MISCELLANEOUS MD RENT ROLLS, MSS 27, 28, 682, 1065, 1999, 2439, The Society, Baltimore, MD.
_RENT ROLLS OF MD, 1658–1762, published in MD Historical Magazine, Volume 19 (1924) pages 341–69; Volume 20 (1925) pages 22–33, 183–99, 273–96; Volume 21 (1926) pages 285–94, 336–56; Volume 23 (1928) pages 26–39, 182–93, 265–78, 373–78; Volume 24 (1929) pages 43–45, 132–45, 228–37; Volume 25 (1930) pages 209–18; Volume 26 (1931) pages 33–42, 171–82, 264–83.
_R. B. Clark, Jr. and S. S. Clark, BALTIMORE COUNTY, MD, TAX LISTS, 1699–1706, The Authors, Washington, DC, 1964.
_MD RENT ROLLS: BALTIMORE (1700–7) AND ANNE ARUNDEL (1705–24) COUNTIES, Genealogical Publishing Co., Baltimore, MD, 1976.

_A. W. Burns, MD RENT ROLLS, The Author, Annapolis, MD, 1939, 2 volumes. Use with care.

When the Revolutionary war set in, the proprietor lost control of the land which made up MD, and rents were no longer paid. The new state of MD moved to begin assessing and collecting taxes to support the governmental operations. There were taxes collected and recorded in the counties, an overall state tax of 1783, a federal tax of 1798, and federal taxes to support the Civil War 1862-73. The state tax of 1783 attempted to list all heads of household, with information on land, slaves, livestock. The existing records cover most MD counties, and the originals and two indexes are at the MSA.

_MSA, MD TAX ASSESSMENT OF 1783, with INDEXES, one by the land owner, and one by the tract of land, The Archives, Annapolis, MD. Photocopy in MHS. Also on microfilm at FHL (FHC).

_R. W. Barnes and B. S. Carothers, 1783 TAX LIST OF BALTIMORE COUNTY, MD. Carothers, Lutherville, MD, 1978. Index to MD TAX LIST, 1783, Historic Publications, Philadelphia, PA, 1970.

_B. S. Carothers, 1783 TAX LIST OF MD: CECIL, TALBOT, HARFORD, AND CALVERT COUNTIES, The Author, Lutherville, MD, 1977.

The federal tax of 1798 was levied on windows, slaves, and some possessions. Copies are in MSA and MHS. There are three parts to the records: Part A (lists dwellings and outbuildings, name of occupant, name of owner, location and description of buildings, and value), Part B (lists lands, lots, wharves, other buildings, name of occupant, name of owner, descriptions, name of adjoining landowners, acreage, and value), and Part C (superintendent or owner of slaves, number of slaves, number of taxable slaves).

_MSA, FEDERAL DIRECT TAX OF 1798 ON MD, with INDEX FOR ANNE ARUNDEL COUNTY, The Archives, Annapolis, MD. No indexes for other available counties (Baltimore, Calvert, Charles, Harford, Prince George's, Queen Anne's, St. Mary's, Somerset, Talbot) and Baltimore City. At MSA, MHS, and FHL (FHC).

During and just after the Civil War (1862-73), the federal government imposed and collected taxes to help pay for the war. These taxes applied to goods and services for production and distribution, and included taxes on personal property, income, and licenses. The MD records for 1862-66 are on microfilm:

_National Archives, INTERNAL REVENUE ASSESSMENT LISTS FOR MD, 1862-66, Microfilm M771, the Archives, Washington, DC, 21 rolls.

This microfilm is available at NA, and NARB. Records of the years beyond 1866 are in Record Group 58 at the NA.

Tax records for MD counties date back into the 1780s, but some have been lost. They may be found in the counties and in MSA. Those for Baltimore City are also in the Baltimore City Archives. Those readily available include: Allegany (1792-1928), Anne Arundel (1827-31, 1841-9,

1876-), Baltimore City (1798-1896), Baltimore (1804-1928 erratic, many years missing), Calvert (1882-), Caroline (1866, 1897-1938), Carroll (1837-), Cecil (1782-, some years missing), Charles (1923-), Dorchester (1850-), Frederick (1798-), Garrett (1867, 1873-, many years missing), Harford (1858-), Howard (1840-), Kent (1804-), Montgomery (1798-), Prince George's (1793-, many years missing), Queen Anne's (1824/41/48/49/65/85/94/95/98,1900, 1922-), St. Mary's (1793-1826, 1876-), Somerset (1793-1896), Talbot (1798-1840, 1876-), Washington (1862-76, 1902-14, 1924-8), Wicomico (1866-), Worcester (1896-). Tax records can be exceptionally useful since they have the potential to indicate deaths, estate settlements, property transfers, and dates on which persons come of age. The tax records available for each of the counties are indicated in the detailed county sections of Chapter 4. Some published tax data are to be found in:
_R. J. Cox, BALTIMORE CITY 1797 SPECIAL TAX LIST, National Genealogical Society quarterly, Volume 66, No. 3 (September, 1978).
_R. J. Cox, A NAME INDEX TO THE BALTIMORE CITY TAX RECORDS, 1798-1808, Department of Legislative Reference, Baltimore, MD, 1981. [5750 names.]
_D. W. Nead, THE PA GERMAN IN THE SETTLEMENT OF MD, Genealogical Publishing Co., Baltimore, MD, 1980. Includes tax lists.
_MHS, MD MANUSCRIPT TAX LISTS, Manuscripts MSS 55, 74, 199, 221, 231, 508, 714, 792, 807, 838, 1028, 1117, 1134, 1233, 1565, 1675, 1929, 1999, 2000, 2139, G5048, The Society, Baltimore, MD.
A somewhat related set of listings of citizens in Baltimore can be accessed in the Baltimore City Archives (BCA):
_BCA, VOTER REGISTRATION RECORDS OF BALTIMORE CITY, 1830s and 1880s, The Archives, Baltimore, MD.

34. Will and probate records

The probate process has to do with the settlement of a person's estate, including provisions for orphaned children. Sometimes a will is involved (testate), and sometimes not (intestate). Some or all of the following records will be generated: bond of the executor or the administrator, inventory of the estate, account of expenses of administering the estate, distribution of the balance (remainder) of the estate, guardian accounts and bonds and dockets, orphans' indentures, and actions of the probate court (testamentary proceedings, papers, and dockets). Estates were probated by the Secretary of the Province (or his clerk) until 1671, and then by the MD Prerogative Court 1672-1777. As of 1692, there was a representative of the central Prerogative Court in each county. Records were kept both in the Prerogative Court and in the counties beginning at this time. The counties were required to file duplicates of their records with the Prerogative Court. In 1777, an Orphans' Court (probate court) was established in each county, and all probate activity took place in the counties from then on. In 1851, a separate Orphans' Court was established for Baltimore City. Probate records are usually of exceptional value to genealogists since they often reveal parent–child connections. A detailed discussion of the history of colonial MD probate arrangements is given in:

_E. Hartsook and G. Skordas, LAND OFFICE AND PREROGATIVE COURT RECORDS OF COLONIAL MD, Hall of Records Commission, Annapolis, MD, 1946.

The keys to colonial MD will and probate records are two card indexes in MSA:

_MSA, CONSOLIDATED CARD INDEX OF PROBATE RECORDS: WILLS, INVENTORIES, ACCOUNTS, BALANCE BOOKS, AND TESTAMENTARY PAPERS, 1634–1777, The Archives, Annapolis, MD.
_MSA, CARD INDEX TO TESTAMENTARY PROCEEDINGS, MINUTES OF THE PREROGATIVE COURT, 1657–1777, The Archives, Annapolis, MD.

The first index leads to recorded wills (1635–1777), original wills (1666–1777), inventories (1638–42, 1657–1777), accounts (1638–42, 1657–1777), balance books (1751–77), and testamentary papers (1659–1777). The records are indexed by the name of the decedent (the person who has died), except the accounts, which are indexed by decedent, executor, and administrator. The second index leads to the records of the actions of the Prerogative Court. Every name found in the records is indexed. In addition to these indexes and the original records to which they refer, there are several published works which cover sizable portions of these colonial probate materials:

_J. M. Magruder, Jr., and L. E. Magruder, INDEX OF MD COLONIAL WILLS, 1634–1777, Genealogical Publishing Co., Baltimore, MD, 1986.
_J. B. Cotton, THE MD CALENDAR OF WILLS, 1634–1743, Genealogical Publishing Co., Baltimore, MD, 1968. Abstracts of wills.
_A. W. Burns, ABSTRACTS OF MD WILLS, 1744–73, The Author, Annapolis, MD, 1938–45, 15 volumes. Use with care.
_J. M. Magruder, Jr., MD COLONIAL ABSTRACTS: WILLS, ACCOUNTS, AND INVENTORIES, 1772–77, Genealogical Publishing Co., Baltimore, MD, 1968.
_INDEX TO INVENTORIES OF ESTATES, 1718–77, Hall of Records Commission, Annapolis, MD, 1947.
_V. L. Skinner, Jr., ABSTRACTS OF THE INVENTORIES OF THE PREROGATIVE COURT OF MD, 1769–, Family Line Publications, Westminster, MD, 1983.
_R. W. Barnes and B. S. Carothers, INDEX TO BALTIMORE CITY WILLS, 1659–1850, Carothers, Lutherville, MD, 1979.
_R. B. Clark, Jr., INDEX TO COLONIAL MD WILLS TO 1777, TWELVE COUNTIES, The Author, St. Michaels, MD, 1982.

_W. F. Cregar, INDEX TO MD WILLS, APPROX. 1666-1781, typescript at
   MHS, Baltimore, MD, 1949. Also on microfilm at FHL.
_MHS, MD COLONY COURT AND PROBATE RECORDS, COUNCIL PRO-
   CEEDINGS, 1634-1774, Hall of Records Commission, Annapolis, MD,
   1963.
_MD GLEANINGS IN ENGLAND: WILLS FROM THE PREROGATIVE COURT
   OF CANTERBURY, MD Historical Magazine, Volumes 1-5, 1906-10.
_A. W. Burns, ABSTRACTS OF RECORDS OF THE PREROGATIVE COURT,
   The Author, Annapolis, MD, 1930s-1970s, over 35 volumes. Use with
   care.
The records above are in MSA which also has the most important published
volumes. The MHS, MSLL, and the FHL (FHC) have most of the published
works, and FHL (FHC) has microfilms of some of the original records.

   The MSA have probate records and indexes for the MD counties
either as originals or microfilm copies. Remember that the counties had
exclusive probate jurisdiction after 1777. These records include wills,
accounts, administrations, bonds, dockets, guardian accounts and bonds,
inventories, papers, petitions, and proceedings. Some date back very early
because the colonial counties have duplicates of some of the colonial Prerogative Court records. The holdings at the MSA for the MD counties (and
Baltimore City) are: Allegany (1789-1964), Anne Arundel (1777-1980),
Baltimore City (1635-1960), Baltimore (1635-1969), Calvert (1882-
1982), Caroline (1679-1970), Carroll (1837-1987), Cecil (1670-1988),
Charles (1665-1980), Dorchester (1688-1987), Frederick (1748-
1988), Garrett (1872-1963), Harford (1774-1965), Howard (1840-
1983), Kent (1664-1984), Montgomery (1777-1978), Prince George's
(1696-1987), Queen Anne's (1706-1987), St. Mary's (1658-1976),
Somerset (1664-1984), Talbot (1664-1986), Washington (1749-1989),
Wicomico (1867-1989), Worcester (1666-1983). Many of these records
are on microfilm at FHL (FHC). Detailed listings of those that are available
at MSA and at FHL, are given in Chapter 4. There are also some published
volumes of county probate records or indexes. Among them are:
_R. W. Barnes, ABSTRACTS OF BALTIMORE COUNTY ADMINISTRATION
   ACCOUNTS, LIBERS 6-8, Carothers, Lutherville, MD, 1975, 3
   volumes.
_L. O. Howard and M. M. Trice, GUARDIANSHIPS AND INDENTURES IN-
   VOLVING ORPHANS AS ABSTRACTED FROM PROCEEDINGS OF THE
   BALTIMORE ORPHANS' COURT, 1778-92, Carothers, Lutherville, MD,
   1975-6, 2 volumes.
_J. Hume, INDEXES TO THE WILLS OF THE COUNTIES OF ALLEGANY
   (1784-1860), GARRETT (1872-1960), HARFORD (1774-1960),
   HOWARD (1840-1950), KENT (1642-1960), ST. MARY'S (1662-
   1960), AND SOMERSET (1664-1955), Tuttle, Rutland, VT, 1970, 4
   volumes.

_R. W. Barnes and B. S. Carothers, INDEX TO BALTIMORE CITY WILLS, 1659–1850, Carothers, Lutherville, MD, 1979.

_A. W. Burns, ABSTRACTS OF WILLS OF BALTIMORE COUNTY, MD, 1782–1850, The Author, Washington, DC, 1954–67, 23 volumes. Use with care.

_R. B. and S. S. Clark, CALVERT COUNTY, MD, WILLS, 1654–1700, The Authors, St. Michaels, MD, 1974.

_V. L. Skinner, Jr., CAROLINE COUNTY, MD, INDEX TO WILLS AND AD-MINISTRATIONS, 1680–1817, The Author, Brookeville, MD, 1980.

_R. T. Dryden, SOMERSET COUNTY, MD, WILL BOOK, INCLUDING AC-COUNTS AND INVENTORIES, 1678–1749, The Author, San Diego, CA, no date.

_R. T. Dryden, SOMERSET COUNTY, MD, WILLS, 1750–72, The Author, San Diego, CA, no date.

_B. and L. D. Barron, INDEX, WILLS OF WASHINGTON COUNTY, MD, 1776–1890, Traces, Center, MO, 1982.

_R. T. Dryden, WORCESTER COUNTY, MD, ADMINISTRATIVE BONDS AND INVENTORIES, 1783–90, The Author, San Diego, CA, no date.

Your attention needs to be drawn to an index to MD probate records for 1777–1854 in the MSA. It is quite incomplete, but even so could save you considerable research time.

_MSA, CARD INDEX OF MD PROBATE RECORDS, 1777–1854, The Archives, Annapolis, MD.

Key to Abbreviations

A	=	Agricultural census records
AGLL	=	American Genealogical Lending Library
B	=	Baltimore police census
BCA	=	Baltimore City Archives (Baltimore)
C	=	Civil War Union veterans census
DAR	=	Daughters of the American Revolution
E	=	Early census–like lists
FHC	=	Family History Center(s)
FHL	=	Family History Library (Salt Lake City)
FHLC	=	Family History Library Catalog
I	=	Industrial census records
IGI	=	International Genealogical Index
LGL	=	Large genealogical libraries
LL	=	Local library(ies) in MD
LR	=	Local repositories
M	=	Mortality census records
MHS	=	MD Historical Society (Baltimore)
MSA	=	MD State Archives (Annapolis)
MSLL	=	MD State Law Library (Annapolis)
NA	=	National Archives (Washington)
NARB	=	National Archives, Regional Branch(es)
P	=	Revolutionary War pensioner census
R	=	Regular census records
RL	=	Regional library(ies) in MD
S	=	Slaveholder census
SASE	=	Long, self-addressed, stamped envelope

Chapter 3

RECORD LOCATIONS

1. Introduction

The purpose of this chapter is to describe for you the major genealogical record repositories for MD records. These repositories are of two major types, libraries and archives. In general, libraries hold materials which have been published in printed, typescript, photocopied, and microfilm (microcard, microfiche) forms. Archives, on the other hand, are repositories for original records, largely in manuscript (hand-written) form, but also often as microfilm copies. Usually, libraries will have some original materials, and archives will have some published materials, but the predominant character of each is as indicated. When visiting and making use of the materials of repositories, there are several rules which almost all of them have. (1) You are required to check all overcoats, brief cases, and packages. (2) You are required to present some identification and to sign a register or fill out a form. (3) There is to be no smoking, no eating, no loud talk, and the use of pencils only. (4) All materials are to be handled with extreme care, with no injury to or defacing of any of them. (5) Materials are usually not to be returned to the stacks or drawers from which they came, but are to be returned to designated carts, tables, or shelves. (6) Upon leaving you should submit all materials for inspection and/or pass through security devices.

As mentioned at the beginning of Chapter 2, the major repositories for MD genealogical materials are the MD Historical Society Library (MHS), the Enoch Pratt Free Library, the Peabody Collection, the Baltimore City Archives (BCA), (all four in Baltimore), the MD State Archives (MSA), the MD State Law Library (MSLL), (both in Annapolis), the Genealogical Society of Utah Family History Library (FHL) in Salt Lake City and its numerous Family History Center branches (FHC) all over the world, the National Archives (NA) in Washington and its Regional Branches (NARB) in several cities, regional libraries (RL) in various MD cities and towns, local libraries (LL) in many MD cities and towns, and county court houses, city halls, and other local repositories (LR) in MD cities and towns. Please note that the abbreviation LR refers to county court houses, city halls, town halls, and other local repositories in cities and towns of MD. These other local repositories can include historical societies, genealogical societies, record archives and institutes, museums, cemetery offices, organizations, mortuaries, and newspaper offices.

Libraries and archives have finding aids to facilitate locating the records which they hold. These aids are usually alphabetically arranged lists or indexes according to names or locations or subjects or authors or titles, or combinations of these, or they may be by dates. They consist of computer catalogs, card catalogs, microform catalogs, printed catalogs, typed catalogs and lists, various indexes, inventories, calendars, and tables of contents. In using these aids, especially computer, card, and microform catalogs, they must be searched in as many ways as possible to ensure that you extract everything from them. These ways are by name, by location, by subject, by author, by title, and sometimes by date. Sometimes certain catalogs are arranged by only one or two of these categories, but otherwise be sure and search them for all that are applicable. To help you to recall these categories, remember the word SLANT, with S standing for subject, L for location, A for author, N for name, and T for title. This is not, however, the order in which they should be searched for the maximum efficiency. They should be searched N–L–S–A–T. First, search the catalog for N(name), that is, for the surnames of all your MD forebears. Second, search the catalog for L(location), that is, look under all places where your ancestor lived (MD colony, MD state, region, county, city, town, village), but especially the county, city, and town. Examine every entry in order to make sure you miss nothing. Third, look under appropriate S(subject) headings, such as the titles related to the sections in Chapter 2 [Bible, biography, birth, cemetery, census, church denomination, church name, court, Daughters of the American Revolution, death, divorce, emigration, ethnic group name (such as Germans, Huguenots, Irish), genealogy, historical records, immigration, marriage, US–history–Revolutionary War, US–history–War of 1812, US–history–Civil War, naturalization, newspaper, MD (colony), pensions, tax, will], but never neglecting these [biography, deeds, epitaphs, family records, genealogy, registers of births etc., wills]. Then finally, look under A(author) or T(title) for books mentioned in the sections of Chapter 2 which you need to examine.

When you locate references in finding aids to materials you need to examine, you will usually find that a numbered or alphabetized or combined code accompanies the listing. This is the access code which you should copy down, since it tells you where the material is located. For books it will usually be a code which refers to shelf positions. For microfilms, it usually refers to drawers and reel numbers. For manuscripts, it usually refers to folders, files, or boxes. In some repositories, the materials will be out on shelves or in cabinets to which you have access. In other repositories you will need to give the librarian or archivist a call slip on which you have written the title and code for the material so that it can be retrieved for you. In the microfilm areas of repositories you will find microform readers which attendants can help you with, if necessary.

Never leave a library or archives without discussing your research with a librarian or archivist. These people are trained specialists who know their collections and the ways for getting into them. And they can often suggest innovative approaches to locating data relating to your progenitors. They also can usually guide you to other finding aids. When you do discuss your work with librarians and archivists, please remember that they are busy people with considerable demand on their time. So be brief, get to the point, and don't bore them with irrelevant detail. They will appreciate this, and you and others will get more and better service from them.

In general, you cannot expect to do much of your genealogy by cor-responding with libraries and archives. The reason is that the hard-working professionals who run these repositories have little time to give to answer-ing mail. This is because of the heavy demands of serving the institutions which employ them, of maintaining the collection, and of taking care of patrons who visit them. Some simply cannot reply to mail requests. Others will answer one brief question which can be quickly looked up in a finding aid, but none of them can do even brief research for you. If you do write them, make your letter very brief, get right to the point, enclose an SASE, and be prepared to wait. Repositories will generally not recommend re-searchers you can hire, but they will sometimes provide you with a list of researchers. Such a list will bear no warranty from the repository, and they in no way have any responsibility toward either you or the researcher, be-cause they are not in the business of certifying searchers.

2. The MD Historical Society Library

The Museum and Library of MD History are sponsored by the MD Historical Society, and are located in the Society's com-plex of buildings at 201 West Monument Street, Baltimore, MD 21201. Of chief concern to genealogists is the Library, which will hereafter be referred to as the MD Historical Soci-ety Library, and will be abbreviated simply as MHS. The telephone number is 1-(301)-685-3750, and the hours are 10:00 am to 4:30 pm Tuesday through Friday, and 9:00 am to 4:30 pm Saturday, with exceptions for holidays. Times are subject to change, however, so please call before going. The MHS is located in the historic and scenic Mount Vernon district just about 14 blocks north of the Inner Harbor and the Harborplace, with its shops, restaurants, and boat excursions. Baltimore blocks are short, and so there are a number of accommodations within walking distance, or you can ride the convenient, frequent, inexpensive downtown Trolley. Among the nearer lodgings are the Peabody Court [612 Cathedral Street, Balti-more, MD 21201, Phone 1-(800)-732-5301, expensive], the Comfort Inn at Mt. Vernon [24 West Franklin Street, Baltimore, MD 21201, Phone 1-(800)-228-5150, moderate], the Shirley-Madison Inn [205 W. Madison Street, Baltimore, MD 21201, Phone 1-(301)-728-6550, moderate], the Tremont Hotel [8 East Pleasant Street, Baltimore, MD 21202, Phone 1-(301)-576-1200, expensive], and the Tremont Plaza [222 St. Paul Place, Baltimore, MD 21202, Phone 1-(301)-727-2222, expensive]. It is best to park at your hotel and to walk or take the Trolley to the MHS. There are numerous restaurants, snack shops, and specialty food places near MHS for lunch. The people at MHS will give you a list and a map. Only a few blocks away from the MHS, you will find two other genealogical repositories. They are the Enoch Pratt Free Library [400 Cathedral Street] and the Peabody Collection of the Eisenhower Library of Johns Hopkins University [17 East Mount Vernon Place]. Another repository of interest to those who have Baltimore ancestors is the Baltimore City Archives (BCA), somewhat farther away [211 East Pleasant Street], so you can ride the Trolley, the bus, or take a cab there.

When you enter the MD Historical Society building, go to the check-in desk directly ahead of you, sign in, pay the small daily fee of a few dollars, then take the elevator to the second floor. Enter the Library anteroom through the door to your right, and present your fee receipt at the Reception Desk. Sign in, let them look at the materials you are bringing in, obtain a guide folder from them, and step through the entry door. Hang your coat and hat on the rack in the room on your left, and then glance around a bit to get your bearings. You will find yourself in a large, long room with research tables in the center. Immediately to your right is the reference desk, and immediately to your left (where you hung your coat and hat) is the entrance foyer to the Manuscripts Division. Along the left and right walls you will see rows and rows of book stacks. Those on the near left hold genealogical and historical books for some other states, and on the far left for MD. The MD holdings continue on the far right, and on the near right there are volumes of collected and family genealogies, followed by genealogical journals. At the back of the room are several reference bookcases, with many MD reference books, census indexes, biographical volumes, Filby and Meyer passenger list indexes, histories, and a complete file of the MD Historical Magazine. Flanking this file at the far end of the large room, you will observe two doors (on the right and on the left), both opening into a medium-sized room which is basically a finding aids room. It contains indexes, alphabetical files, vertical files, inventory notebooks, and document lists. Beginning on the left and moving to the right, you will see these finding aids, all of which sit out in the room (away from the walls):

_F1. DIELMAN-HAYWARD FILE, biographical information on MD people taken from newspapers and other sources, 1790-, arranged alphabetically, look under name.

_F2. WILKINS FILE, name index to miscellaneous tax, census, cemetery, obituary, genealogical, and immigration records, and many MD state and county histories. Alphabetically arranged, search by name.

_F3. SUBJECT FILE, vertical files, heraldry file, newspaper clippings, and other specialized files. Search by subject, location, and name.

_F4. FILING CASE A, large number of unpublished genealogical data, indexed in Genealogy Index (see later), contained in numerous boxes which are alphabetically arranged. Search by name and through use of Genealogy Index (see later).

_F5. MAP FILES AND FINDING AIDS, at the near end of FILING CASE A, search by location. Other maps on top of MICROFORM cabinets and in reference bookcases.

_F6. MICROFORM FILING CASE, contains microfilms or microfiche of MD newspapers, MD passenger lists, Baltimore city directories, MD church records, MD censuses, and the International Genealogical Index.

_F7. INTERNATIONAL GENEALOGICAL INDEX, microfiche index to numerous MD birth and marriage data and other genealogical information, search by name.

In between Filing Case A and the Microforms cabinets are microform readers.

Along the right wall are five further essential finding aids in card index cabinets:

_F8. NORRIS-HARRIS CHURCH REGISTER FILE, abstracts of genealogical data from many of the church records at MHS, arranged alphabetically by name, search by name

_F9. GENEALOGY INDEX, a finding aid to all the numerous unpublished genealogical information in MHS, arranged alphabetically by name, search by name. Items labelled G or CHARTCASE should be requested from a staff member, others are in Filing Case A.

_F10. NEWSPAPER HOLDINGS LIST, card file, search by location.

_F11. MD SOLDIERS OF THE REVOLUTION, card file, look under name.

_F12. HERALDRY INDEX, leads to materials in the Heraldry File, which is in the Subject File case, search by family name.

_F13. MAIN CARD CATALOG, key to the published volumes in the MHS, search by name, location, subject, author, and title.

Three other valuable areas in this back room are to be noted. In the center of the back wall is a large set of shelves bearing the MHS collection of published church records. In the center of the front wall is a set of indexes to the MD Historical Magazine:

_F14. CARD INDEXES TO THE MD HISTORICAL MAGAZINE, one for Volumes 1-50, another for 51-to-date, search by name, location, and subject.

In the near right corner are three further reference works:

_F15. F. Rider's AMERICAN GENEALOGICAL BIOGRAPHICAL INDEX, Series 1, Volumes 1-48 (1942-52), and Series 2, over 180 volumes (1952-), Godfrey Memorial Library, Middletown, CT. [Over 13 million entries.]

_F16. MD CHURCH RECORD DIRECTORIES, list church records available at MHS, MSA, and some other repositories, listings by county. These directories sit on a cart. Also see book by Kanely.

_F17. MD CEMETERY RECORD DIRECTORY, lists cemetery records and where they may be found. The directory sits on the same cart as the church record directories.

Now the Manuscripts Division will be discussed. You will recall that the entrance to this division is just to the left as you enter the library from the anteroom where you registered. There are three major keys to the holdings of the Manuscripts Division, all of them being published volumes:

_F18. A. J. M. Pedley, THE MANUSCRIPT COLLECTIONS OF THE MD HISTORICAL SOCIETY, MHS, Baltimore, MD, 1968. Search the index by name, location, event, and subject.

_F19. R. J. Cox and L. E. Sullivan, GUIDE TO RESEARCH COLLECTIONS OF THE MHS, MHS, Baltimore, MD, 1981. Search the index by name, location, event, and subject.

_F20. D. M. Ellis and K. A. Stuart, THE CALVERT PAPERS, CALENDAR AND GUIDE TO THE MICROFILM EDITION, MHS, Baltimore, MD, 1989. Look carefully at listings to find records which might refer to your ancestor.

Among the very useful records in the Calvert microfilms are rent receipts (1633-1765); land office accounts (1735-61); land grants for Anne Arundel (1701-38), Baltimore (1722), Calvert (1636-59), Cecil (1721-54), Charles (1636-59), Dorchester (1665-83), Kent (1744), Prince George's (1729-45), St. Mary's (1634-81), and Talbot (16789-84) Counties; land warrants (1720-21); land patent forms (1658-1761); alienation fees (1752-3); quit rents for Anne Arundel (1651-1762), Baltimore (1658-1761), Calvert (1651-1759), Cecil (1658-1762), Charles (1642-1762), Dorchester (1659-1762), Frederick (1760-62), Kent (1640-1761), Prince George's (1650-1761), Queen Anne's (1640-1762), St. Mary's (1639-1762), Somerset (1663-1762), Talbot (1658-1761), and Worcester (1658-1761) Counties; and 1750 debt books for Anne Arundel, Baltimore, Charles, Frederick, and Prince George's Counties.

When you locate references in any of the finding aids to records which you want, obtain them for yourself from the book stacks, file drawers, microfilm cabinets, or reference shelves. In some cases, most particularly manuscripts, you will need to request the materials from staff members.

Now that you have seen the 20 major indexes, lists, inventories, and other finding aids (F1-F20) in the MHS, we can recommend to you the best order in which to use them the first time you visit (or have a hired researcher visit). Practically all of the printed materials, most of the typescript materials, many of the microform materials, and most of the private manuscript materials mentioned in Chapter 2 are in MHS and can be located by using these finding aids. First, search the following items for all MD surnames of interest to you: F1-F4, F6-F9, F11-F15, F18-F19. Also, use the census indexes, then the main card catalog (F13) to locate (according to author and/or title) the MD genealogical compilations listed in the 2nd paragraph of Section 18 of Chapter 2 (genealogical indexes and compilations for MD). Check for your progenitor's name in every one of them. By the time you have completed this first step, you will probably know the county of your ancestor. So, second, you can proceed to examine the pertinent finding aids for the places where your ancestor lived in MD. Under these places, you will find listings of many sorts of records which are available for your further searching. These should be examined for the pertinent locations where your ancestor lived: MD-Colony, MD-State, any applicable region (Eastern Shore, Western Shore, Western MD, Delmarva Peninsula, etc.), the county, the city, the town. Examine every card or listing under each of the locations. Write down from the cards and listings the finding information on all promising materials, then find them and search them for ancestor data. The catalogs, indexes, and other finding aids for this second endeavor are: F3, F5, F6-F7, F10, F13-F14, F16, F17-F20. Third, you should check the appropriate items for special subjects in which you are interested: F3, F13-F14, F-18-F20. The headings of the sections in Chapter 2 will suggest some of the better possibilities, and others were suggested to you in Section 1 of this chapter. Fourth, look carefully at the large number of books and other items listed in the many sections of Chapter 2. If you have not checked them for information on your ancestor, locate these MHS holdings by author or title in the MAIN CARD CATALOG (F13), and examine them.

3.Other Baltimore repositories

In addition to the MHS, there are several other repositories in Baltimore which have genealogical materials. The first of these is the Enoch Pratt Free Library, Baltimore's principal public library. It is just a half block east and three blocks south of the MHS. The address is 400 Cathedral Street, Baltimore, MD 21201, the telephone number is 1-(301)-396-5430, and the hours are 10:00 am to 9:00 pm Monday-Wednesday, 10:00 am to 5:00 pm Thursday-Friday, 9:00 am to 5:00 pm Saturday, and 1:00 pm to 5:00 pm Sunday. The library is closed on Sunday during the summer. The library has good holdings of MD colonial, state, and local history, some very useful biography and vertical file materials, an exceptionally rich newspaper collection, MD census records, Baltimore city directories, a sizable map collection, and a fine Afro-American collection. Two areas are important to family researchers: the Maryland Room on the north end of the 2nd floor, and the Microform Center in the southwest corner of the 1st floor. Among the major finding aids and sources in the MD Room are:

_COMPUTERIZED MD UNION CATALOG, listings of over 5 million holdings in 98 MD libraries, including most the Pratt Library's materials. Contains two sections, an old catalog (pre-1972), a new catalog (after 1971). Be sure and search both. Search the catalog by name, location, subject, author, title, or any word.

_ENOCH PRATT FREE LIBRARY MICROFICHE CATALOG, contains two
    sections, one pre-1972, one post-1971. Search both sections by
    name, location, subject, author, and title.
_BIOGRAPHY FILE, many items including references to vertical file (bio-
    graphical, cemetery, church, etc.) and material taken from numerous
    sources (biographical volumes, newspapers, histories). Search by
    name.
_QUERY FILE, many subject-oriented data including vertical file referenc-
    es. Search by subject, location, name, institution, organization.
_AFRO-AMERICAN COLLECTION, 4 large vertical file cabinets, Afro-
    American biography-query card index, large book collection.
_MD NEWSPAPER PROJECT LISTINGS, The Project, McKeldin Library,
    University of MD, College Park, MD, 1991. Lists holdings of original and
    microfilmed MD newspapers in numerous repositories, including the
    extensive Pratt Library holdings. Look under name of city or town.
_CARD CATALOG MAP INDEX, by county, city, town, and geographical
    feature (river, lake, valley, etc.).
_CARD INDEX TO MD HISTORICAL MAGAZINE, Volumes 1-52, 1906-57.
The chief genealogical items in the Microform Center are:
_Baltimore, MD city directories, 1752, 1796-1901.
_MD censuses (1790-1910) and indexes to them.
_Microfilmed newspapers.

    The second of the other repositories in Baltimore is the Peabody
Collection of the Eisenhower Library of Johns Hopkins University. This
facility is to be found at 17 East Mount Vernon Place, Baltimore, MD
21202, just four short blocks east of the MHS. It is open 9:00 am to 5:00
pm Monday-Saturday, with closing on Saturday in the summer. The Peabody Collection is remarkably strong on English genealogical sources, and
it has many published works relating to MD genealogy. There is also a
vertical file containing useful references. The two keys to practically all of
the genealogical holdings are:
_GENEALOGY CARD CATALOG (for materials before 01 Feb 1989),
    search by name, location, subject, title, and author.
_JANUS COMPUTER CATALOG (for materials after 31 Jan 1989), search
    by name, location, subject, author, title, and keyword.

    The third of the other repositories in Baltimore is the Baltimore City
Archives (BCA). Please recall that many Baltimore City records are in MSA,
but BCA holds some valuable materials. The BCA is located at 211 East
Pleasant Street, Baltimore, MD 21202. This is roughly 5 blocks south and
6 blocks east of the MHS. The telephone number is 1-(301)-396-4863,
and the hours are 8:30 am to 4:30 pm Monday-Friday. A very good guide
to the collection is available from them for a few dollars:
_GUIDE TO THE RECORDS IN THE BALTIMORE CITY ARCHIVES, The
    Archives, Baltimore, MD, 1991.

Among the holdings of value to genealogical researchers are:
_CARD INDEX TO RECORDS COMPILED BY THE WPA IN THE 1930s, over
    220,000 entries. Name index to city records 1756-1938.
_CARTOGRAPHIC RECORDS, 1730-present
_CENSUS INDEXES, 1790-1860, 1880, 1900-20, arranged alphabeti-
    cally
_CITY COUNCIL, 1797-present, with some indexes
_CITY DIRECTORIES, 1796-1964, arranged alphabetically
_CIVIL WAR RECORDS, 1861-67, with indexes
_CORONERS' INQUESTS, with indexes
_EARLY RECORDS, 1756-97
_HARBOR RECORDS, 1797-1951
_INTERMENTS, 1834-40, with indexes
_NATURALIZATIONS, 1797-1951, with indexes
_PASSENGER ARRIVALS, 1820-1952, with indexes
_POLICE CENSUS, 1868
_PROPERTY TAX RECORDS, 1798-1808, 1837-46, 1856/61/66-67/
    76/86/96/1905/07
_QUERY FILE CARD INDEX
_SCHOOL RECORDS CARD INDEX
_TAX APPEAL COURT RECORDS,D 1841-1947
_TOWN COMMISSIONERS' RECORDS, 1729-97
_VOTER LISTS, 1838, 1839, 1868, 1877-89, with some indexes
_WAR OF 1812 RECORDS, 1813-14

4. MD State Archives (MSA)

The MD State Archives (MSA) is the official repository for the preservation of the colonial, state, county, and local records of MD from the beginning of MD to the present. The MSA holds a remarkably rich collection of original, microfilmed, and published records pertinent to MD genealogical research, along with a wealth of indexes and other finding aids. The Archives is located in the Hall of Records Building, 350 Rowe Blvd., Annapolis, MD 21401. The telephone numbers are 1-(301)-974-3914 and 1-(301)-974-3916. They are open 8:30 am to 4:30 pm, Monday through Saturday, except on state holidays (January 1, 15, 3rd Monday in September, 2nd Monday in October, 1st Tuesday in November of even-numbered years, November 11, Thanksgiving Day, December 25). If one of these holidays falls on Sunday, the MSA is closed the following Monday. If one of these holidays falls on Friday or Saturday, the MSA is closed both days. The above times are subject to change, so never go to the MSA without writing or calling them about your planned visit.

There is a parking lot adjacent to the Archives, but be sure and register your presence there when you check in. The nearest lodgings are about a mile away, and in good weather it is not a difficult walk. If you do not wish

to walk, the Shuttle bus route runs out there in a few minutes and at low cost. Accommodations include the Loew's Annapolis Hotel [126 West St., Annapolis, MD 21401; Phone 1-(301)-263-7777 or 1-(800)-333-3333], Annapolis Hilton Inn [Compromise and St. Mary's Streets, Annapolis, MD 21401; Phone 1-(301)-268-7555 or 1-(800)-445-8667], Maryland Inn [16 Church Circle, Annapolis, MD 21401; Phone 1-(301)-263-2641 or 1-(800)-847-8882], Governor Calvert House [58 State Circle, Annapolis, MD 21401; Phone 1-(301)-263-2641 or 1-(800)-847-8882], Gibson's Lodgings [110 Prince George St., Annapolis, MD 21401; Phone 1-(301)-268-5555], and Prince George Inn [232 Prince George St., Annapolis, MD 21401; Phone 1-(301)-263-6418]. Eating places for lunch near the Archives include the New Canton (111 Ridgely Avenue), the MD Department of Natural Resources Cafeteria (just across Rowe Blvd. in the Tawes State Office Building), and the soup, salad, and deli service in Graul's Supermarket (607 Taylor Ave.). The local tourist office will send you a guide to scenic Annapolis, a restaurant list, an accommodation list, and a bus map, if you will write them:
_The Greater Annapolis Chamber of Commerce, 152 Main St., Annapolis, MD 21401. Phone 1-(301)-268-7676.

Before visiting the MSA, there are several guides which you should order from them. Then, you should make yourself thoroughly acquainted with their contents. Such a procedure will save you an immense amount of time and will permit you to go to work almost immediately upon your arrival. These guides are:
_MSA, GUIDE TO THE FINDING AIDS AT THE MSA, The Archives, Annapolis, MD, latest edition. Free, but send $1 postage.
_MSA, A GUIDE TO THE INDEX HOLDINGS AT THE MSA, The Archives, Annapolis, MD, latest edition. About $6, write for price.
_MSA, A GUIDE TO GOVERNMENT RECORDS AT THE MSA, The Archives, Annapolis, MD, latest edition. About $18, write for price.

Upon arrival at the MSA, you will report at the registration desk, where you will fill out a registration form, show some identification, read and sign an agreement to abide by their rules, sign the log book, and receive an identification badge, a locker assignment, and a desk assignment. The lockers are in the region of the registration desk, as are the rest rooms. You are required to store all pens, books, bags, handbags, briefcases, carrying cases, parcels, and overcoats in your locker. Only pencils, paper, and a small quantity of research materials may be taken into the Search Room. They all must be submitted for inspection upon your departure, at which time, you must log out. Permission must be obtained to bring in computers, typewriters, recorders, and photo equipment. Personal copiers are forbidden. When you enter the Search Room, you will find yourself in a very large room filled with 48 research desks, 5 shelves bearing reference volumes, a map case and table, 2 book return carts, a circulation desk, 15 cabinets and tables carrying 124 INDEXES, several places with COMPUT-ERS, and a GUIDE TABLE. Off to your right, there are 2 doors, one into the Microfilm Reader Room, and another into the Microfilm Reference Room, which contains numerous microfilm storage cabinets and the MICROFILM GUIDE TABLES. The four items capitalized in this paragraph are the keys to the entire contents of the MSA: (1) INDEXES, (2) COMPUTERS, (3) GUIDE TABLE, (4) MICROFILM GUIDE TABLES.

These key items will now be described. The 124 INDEXES include both card indexes and indexes in volumes. Each is numbered to facilitate you finding it. They are numbered 1 through 143, but some of the numbers are unassigned. The indexes are as follows:

_1. Probate records 1634-1777
_2. Testamentary (probate) proceedings 1634-1777
_3. Probate records 1777-1854, very incomplete
_5. Records which imply marriages, Hodges 1674-1851
_6. Marriage licenses and records 1650-95, 1776-1886, incomplete
_7-26. Baltimore City and County marriage licenses 1777-1851
_27. Church records - marriages 1686-1958, for only 15 churches
_28. Church records - births and baptisms 1663-1967, for only 15 churches
_29. Church records - deaths and burials 1663-1967, for only 15 churches
_30. Birth records 1649-1715, 1804-77, 1898-1923, incomplete
_31. Death records 1655-95, 1898-1930, incomplete
_32. Family Bible and tombstone records, refers to manuscript and published records
_33. Anne Arundel miscellaneous records 1704-05, 1788-1867
_34. Anne Arundel certificates of freedom 1805-64
_35. Anne Arundel freedom records, owners 1785-1867
_36. Dorchester black records 1806-68
_37. Dorchester slave owners 1806-68
_38. Prince George's freedom and slave data 1806-69
_39. Queen Anne's certificates of freedom - free blacks 1807-64
_40. Queen Anne's certificates of freedom - owners 1807-64
_41. Provincial naturalizations 1634-1776
_42. Naturalizations in Eastern and Western Shore General Courts and some other courts 1777-1917
_43. Naturalizations in Baltimore County 1796-1851 and Baltimore City 1796-1933
_44. Baltimore county naturalizations 1852-1918
_45. Colonial muster and pay rolls 1732-72
_46. Censuses of 1776 and 1778
_47. Oaths of fidelity 1778
_48. Revolutionary War pensions 1775-
_49. Revolutionary War papers 1775-89

_127. Montgomery land records 1777–1845
_129–130. Queen Anne's land records 1706–1854
_131. Somerset land records 1665–1841
_132. Talbot land records 1662–1833
_133. Washington land records 1776–1836
_134–135. Worcester land records 1742–1844
_136. Provincial court judgments 1658–1778
_137–139. Provincial and general court deeds 1658–1815
_140. Land warrants and assignments 1634–1751
_141. Land caveats and records 1739–1964
_142. US courts of MD naturalizations 1797–1906, 1925–51
_143. Provincial court judgments 1679–1717

Please note the following classifications of the above indexes (the index numbers are in parentheses):
_Baltimore marriage indexes, 1777–1848 (5–27)
_Bible and cemetery records listings (32)
_Births, 1649–1715, 1804–77, 1898–1923 (30)
_Black records, 1805–69 (34–40)
_Chancery court, 1713–1851 (59–61)
_County land (33, 69–80, 115, 117–118, 120–123, 125, 127, 129–135)
_County probate (3, 82–84, 119, 124, 126)
_Deaths, 1655–95, 1898–1930 (31)
_Library Catalog up to 1975 (101)
_Maps, plats, and atlases (111–113)
_Marriage indexes, 1674–1886 (5–6)
_MD Historical Magazine indexes (102–105)
_Military records indexes 1732–1865 (45–53)
_Naturalizations indexes 1634–1973 (41–44, 142)
_Provincial court and general courts indexes, 1658–1815 (136–139, 143)
_Provincial land indexes 1634–1985 (54–58, 64, 140–141)
_Provincial probate indexes (1–2)
_Special collections (108–109)
_Tax list indexes, 1783 (65–66)

The COMPUTERS are connected into a number of very large data bases which function as detailed indexes. You may call up any word (like Wicomico or assessment) or any two-word phrase (such as Anne Arundel or rent rolls), and the computer will bring to the screen all occurrences of the word or the phrase in the data base. Among the most useful data bases on the computer which are pertinent to genealogical research are these:
_DB1. ADMIRALTY: MD Admiralty Court records 1776–87
_DB2. BA–BCPAP: Chancery papers of Baltimore County Court 1815–51, and Baltimore City Superior Court 1851–70
_DB3. LIBRARY: Catalog of published works in MSA up to present; see Index 101

_DB4. MAPS: Maps in MSA; see Index 111
_DB5. PLATS: Provincial, state, and some county plats 1724-1962; see Indexes 112-113
_DB6. PROV-PAP: Miscellaneous provincial papers in MSA 1714-77
_DB7. SERIALS: List of periodicals in MSA
_DB8. SERIES: Detailed list of governmental records in MSA and dates of them [original and microfilm records for the colony, state, counties, cities, towns of MD]; Updated version of A GUIDE TO GOVERNMENT RECORDS AT THE MSA, The Archives, Annapolis, MD, latest edition.
_DB9. SPECCOL: List of private papers, manuscripts, and records; see Index 108
_DB10. SPECCOLM: Miscellaneous microfilms [church records, state documents, 1798 tax, marriage records, published genealogies, census records, private manuscripts, military records, published books, maps, atlases, newspapers, debt books, cemetery records, surveys]; see Index 109
_DB11. TOPIC: Special topics [newspaper clippings, magazine articles, pamphlets, announcements, brochures, personal letters, notable events, buildings, sites]
_DB12. CHANCERY: Chancery Court papers 1770-1851; see Indexes 59-63
_DB13, SCHARF: The Scharf historical collection [large amount of data on MD history]

There are other data bases on the COMPUTERS, and more are being added. By far the most useful to you are DB3 and DB8. DB3. LIBRARY functions as a card catalog of books in MSA. You can enter any word or group of words and there will be displayed on the screen all books whose reference citations contain the word or group of words. Each reference citation includes the author, the title, the subject matter of the book, and the geographical location to which it applies. Hence, you can enter the name of an author and see all his/her books; enter the word marriage and see all books whose titles contain the word marriage or whose descriptions contain the word marriage; enter the words Harford County and you will get all volumes relating to Harford County. DB8. SERIES is a data base which contains a very detailed list of the colonial, state, county, and municipal records held by MSA, both as originals and microfilms. These listings may be called up by a word or a two-word phrase. This lets you see all will records by entering the word wills. Or you can see all Allegany wills by entering those two words. Or you can view all Allegany County records by entering Allegany County. Or all provincial court records by entering provincial court.

The GUIDE TABLE holds numerous guides in blue notebooks. They describe in detail the large holdings in MSA in original colony, state, county, and municipal records, as well as some very important private records (chiefly church records and special manuscript collections). These guides are as follows:

_G1. COUNTY AGENCY SERIES GUIDES, one guide for each of MD's counties and one for Baltimore City, list original records held by MSA, contained in 34 notebooks.

_G2. MUNICIPAL AGENCY SERIES GUIDES, one guide for each of Annapolis, Cambridge, Charlestown, Chevy Chase, Denton, Easton, Fishing Creek, Islington, Leonardtown, and Vienna, list original records held by MSA, contained in 2 notebooks.

_G3. STATE AGENCY SERIES GUIDES, index of the MD state agencies in the first notebook, list original colony and state records held by MSA, contained in 20 notebooks.

_G4. GUIDES TO ORIGINAL STATE BIRTH AND DEATH RECORDS, list original records held by MSA, pertain to records of Baltimore City after 1874 and county records after 1897.

_G5. GUIDES TO ORIGINAL LOCAL BIRTH AND DEATH RECORDS, list original records held by MSA, listed by county.

_G6. GUIDES TO CHURCH RECORDS, listed by denomination, then by county, list records held by MSA, contained in 10 notebooks. Major denominations represented are Baptist, Church of God, Evangelical Lutheran, Lutheran, Methodist, African Methodist Episcopal, Protestant Episcopal, Moravian, Presbyterian, Quaker, United Church of Christ, Roman Catholic. Those which are underlined are very large collections.

_G7. GUIDES TO SPECIAL COLLECTIONS, in MSA, listed by name of special collection (private manuscripts, papers, and/or records), gives brief inventory of contents of each, contained in 4 notebooks.

The MICROFILM GUIDE TABLES holds many guides to microfilm records in a set of blue notebooks. They describe in detail the large holdings of MSA of microfilmed colony, state, county, and some private records of MD. These guides are as follows:

_M1. GUIDES TO MSA HOLDINGS OF COUNTY RECORDS ON MICRO-FILM one for each county and one for Baltimore City, list microfilmed records held by MSA, contained in 7 notebooks. [Guides available from MSA for $5 each.]

_M2. GUIDES TO STATE AGENCY MICROFILMED RECORDS IN MSA, index of state agencies in first volume, index of record types in first volume, list microfilmed records held in MSA, contained in several notebooks.

_M3. GUIDE TO MISCELLANEOUS MICROFILMS IN MSA, microfilms of such items as the published Archives of MD, special private collections, state papers, family papers, contained in 1 notebook.

_M4. GUIDE TO NEWSPAPERS IN THE MSA, consists of two volumes contained in 1 notebook. They are L. White and others, A GUIDE TO THE MICROFILM COLLECTION OF NEWSPAPERS AT THE MSA, The Archives, Annapolis, MD, 1990; and MD Newspaper Project, NEWSPAPERS LOCATED AT THE MSA, The Project, College Park, MD, 1990.

_M5. GUIDE TO MD CITY DIRECTORIES AND US CENSUSES ON MICRO-
FILM AT THE MSA, contained in one notebook.
_M6. GUIDE TO BIRTH AND DEATH RECORDS AND INDEXES ON MICRO-
FILM AT THE MSA, contained in 2 notebooks.
The contents of guides G1-G5, M1-M2, and M6 are largely in DB8 and
printed out in A GUIDE TO GOVERNMENT RECORDS AT THE MSA, The
Archives, Annapolis, MD, latest edition.

The 124 INDEXES (1-3, 5-84, 101-115, 117-143), the 13 COM-
PUTER DATA BASES (DB1-DB13), the 7 sets of guides on the GUIDE
TABLE (G1-G7), and the 6 sets of guides on the MICROFILM GUIDE TA-
BLES (M1-M6) will lead you to the holdings of the MSA (original, microfilm,
published). You have probably noticed that several of these finding aids
deliver practically the same information. For example, Index 101 and DB3
both list published works in MSA, but 101 is incomplete. Or you may have
discerned that DB8 and the book A GUIDE TO GOVERNMENTAL RECORDS
AT THE MSA list practically everything in the combined G1-G2-G3-G4-
G5-M1-M2-M6. When you discover a record in any of these finding aids
(1-3, 5-84, 101-115, 117-143, DB1-DB13, G1-G7, M1-M6) that you
wish to consult, copy the reference numbers accompanying the listing. If
the record is a book, check the reference shelves for it. If you do not find it,
request it at the request desk. If the record is a microfilm, proceed to locate
it in the microfilm cabinets (in the microfilm room), then take it next door to
the microfilm reader room. For all other materials, request them at the
request desk.

Now that you have read about the abundant indexes and record finding lists in the MSA, here is one comprehensive way to proceed with your
search. First, examine the following for your ancestor's name: DB3. Then
use DB3 to locate (by author or title) as many as possible of the large indexes listed in the 2nd paragraph of Section 18 of Chapter 2 (census, indexes,
military microfilms, large MD genealogical compilations, Passano, MD
GENEALOGIES, Brumbaugh, Virdin, passenger lists, Barnes, Baltimore
City directories, Coldham, Skordas, Magruder, MD ARCHIVES indexes,
Burns, Wright, Parran, Newman, index of MD GENEALOGICAL SOCIETY
BULLETIN, Cotton, Clark, Bromwell, etc.). Examine all of these carefully
for references to your forebear, and if indicated, consult the original records to which they lead you. Then continue your search for your forebear's name in these finding aids: 1-26, 30-31, 41-63, 65-66, 81,
102-104, 136-143. By this time, you will probably have located your
ancestor, discovered her/his county, and quite likely gathered other data.
Then, second, proceed to examine the pertinent finding aids for the places
where your progenitor lived in MD. Under these places you will find listings
of many sorts of records which are available for your further searching.

These listings should be examined for the pertinent locations where your ancestor lived: MD-Colony, MD-State, any applicable region (Eastern Shore, Western Shore, Western MD, Delmarva Peninsula, etc.), the county, the city, the town. Examine every card or listing under each of the locations. Write down from the cards or listings the finding information on all promising materials, then find them and search them for ancestor data. The finding aids for this second endeavor are: DB8 (and/or the book A GUIDE TO GOVERNMENT RECORDS AT THE MSA), DB3, DB4-DB5, DB7, DB9-DB11, G6-G7, M3-M5, 32, 203-204, 108-109. Third, check the following items for any special subjects in which you are interested: DB3, DB8, 79-81, 106-107, 110-114, DB1, DB6, DB9-DB11, DB13, G7, M4-M5. Fourth, review Chapter 2, look at the many books and other reference items mentioned there, and seek out those which might list your progenitor, and which you have not yet seen. Locate them by author or title in DB3, and look into them.

Some small amount of searching can be requested by mail from the MSA. For a non-refundable $15 fee, they will devote up to one hour of time answering one or two questions by searching their indexes. For each question, you must provide four pieces of information: (1) full name of the person, (2) the MD county in which the person lived, (3) the type of record being sought, and (4) an approximate date (plus or minus 15 years) of the record. Make your letter brief and to-the-point, send no more than $15, recognize that only indexes will be examined, and remember that success cannot be guaranteed. You are paying for the work they must do, whether they find your information or not. If you require detailed research, MSA will provide you with a list of professional genealogists. However, MSA does not and cannot recommend or guarantee researchers, since this is not part of their mission.

Now, we have the pleasure of telling you something absolutely marvelous. The MSA will lend practically any of their vast collection of microfilmed records to any library in the US which maintains an interlibrary loan department. This means that your local library may borrow for you the microfilms you need. Your local library may make a small charge in addition to the postage, but the MSA offers this service free. The best book which lists the governmental (state, colony, county, city, town) records which MSA has on microfilm is the following volume:
_MSA, A GUIDE TO GOVERNMENTAL RECORDS AT THE MSA, The
    Archives, Annapolis, MD, latest edition.
There is no comparable listing of non-governmental records, so you will need to request those you need by name. Practically all of the microfilmed church records at MSA are listed in
_E. A. Kanely, DIRECTORY OF MD CHURCH RECORDS, Family Line Publi-
    cations, Silver Spring, MD, 1988.

All are available from them except the Catholic, for which special permission from the Archdiocese is required.

5. The MD State Law Library (MSLL)

Just across Rowe Boulevard from the MSA, you will find the MD State Law Library (MSLL). It is located on the 1st floor of the MD Courts of Appeal Building at 361 Rowe Boulevard, Annapolis, MD 21401-1697. The hours are 8:30 am to 4:30 pm Monday, Wednesday, and Friday, 8:30 am to 9:00 pm Tuesday and Thursday, and 9:00 am to 4:00 pm Saturday, except for holidays. The telephone number is 1-(301)-974-3395. Even though law is the primary focus of the library, they have excellent collections in the areas of MD genealogy, MD history, and government documents. They have an active on-going policy of acquiring all newly published volumes relating to MD history and MD genealogy. A useful pamphlet describing many of their major genealogical reference works is available from them:
_MSLL, SOURCES OF BASIC GENEALOGICAL RESEARCH IN THE MSLL, A SAMPLER, The Library, Annapolis, MD, latest edition.
Their extensive holdings of books include volumes on the following: MD censuses and indexes, MD military records, MD immigration and naturalization records, MD newspaper abstracts, MD Archives (72 volumes), and MD biography records. They also have some MD newspapers and a number of MD genealogical and historical periodicals.

When you enter the library, check in at the desk just ahead of the entry doors. Then walk to your right, and go into the Genealogy/Government Documents Area. In the stacks to your left, you will find the MD materials. They carry call numbers chiefly MD920 through MD976, and CS2 through CS2481. There is a separate section for each MD county, and the book shelves are labelled to assist you. Behind the genealogy book stacks on the left wall is the key to the genealogical contents of the MSLL:
_MD CARD CATALOG, search by name, location, subject, title, author.

6. Family History Library (FHL) and Its Branches (FHC)

The largest genealogical library in the world is the Family History Library of the Church of Jesus Christ of Latter-Day Saints (FHL), often referred to as Mormon Library or the LDS Library. This repository holds well over 1.7 million rolls of microfilm plus more than 175,000 books, all genealogical material. It is located at 35 North West Temple, Salt Lake City, UT 84150. The library opens every day except Sunday and holidays at 7:30 am. It closes at 5 pm Saturday, 6 pm Monday, and 10 pm Tuesday through Friday. The general telephone number is 1-(801)-521-0130.

The basic key to the library is a massive index called the Family History Library Catalog (FHLC), a set of microfiche (with five sections: surname, locality, subject, author–title, foreign–language–locality). In addition to the main library, the Church maintains a large number of branches called Family History Centers (FHC) all over the world. Each of these has microfiche copies of the Family History Library Catalog (FHLC), plus several other major indexes, plus forms for borrowing microfilm copies of the records at FHL. This means that the astonishingly large holdings of the FHL are available on loan through each of its numerous FHC (Family History Centers or Branch Libraries of the FHL).

The Family History Centers in the state of MD are:
_Family History Center, 1875 Ritchie Highway, Annapolis, MD 21401.
_Family History Center (Baltimore), 1400 Dulaney Valley Road, Lutherville, MD 21093.
_Family History Center (Seneca), 4100 St. John's Lane, Ellicott City, MD 21043.
_Family History Center (Silver Spring), 1000 Stoneybrook Drive, Kensington, MD 20795.
_Family History Center, 199 North Place, Frederick MD 21701.
When you get ready to visit these FHC or any of the hundreds of others we will soon mention, call them or write them (including an SASE) inquiring about open hours and exact locations.

Other FHC are to be found in the cities listed below. They may be located by looking in the local telephone directories under the listing CHURCH OF JESUS CHRIST OF LATTER DAY SAINTS or in the yellow pages under CHURCHES–LATTER–DAY SAINTS.
_In AL: Birmingham, Huntsville, in AK: Anchorage, Fairbanks, in AZ: Campe Verde(Cottonwood), Flagstaff, Globe, Holbrook, Mesa, Page, Phoenix, Prescott, St. David, Safford, St. Johns, Show Low, Snowflake, Tucson, Winslow, Yuma, in AR: Little Rock,
_In CA: Anaheim, Bakersfield, Barstow, Blythe(Needles), Camarillo, Cerritos(Santa Fe Springs, Lakewood), Covina (West Covina), Cypress-(Buena Park), El Centro, Escondido, Eureka, Fairfield, Fresno, Garden Grove, Glendale, Gridley, Hacienda Heights, Hemet, La Crescenta(La Canada), Lancaster, Long Beach, Los Angeles(Alhambra, Canyon Country), Menlo Park, Mission Viejo, Modesto, Monterey(Seaside), Napa, Newbury Park, Oakland, Orange, Palmdale, Palm Springs(Cathedral City), Pasadena(East Pasadena), Redding, Ridgecrest, Riverside, Sacramento(Carmichael), San Bernardino, San Diego, San Jose, San Luis Obispo, Santa Barbara(Goleta), Santa Clara, Santa Maria, Santa Rosa, Simi Valley, Southern CA(Los Angeles), Stockton, Upland, Ventura, Whittier,
_In CO: Arvada, Boulder, CO Springs, Columbine(Littleton), Cortez, Denver(Northglenn), Durango, Ft. Collins, Grand Junction, LaJara, Littleton,

Meeker(Glenwood Springs), Montrose, Pueblo, in CT: Hartford, in DE: Wilmington(Newark), in FL: Cocoa, Gainesville(Alachua), Hialeah/Ft. Lauderdale, Jacksonville(Orange Park), Lakeland, Marianna, Miami, Orlando(Fern Park), Pensacola, St. Petersburg, Tallahassee, Tampa, West Palm Beach(Boca Raton), in GA: Macon, Marietta(Powder Spring), Sandy Springs(Dunwoody), in HI: Hilo, Honolulu, Kaneohe, Kona(Kailua), Laie,

_In ID: Bear Lake(Montpelier), Blackfoot(Moreland), Boise, Burley, Caldwell, Driggs, Firth, ID Falls, Iona, Lewiston, Malad, Meridian(Boise), Moore(Arco), Nampa, Pocatello, Post Falls, Salmon, Shelley, Twin Falls, Upper Snake River(Rexburg), in IL: Champaign, Chicago Heights(Lossmoor), Naperville(Downers Grove), Rockford, Wilmette, in IN: Fort Wayne, Indianapolis(Greenwood), in IA: Cedar Rapids, Davenport, Des Moines, in KS: Topeka, Wichita, in KY: Hopkinsville(Benton), Lexington, Louisville, in LA: Baton Rouge, Shreveport,

_In MA: Boston(Weston), Foxboro(Hingham), Lynfield, Worcester, in ME: Augusta(Hallowell), in MD: Annapolis, Ellicott City (Seneca), Frederick, Kensington (Silver Spring), Lutherville (Baltimore), in MI: Bloomfield Hills, Grand Blanc, Grand Rapids, Lansing(East Lansing), Midland, Westland, in MN: Minneapolis(Richfield), St. Paul, in MS: Hattiesburg, in MO: Columbia, Kansas City(Shawnee Mission), Liberty, Springfield, St. Louis (Berkeley), in MT: Billings, Bozeman, Butte, Great Falls, Helena, Kalispell, Missoula, in NE: Omaha,

_In NV: Elko, Ely, Fallon, Las Vegas, Logandale, Reno, Sparks, in NJ: East Brunswick, Morristown(Chatham), in NH: Nashua, in NM: Albuquerque-(Los Alamos), Farmington, Gallup, Grants, Los Cruces, Roswell, Santa Fe, in NY: Albany(Loudonville), Buffalo(Williamsville), Ithaca (Vestal), New York City, Plainview(Massapequa), Rochester(Webster), Syracuse, Yorktown(New Canaan, CT), in NC: Asheville(Arden), Charlotte, Fayetteville, Hickory, Kinston, Raleigh(Bailey Road), Wilmington(Hampstead), in OH: Cincinnati, Cleveland(North Olmstead), Columbus(Reynoldsburg), Dayton(Jettering), Kirtland, Toledo(Maumee), in OK: Norman, Oklahoma City, Tulsa,

_In OR: Beaverton, Bend, Coos Bay, Corvallis, Eugene, Grants Pass, Gresham(Fairview), Klamath Falls, LaGrande, Lake Oswego(West Linn), Medford, Nyssa(Ontario), Oregon City, Portland, Prineville, Roseburg, Salem, The Dallas, in PA: Philadelphia(Broomall), Pittsburgh, Reading, State College, York, in SC: Charleston(Hanahan), Columbia(Hopkins), Greenville, in TN: Chattanooga, Kingsport, Knoxville(Bearden), Memphis, Nashville(Madison), in TX: Austin(Georgetown), Beaumont(Nederland), Corpus Christi, Dallas, El Paso, Hurst, Friendswood, Houston-(Bellaire), Longview, Lubbock, Odessa, Plano(Richardson), San Antonio,

_In UT: Beaver, Blanding, Bountiful, Brigham City, Cache(Logan), Castledale(Orangeville), Cedar City, Delta, Duchesne, Fillmore, Heber City, Hurricane, Kanab, Lehi(Salt Lake City), Loa, Moroni, Mount Pleasant,

Nephi, Ogden, Parowan, Price, Richfield, Roosevelt, Rose Park(Salt Lake City), Sandy, Santaquin, South Jordan(Riverton), St. George, Springville, Tremonton, UT Valley(Provo), Uintah(Vernal), in VA: Annandale, Charlottesville, Fairfax(Springfield), Norfolk(VA Beach), Oakton, Richmond, Roanoke,
In WA: Bellevue, Bellingham(Ferndale), Bremerton, Ephrata(Quincy), Everett, Kennewick, Longview, Moses Lake, Mount Vernon, Olympia, Pasco, Pullman, Puyallup(Sumner), Richland, Seattle, Spokane, Tacoma, Vancouver, Walla Walla, Wenatchee(East Wenatchee), Yakima, in WI: Appleton, Beloit(Belvidere), Milwaukee, in WY: Afton, Casper, Cody, Evanston, Gillette(Sheridan), Green River, Kemmerer, Lovell, Rock Springs, Worland, Wyoming(Cheyenne).
The FHL is constantly adding new branches, so this list will probably be out-of-date by the time you read it. An SASE and a $2 fee to the FHL (address in the 1st paragraph above) will bring you the most-recent listing of FHC.

When you go to a FHC, you need to first look up the MD surnames of interest to you in the following indexes:
_The MD Section of the INTERNATIONAL GENEALOGICAL INDEX (IGI).
_The Surname Portion of the FAMILY HISTORY LIBRARY CATALOG (FHLC).
_THE FAMILY REGISTRY.
_THE ANCESTRAL FILE.
_The AIS INTEGRATED CENSUS INDEXES for 1790/1800/10, for 1820, for 1830, for 1840, and for the 1850 Eastern States.
_The Subject Portion of the FAMILY HISTORY LIBRARY CATALOG (FHLC), under the heading Family Group Records.

The second set of index investigations you should make is to look at all entries under MD, then all entries under the MD counties of interest to you in:
_The Locality Portion of the FAMILY HISTORY LIBRARY CATALOG (FHLC).
You will find extensive listings of these types of records: administrative, business, census, church, county/city histories, court, family histories, genealogical collections, land, military, newspaper, probate, tax, town, vital record (birth, marriage, death), and will. When you find entries which you think are applicable to your progenitor(s), copy down the reference numbers and names of the records. These data will permit the FHC librarian to borrow for you the microfilm(s) containing the detailed information from the FHL. The cost is only a few dollars per roll, and when your microfilms arrive (usually 3-6 weeks), you will be notified so that you can return and examine them. A third action you should take is to ask the FHC librarian for a form (Temple Ordinance Indexes Request) to request from the FHL an examination of the Temple Index Bureau Records and the Family Group Records Archive. The above three actions will lead you to many of the materials

mentioned in Chapter 2 and many of the records listed under the counties in Chapter 4.

In case you happen to visit the FHL in Salt Lake City, UT, you should proceed by examining all the above indexes plus the Computer-Assisted Catalogs, looking under both surnames and localities. Pertinent records can be requested or found on the open shelves. The main and the second floors of the building are where most of the MD records can be found.

7. The National Archives (NA) and Its (NARB)

The National Archives and Records Service (NA), located at Pennsylvania Avenue and 8th Street, Washington, DC 20408, is the central national repository for federal records, many being of importance to genealogical research. The NA does not concern itself with colonial records (pre-1776), state, county, city, or town records. Among the most important NA records which pertain to MD are the following:
_Census records: Federal census records for MD, 1790-1910
_Immigration records: Passenger lists for Baltimore 1820-1952, and for a few other MD ports, 1820, 1849
_Military records: Service, bounty land, pension, claims records, and indexes for the Revolution, War of 1812, Mexican War, Civil War, Spanish-American War
_Naturalization records: For US District and Circuit Courts in MD, 1797-1956
Details on all of these have been given in the pertinent sections of Chapter 2. Further detail on them may be obtained in:
_NA Staff, GENEALOGICAL RESEARCH IN THE NATIONAL ARCHIVES, NA, Washington, DC, 1982.

The numerous records of the NA may be examined in Washington in person or by a hired researcher. Microfilm copies of many of the major records and/or their indexes may also be seen in Regional Branches of the National Archives (NARB) which are located in or near Atlanta (1557 St. Joseph Ave., East Point, GA 30344), Boston (380 Trapelo Rd., Waltham, MA 02154), Chicago (7358 S. Pulaski Rd., Chicago, IL 60629), Denver (Bldg. 48, Federal Center, Denver, CO 80225), Fort Worth (501 West Felix St., Ft. Worth, TX 76115), Kansas City (2312 E. Bannister Rd., Kansas City, MO 64131), Los Angeles (24000 Avila Rd., Laguna Niguel, CA 92677), New York (Bldg. 22-MOT, Bayonne, NJ 07002), Philadelphia (9th and Market Sts., Philadelphia, PA 19107), San Francisco (1000 Commodore Dr., San Bruno, CA 94066), and Seattle (6125 Sand Point Way, NE, Seattle, WA 98115). Take special note of the Philadelphia Branch in Philadelphia, PA. They hold all MD census records, Revolutionary War service, pension, and bounty land records, US Courts of MD 1790–1911, naturalizations in US Circuit and District Courts 1797–1956, records of the MD Continental Loan Office 1777–90, 1798, 1800, Internal Revenue tax records 1862–66, passenger lists for Baltimore 1820–1952, MD Union and Confederate service records 1861–65, papers of the Continental Congress 1774–89, and the MD census of manufactures 1820.

Many of the NA records pertaining to MD, as was noted in detail in Chapters 2 and 3, are also available at MSA, MHS, and the FHL (FHC), and some are available at LGL and RL. In addition, practically any local library in the US can borrow NA microfilms for you from AGLL (American Genealogical Lending Library, PO Box 244, Bountiful, UT 84010). Or you may borrow from them directly. Included are NA census records (1790–1910), military records (Revolutionary War, War of 1812, Mexican War, Civil War), and passenger lists (1820–97).

8. Regional libraries (RL)

In the state of MD there are a number of regional libraries (RL) and larger county and city libraries which have good genealogical collections. Their holdings are larger than most local libraries (LL), but are smaller than the holdings of MSA and MHS. As might be expected, the materials in each RL are best for the immediate and surrounding counties. Among the better of these RL for genealogical research are the following (listed in order of the cities where they are found):

_(Cambridge) Dorchester County Public Library, 303 Gay Street, Cambridge, MD 21613. Tel: 1–(301)–228–7331. Eastern Shore.
_(Easton) Talbot County Free Library, MD Room, 100 West Dover Street, Easton, MD 21601. Tel: 1–(301)–822–1626. Eastern Shore.
_(Frederick) C. Burr Artz Library, 110 East Patrick Street, Frederick, MD 21701. Tel: 1–(301)–694–1628. Frederick and adjacent Counties.
_(Hagerstown) Washington County Free Library, Western MD Room, 100 South Potomac Street, Hagerstown, MD 27140. Tel: 1–(301)–739–3250. Western MD.
_(La Plata) Charles County Community College, Southern MD Studies Center, Mitchell Road, La Plata, MD 20646. Tel: 1–(301)–934–2251. Charles, St. Mary's, Calvert, and Prince George's Counties.
_(Leonardtown) St. Mary's County Historical Society Library, 11 Court House Drive, Leonardtown, MD 20650. Tel: 1–(301)–475–2467. St. Mary's, Charles, and Calvert Counties.
_(Salisbury) Wicomico County, Free Library, 122–126 South Division Street, Salisbury, MD 21801. Somerset, Wicomico, and Worcester Counties.

When a visit is made to any of these libraries, your first endeavor is to search the main catalog. You can remember what to look for with the acronym SLANT (standing for Subject, Locality, Author, Name, and Title) and by searching the categories out in the order: name–locality–subject–author–title. This procedure should give you very good coverage of the library holdings which are indexed in the main catalog. The second endeavor at any of these libraries is to ask about any special indexes, catalogs, collections, lists, finding aids, or materials which might be pertinent to your search. You should make it your aim particularly to inquire about Bible, cemetery, church, map, manuscript, military, mortuary, and newspaper materials. In some cases, microform (microfilm, microfiche, microcard) records are not included in the regular catalog but are separately indexed. It is important that you be alert to this possibility.

9. Large genealogical libraries (LGL)

Spread around the US there are a number of large genealogical libraries (LGL) which have at least some major MD genealogical source materials. In general, those of these LGL which are nearest to MD are the ones which have the better MD collections. The fourteen libraries which are probably those which have the largest genealogical collections in the US are:

_Family History Library (FHL) of the Genealogical Society of UT, 35 North West Temple St., Salt Lake City, UT 84150.
_Public Library of Fort Wayne and Allen County, 301 West Wayne St., Fort Wayne, IN 46802.
_New England Historic Genealogical Society Library, 101 Newbury St., Boston, MA 02116.
_NY Public Library, 5th Avenue and 42nd St., New York, NY 10022-1939.
_Library of Congress, First and Second Sts. at East Capitol St. and Independence Ave., Washington, DC 20540.
_NY Genealogical and Biographical Society Library, 122-126 East 58th St., New York, NY 10022.
_Library of the National Society of the Daughters of the American Revolution, 1776 D St., Washington, DC 20006-5392.
_Western Reserve Historical Society Library, 10825 East Blvd., Cleveland, OH 44106.
_Detroit Public Library, 5201 Woodward Ave., Detroit, MI 48202.
_Newberry Library, 60 West Walton St., Chicago, IL 60610.
_State Historical Society of WI Library, 816 State St., Madison, WI 53703.
_Dallas Public Library, 1515 Young St., Dallas, TX 75201.
_Los Angeles Public Library, 630 West 5th St., Los Angeles, CA 90071.
_Public Library of Cincinnati and Hamilton County, 800 Vine Street, Library Square, Cincinnati, OH 45202-2071.

Among other large libraries which have good genealogical collections are the following:

In AL: Birmingham Public Library, Davis Library at Samford University in Birmingham, in AZ: Mesa FHC, AZ State Library in Phoenix, Phoenix Public Library, in AR: Central AR Library in Little Rock, AR State Library in Little Rock, in CA: see above, San Diego Public Library, CA Genealogical Society in San Francisco, CA State Library (Sutro) in San Francisco, San Francisco Public Library, in CO: Denver Public Library,

In CT: CT Historical Society in Hartford, CT State Library in Hartford, Godfrey Memorial Library in Middletown, in DC: see above, in FL: Miami-Dade Public Library, Orange County Library in Orlando, FL State Archives in Tallahassee, Tampa-Hillsborough County Public Library, in GA: Atlanta-Fulton Public Library, GA Department of Archives in Atlanta, Washington Memorial Library in Macon, in HI: HI State Library in Honolulu,

In ID: ID State Historical Society Library in Boise, Ricks College Library in Rexburg, in IL: see above, IL State Historical Society in Springfield, in IN: see above, IN State Library in Indianapolis, Valparaiso Public Library, in IA: IA State Historical Society in IA City, in KS: KS State Historical Society Library in Topeka, Wichita Public Library, in KY: KY Historical Library in Frankfort, Filson Club Library in Louisville,

In LA: LA State Library in Baton Rouge, New Orleans Public Library, in ME: ME State Library in Augusta, ME Historical Society in Portland, in MD: MD Historical Society in Baltimore, in MA: Boston Public Library, in MI: see above, Library of MI in Lansing, in MN: Minneapolis Public Library, MN Historical Society Library in St. Paul, in MS: MS Department of Archives and History in Jackson, in MO: Mid-Continent Public Library in Independence, Kansas City Public Library, St. Louis County Library,

In MT: MT Historical Society in Helena, in NE: NE State Historical Society in Lincoln, in NV: Las Vegas FHC, NV Historical Society Library in Reno, in NH: NH Historical Society in Concord, NH State Library in Concord, Manchester City Library, in NJ: Joint Free Public Library and Morristown and Morris Township, NJ Historical Society in Newark, NJ State Library in Trenton, in NM: Albuquerque Public Library,

In NY: see above, NY State Library in Albany, Buffalo and Erie County Public Library, Rochester Public Library, Onondaga County Public Library in Syracuse, in NC: Public Library of Charlotte, NC State Library in Raleigh, in ND: Red River Valley Genealogy Society in West Fargo, in OH: see above, State Library of OH in Columbus, in OK: OK Metropolitan Library in Oklahoma City, Oklahoma Historical Society in Oklahoma City,

In OR: Genealogical Forum of OR in Portland, Multnomah County Library in Portland, in PA: State Library of PA in Harrisburg, Historical and Genealogical Society of PA in Philadelphia, Carnegie Library of Pittsburgh, in RI: Westerly Public Library, in SC: South Caroliniana Library in Columbia, Greenville County Library in Greenville, in SD: SD State Archives in Pierre, in TN: Knox County Public Library in Knoxville, Memphis and Shelby County Public Library, TN State Library and Archives in Nashville,

_In TX: see above, TX State Library in Austin, Fort Worth Public Library, Clayton Library of the Houston Public Library, in UT: see above, Brigham Young University Library in Provo, in VT: Genealogy Library of the Bennington Museum, in VA: National Genealogical Society Library in Arlington, VA State Library and Archives in Richmond, in WA: Seattle Public Library, Spokane Public Library, Tacoma Public Library, in WV: WV Archives and History Library in Charleston, in WI: see above, Milwaukee Public Library, in WY: Laramie County Library in Cheyenne.

---

10. Local libraries (LL) and local repositories (LR)

Listed under the MD counties in Chapter 4 are the most important local libraries (LL) in the state. These are libraries which have indicated in published compilations (such as the American Library Association Directory, Directory of American Libraries with Genealogical or Local History Collections) that they have genealogical holdings. There are several types of local libraries in MD: system libraries (serving several towns), county libraries, city libraries, town libraries, local historical society libraries, college and university libraries, county historical society libraries, county archives, local genealogical society libraries, local museum libraries, historical park libraries, and private libraries. As you might imagine, these institutions are of a wide variety, some having sizeable genealogical materials, some having practically none. Many of the LL (particularly the town ones) are affiliates of a nearby larger library which has much greater holdings. What is of importance, however, is that you not overlook any LL in your ancestor's region, county, city, or town. Sometimes they will have local records or collections available nowhere else. This is particularly true for Bible, cemetery, church, manuscript, and newspaper records. It is also sometimes the case that counties, cities, and towns have turned older records over to LL, especially the county historical societies. You will almost inevitably find local librarians to be very knowledgeable concerning genealogical sources in their areas. Further, they are also usually acquainted with people in the county who are experts in the region's history and genealogy. Thus, both local libraries and local librarians can be of inestimable value to you.

When you visit a LL, the general procedure described previously should be followed. First, search the card (computer) catalog or catalogs. Look under the headings summarized by SLANT: Subject, Location, Author, Name, Title, doing them in the order N-L-S-A-T. Then, second, inquire about special indexes, catalogs, collections, materials, manuscripts, finding aids, and microforms. Third, ask about any other local sources of data such as cemetery records, church records, maps and atlases, genealogical and historical societies, museums, mortuary records, and old newspapers, plus indexes to all of these. Every local area in MD has many other

local repositories (LR) which must not be missed. These are the appropriate offices related to the records just mentioned: offices of cemeteries,
churches, societies (DAR, Masonic Lodge, GAR, etc.) mortuaries, and
newspapers.

If you choose to write to a LL, please remember that librarians are
very busy people. Always send them an SASE and confine your questioning
to one brief straight-forward item. Librarians are usually glad to help you if
they can employ readily-available indexes to answer your question, but you
must not expect them to do research for you. In case research is required,
they can often provide you with a list of researchers which you may hire, but
which they do not guarantee.

Key to Abbreviations

A	=	Agricultural census records
AGLL	=	American Genealogical Lending Library
B	=	Baltimore police census
BCA	=	Baltimore City Archives (Baltimore)
C	=	Civil War Union veterans census
DAR	=	Daughters of the American Revolution
E	=	Early census-like lists
FHC	=	Family History Center(s)
FHL	=	Family History Library (Salt Lake City)
FHLC	=	Family History Library Catalog
I	=	Industrial census records
IGI	=	International Genealogical Index
LGL	=	Large genealogical libraries
LL	=	Local library(ies) in MD
LR	=	Local repositories
M	=	Mortality census records
MHS	=	MD Historical Society (Baltimore)
MSA	=	MD State Archives (Annapolis)
MSLL	=	MD State Law Library (Annapolis)
NA	=	National Archives (Washington)
NARB	=	National Archives, Regional Branch(es)
P	=	Revolutionary War pensioner census
R	=	Regular census records
RL	=	Regional library(ies) in MD
S	=	Slaveholder census
SASE	=	Long, self-addressed, stamped envelope

Key to Abbreviations

A	=	Agricultural census records
AGLL	=	American Genealogical Lending Library
B	=	Baltimore police census
BCA	=	Baltimore City Archives (Baltimore)
C	=	Civil War Union veterans census
DAR	=	Daughters of the American Revolution
E	=	Early census–like lists
FHC	=	Family History Center(s)
FHL	=	Family History Library (Salt Lake City)
FHLC	=	Family History Library Catalog
I	=	Industrial census records
IGI	=	International Genealogical Index
LGL	=	Large genealogical libraries
LL	=	Local library(ies) in MD
LR	=	Local repositories
M	=	Mortality census records
MHS	=	MD Historical Society (Baltimore)
MSA	=	MD State Archives (Annapolis)
MSLL	=	MD State Law Library (Annapolis)
NA	=	National Archives (Washington)
NARB	=	National Archives, Regional Branch(es)
P	=	Revolutionary War pensioner census
R	=	Regular census records
RL	=	Regional library(ies) in MD
S	=	Slaveholder census
SASE	=	Long, self–addressed, stamped envelope

Chapter 4

RESEARCH PROCEDURE AND COUNTY LISTINGS

1. Introduction

Now that you have read Chapters 1–3, you should have a good idea of MD history, its genealogical records, and the locations and availabilities of these records. The emphasis in the first three chapters was on records at levels higher than the county. Detailed information on national, state–wide, and regional records was given, but county records were normally treated only in general. We now will turn our focus upon the county records (including those of Baltimore City, MD's pseudo–county). We will also emphasize non–governmental records available at the county level (Bible, biography, cemetery, directories, histories, DAR, ethnic, maps, periodicals, genealogies, manuscripts, mortuary, newspaper). The reason for all this attention to county records is that these records are likely to contain more information on your ancestors than any other type. Such records were generally recorded by people who knew your forebears, and they relate to the personal details of his/her life.

In the state of MD, some of the original governmental records of the counties and cities, remain within the counties, but most have been transferred to the MSA. Many of these original governmental records and some non–governmental records have been microfilmed by the FHL, and the microfilms are available at FHL, and by interlibrary loan through the many FHC throughout the US. Some of these original governmental records and numerous non–governmental records have been published either in printed volumes or as typescripts. Most of these publications are available in MHS and MSLL and many are in FHL (FHC). Some are available in LGL, and those pertinent to their regions are available in RL and LL.

Chapter 4 will deal with county and city records in detail. We will first discuss procedures for finding the county in which your MD progenitor(s) lived. This is important because knowing that your ancestors were simply from MD is not enough to permit genealogical research. You need to know the county or city since many genealogically–applicable records were kept on a local basis, and since you will often find more than one person in MD state bearing the name of your forebear. In such a case, the county/city location will often let you tell them apart. After discussing ways to find the county, we will second suggest approaches for doing genealogy in MD, recommending the order in which the various repositories should be used.

2. Locating the county

As you will recall from Chapter 1, MD record-keeping began with the settlement of the proprietorship in 1634. When a second county (Kent) was added to the original county (St. Mary's), record-keeping started being shared by the county governments and the colony government. As time went on, the population increased, the number of counties increased, and more and more of the keeping of records was gradually shifted to the counties. It is, therefore, of considerable importance for you to know your MD progenitor's county in order to direct yourself efficiently to all the proper records. It is also important because the local county officials probably knew your ancestor personally, and further, kept more detailed records on him, his family, his property, and his activities than did the colony or state. If you happen to know your ancestor's county, you may skip the remainder of this section. If not, your first priority must be a search for the county. The most efficient method for discovering the county depends on the time period during which your forebear lived in MD. We will discuss county-finding techniques for four periods of time in MD history: (a) 1634–1700, (b) 1700–90, (c) 1790–1895, and (d) 1895–present.

If your forebear's time period was 1620–1700, you should look in the following major sources for your progenitor's name. Items more generally available (indexes in FHC; published and microfilm indexes in LGL) will be listed before those available chiefly in MD repositories (MHS, MSA), or available by ordering from FHL through FHC.

_(1) INTERNATIONAL GENEALOGICAL INDEX (IGI), MD SECTION; FAMILY SEARCH; ANCESTRAL FILE; FAMILY GROUP RECORDS COLLECTION; TEMPLE INDEX BUREAU; all available at FHL, all available at or through FHC, IGI available at MHS.

_(2) TEMPLE INDEX BUREAU, at FHL, obtain order blank from FHC to have it searched.

_(3) F. Rider, AMERICAN GENEALOGICAL [–BIOGRAPHICAL] INDEX, Godfrey Memorial Library, Middletown, CT, 1942–, 2 series, 1st containing 48 volumes, 2nd containing over 170 volumes.

_(4) M. Kaminkow, GENEALOGIES IN THE LIBRARY OF CONGRESS, Magna Carta, Baltimore, MD, 1972-7, 3 volumes; plus A COMPLEMENT TO GENEALOGIES IN THE LIBRARY OF CONGRESS [GENEALOGIES IN OTHER LIBRARIES], Magna Carta, Baltimore, MD, 1981.

_(5) MD GENEALOGIES, A CONSOLIDATION OF ARTICLES FROM THE MD HISTORICAL MAGAZINE, Genealogical Publishing Co., Baltimore, MD, 1980, 3 volumes.

_(6) E. P. Passano, AN INDEX TO THE SOURCE RECORDS OF MD, GENEALOGICAL, BIOGRAPHICAL, HISTORICAL, The Author, Baltimore, MD, 1940.

_(7) G. M. Brumbaugh, MD RECORDS, COLONIAL, REVOLUTIONARY, COUNTY, AND CHURCH, FROM ORIGINAL SOURCES, Lancaster Press, Lancaster, PA, 1928.

_(8) R. W. Barnes, MD MARRIAGES, 1634-1800, Genealogical Publishing Co., Baltimore, MD, 1975/8, 2 volumes.

_(9) J. M. Magruder, INDEX OF MD COLONIAL WILLS, 1635-1777, Genealogical Publishing Co., Baltimore, MD, 1967.

_(10) G. Skordas, EARLY SETTLERS OF MD, AN INDEX TO NAMES OF IMMIGRANTS COMPILED FROM RECORDS OF LAND PATENTS, 1633-80, Genealogical Publishing Co., Baltimore, MD, 1968.

_(11) P. W. Filby and M. K. Meyer, PASSENGER AND IMMIGRATION LISTS INDEX, Gale Research Co., Detroit, MI, 1981, with ANNUAL SUPPLEMENTS thereafter.

_(12) J. A. and F. L. Wyand, COLONIAL MD NATURALIZATIONS, 1660-1775, Genealogical Publishing Co., Baltimore, MD, 1975.

_(13) R. W. Barnes, BALTIMORE COUNTY FAMILIES, 1659-1759, Genealogical Publishing Co., Baltimore, MD, 1989.

_(14) F. W. Wright, MD EASTERN SHORE RECORDS, 1648-1825, Family Line Publications, Silver Spring, MD, 1972-6, 5 volumes.

_(15) MSA, MD LAND PATENTS INDEX, 1634-1985, Index No. 54, The Archives, Annapolis, MD.

_(16) MSA, MD LAND WARRANTS AND ASSIGNMENTS, 1634-1751, Index No. 140, The Archives, Annapolis, MD.

_(17) MSA, MD PROBATE RECORDS INDEX, 1634-1777, Index No. 1, The Archives, Annapolis, MD.

_(18) MSA, MD TESTAMENTARY (PROBATE) PROCEEDINGS, 1657-1777, Index No. 2, The Archives, Annapolis, MD.

_(19) MHS, NORRIS-HARRIS CHURCH REGISTER INDEX, The Society, Baltimore, MD.

_(20) Enoch Pratt Free Library, BIOGRAPHY FILE (INDEX), MD Room, The Library, Baltimore, MD.

Notice that indexes (1-2) are accessible at or through your local FHC, indexes (3-15) are publications available in most large genealogical libraries (LGL), and indexes (16-21) are to be found at MSA (Annapolis) and the Pratt Library (Baltimore). If these indexes fail to locate your forebear's county, two further steps should be taken: (a) explore other indexes in MSA and MHS [see pertinent sections in Chapter 3], and(b) since there were only 11 counties constituted before 1700, a search of major indexes of all these counties is not a forbidding route to take.

For the time period 1700-90, consult all the above-listed items except No. 10, that is (1-9) and (11-20). In addition, the following indexes should be looked at:

_(21) R. V. Jackson and others, EARLY MD, 1700-09, 1740-49, Accelerated Indexing Systems, Bountiful, UT, 1980-1.

_(22) BALTIMORE CITY DIRECTORIES ON MICROFILM, 1752, 1796, 1799–1901, Research Publications, New Haven, CT. Later volumes in MHS.
_(23) H. Chance, WESTERN MD PIONEERS, LISTS OF MARRIAGES, BIRTHS, AND DEATHS OF 8000 EARLY SETTLERS, Library of PA Historical Society, Philadelphia, PA, 1968.
_(24) MD Historical Society, MUSTER ROLLS OF MD TROOPS IN THE AMERICAN REVOLUTION, Genealogical Publishing Co., Baltimore, MD, 1972.
_(25) NA, GENERAL INDEX TO COMPILED SERVICE RECORDS OF REVOLUTIONARY SOLDIERS, SAILORS, ARMY STAFF, The Archives, Washington, DC, Microfilm Publication M860.
_(26) R. W. Barnes, GLEANINGS FROM MD NEWSPAPERS, and MARRIAGES AND DEATHS FROM BALTIMORE NEWSPAPERS, AND THE MD GAZETTE, 1727–1839, several publishers, Lutherville and Baltimore, MD, 1975–9, 6 volumes.
_(27) R. B. Clark, JR., INDEX TO COLONIAL MD WILLS TO 1777, TWELVE COUNTIES, The Author, St. Michaels, MD, 1982.
_(28) BCA, WPA–HRS INDEX TO BALTIMORE CITY RECORDS, 1756–1938, Baltimore City Archives, Baltimore, MD.
_(29) B. S. Carothers, 1776 CENSUS OF MD, MD OATHS OF FIDELITY, 1778 CENSUS OF MD, The Author, Lutherville, MD, 1972–80, 3 volumes.
_(30) M. J. Clark, COLONIAL SOLDIERS OF THE SOUTH, 1732–74, Genealogical Publishing Co., Baltimore, MD, 1983.

If your ancestor was somewhere in the state of MD during 1790–1898, the best way to find her/him is in the census indexes:
_(31) US Bureau of the Census, MD Genealogical Society, R. V. Jackson and others, INDEXES TO THE 1790–1860, 1880–1900, MD CENSUSES, National Archives, Genealogical Publishing Co., and Accelerated Indexing Systems, Washington, DC, Baltimore, MD, and Bountiful, UT, 1966–91.
Also helpful are military indexes for the War of 1812 and the Civil War:
_(32) NA MICROFILM INDEXES TO COMPILED SERVICE RECORDS OF VOLUNTEER SOLDIERS WHO SERVED DURING THE WAR OF 1812, Microfilm M602, OF VOLUNTEER UNION SOLDIERS, Microfilm M388, and OF CONFEDERATE SOLDIERS, Microfilm M379, The Archives, Washington, DC.
_(33) F. E. Wright, MD MILITIA, WAR OF 1812, Family Line Publications, Silver Spring, MD, 1979–, 8 volumes.
The above–mentioned indexes (1–2), (4–6), (8), (14–15), (19–20), (22), (26), and (28) may also be used, as well as these collections and indexes:
_(34) D. P. Hartzler, MARYLANDERS IN THE CONFEDERACY, Family Line Publications, Silver Spring, MD, 1986.

_(35) MHS, DIELMAN–HAYWARD CARD FILE (INDEX), 1790–, The Society, Baltimore, MD.

_(36) FHL, MICROFILM COPY OF THE HOLDCRAFT COLLECTION, 1800–1977, The Library, Salt Lake City, UT. Chiefly western MD. May be borrowed through FHC.

_(37) MSA, BALTIMORE CITY HEALTH DEPARTMENT BIRTH AND DEATH RECORDS INDEX, 1875–1941, County Microfilms 1133–34.

For progenitors who lived in MD during the years 1898 to the present, your family will probably know the county. If not, the 1900 census index may be helpful (31), as perhaps (1–2), (22), (28), and (35–37). The indexed 1920 census could give you the needed information, as could World War I and World War II records.

_(38) MD War Records Commission, MD IN WORLD WAR I, 1917–19, MILITARY AND NAVAL SERVICE RECORDS, The Commission, Baltimore, MD, 1933, 2 volumes.

_(39) MHS, MD IN WORLD WAR II, REGISTER OF SERVICE PERSONNEL, The Society, Baltimore, MD, 1965, 5 volumes.

However, the best county finding aids are the state–wide birth and death record indexes:

_(40) MSA, MICROFILM AND CARD INDEXES TO MD BIRTH RECORDS, since 1898, The Archives, Annapolis, MD.

_(41) MSA, MICROFILM AND CARD INDEXES TO MD DEATH RECORDS, since 1898, The Archives, Annapolis, MD.

For a charge of $5 each, MSA will examine its birth and death record indexes and provide you with the name of the county. Of exceptional value for this period is the Social Security death index which lists persons who had social security numbers and whose deaths were reported 1937–88:

_Social Security Administration, SOCIAL SECURITY DEATH INDEX, 1937–88, on four compact computer discs, at FHL and FHC.

The work of locating your MD ancestor can generally be done from where you live or nearby. This is because the key items are either indexes or indexed records which means that they can be scanned rapidly. Also many are in published form (books or microfilms) which means that they are in numerous LGL outside of MD as well as being available through FHC. Some can be borrowed from AGLL. Therefore, you should not have to travel too far to find many of the indexes you need. If, however, it is more convenient, you may hire a researcher in Baltimore/Annapolis to delve into the records at MHS, MSA, Pratt Library, and FHC to locate your forebear. This should not cost too much because you can instruct your searcher to look into the indexes which are noted above, and to stop when the county is identified.

3. Research approaches

Having identified the county (or Baltimore City) of your forebear's residence, you are in position to ferret out the details. This means that you need to identify what non-governmental, federal, state (colonial), county, and city/town records are available, then to locate them, and finally to examine them in detail. The most useful non-governmental records have been discussed in Chapter 2 (sections 2-3, 5, 7-9, 12, 16-19, 22, 28, 30-32). The federal records which are most important for consideration also have been treated in Chapter 2 (sections 6, 15, 25-27, 29). State records of the greatest utility for genealogical research are examined in certain sections of Chapter 2 (4, 6, 11, 13-14, 21, 23, 25-27, 29, 33). Colonial governmental records were listed principally in section 10 of Chapter 2, but other sections also deal with them (6, 11, 15, 21, 24, 34). The types of records which were generated by MD counties are listed in Chapter 2 (section 1), and they are discussed in various sections of Chapter 2 (4, 11, 13-14, 21, 23, 27, 29, 33-34). County and city records which have been microfilmed are in FHL (available through FHC) and MSA, and county and city records which have been published (printed and typescript) are in MHS, MSLL, and Pratt Library. Some of these published materials are also located in LGL, RL, and LL. Both the major microfilmed records and the major published records are listed in detail in later sections of this chapter.

The general approach for doing an utterly thorough job of researching a MD ancestor is to follow this pattern:

_1st, check all family sources (oral, records, mementos, Bible)
_2nd, locate your forebear's county (section 2, this chapter)
_3rd, use the nearest LGL (indexes, publications, microfilms)
_4th, use the nearest FHC or the FHL (IGI, Ancestral File, Family Group Records Archives, Temple Index Bureau, Family Registry, FHL surname and locality indexes, integrated census indexes; borrow microfilmed records)
_5th, borrow any major federal records you haven't seen from AGLL (census, military, passenger lists)
_6th, 6a–borrow from the MSA (microfilmed records and microfilmed state, colony, and county documents), then 6b–use the non-microfilmed documents
_7th, use the MHS (original, microfilmed, and published federal, state, colony, and non-governmental records; published and manuscript county and city records)
_8th, use the Pratt Library, Peabody Collection, MSLL, and BCA (published and microfilmed federal, state, colony, county and non-governmental records; published county and city records; manuscripts)

_9th, use LL (indexes, manuscripts, local records), visit offices of cemeter-
ies, churches, mortuaries, newspapers, organizations, use RL (if LL
directs you there)
_10th, use court houses and offices of county record keepers (for local
records not seen)
_11th, use NARB and NA (further federal, military, census, passenger list,
naturalization, and court materials)
_12th, use Church Archives (if church records still not found)
The precise way in which you use this scheme is chiefly determined by how
far you are from Baltimore/Annapolis where MHS, MSA, MSLL, Pratt Library, Peabody Collection, and BCA Library are located. It is in these six
repositories that the best total collection of MD genealogical materials in the
whole world exists (even though they do not have copies of all county and
city records). This small county and city record shortfall means that visits to
the county may be needed. Therefore, the major idea that you must recognize is that eventually you will have to go to Baltimore/Annapolis and perhaps the county, or hire a researcher to go for you. In short, research in
these repositories is an absolute necessity if your ancestor quest is to be
complete.

If you live very far from Baltimore/Annapolis, you should follow the
research procedure essentially as it is. In the 3rd, 4th, 5th, and 6th[6a]
steps (LGL, FHC, FHL, AGLL, MSA-microfilms), just as many items as
possible should be examined, since this will reduce what remains to be
done at the rest of the repositories (non-microfilmed-6th[6b] through
12th), but especially at the county and city offices. It is preferable to visit
FHL rather than FHC, so you should elect that option if you are near enough
to Salt Lake City, UT (where FHL is). You then need to hire a researcher to
go to MSA (for non-microfilmed records), MHS, MSLL, Pratt Library, Peabody Collection, and BCA or go there yourself. Be sure and explain to your
hired researcher exactly what records you have seen so that your money
will not be wasted on duplicated work. Once the 6th, 7th, and 8th steps
have been done, a hired researcher or a personal visit will again be involved
for the 9th and 10th steps (LL and county offices). The 11th step can be
done at the NARB in your region, and the 12th can be conducted by mail.

If you live within range of MD, the 12-step pattern can be modified
substantially. By "within range" is meant that you deem a personal visit to
Baltimore/Annapolis workable within the near future. In such a case, you
can skip the 3rd and 4th steps, then do the 5th by mail, then the 6th through
the 10th by personal visit, and finally the 11th at some NARB (or the NA)
and the 12th by mail.

In selecting a research approach, whether it be one of the above or a
modified one which you design, you ought to think about three items. The
first is expense. You need to balance the cost of a hired researcher over

against the cost of personal visits (to Baltimore/Annapolis and the county): travel, lodging, meals. Also do not forget the costs of borrowing microfilms from your nearest FHC (a few dollars per roll) or the MSA (small fee). Of course, your desire to look at the records for yourself (rather than have a researcher do it) may be an important consideration.

The second item is a reminder about interlibrary loans. With the exceptions of the microfilms of FHL (available through FHC), those of the MSA, and those of AGLL (available personally or through your local library), very few libraries and practically no archives will lend out genealogical materials. The third item is also a reminder. Correspondence with librarians, governmental officials, and archivists is of very limited use. The reason is that these helpful and hard-working state, local, and private employees do not have time to do any detailed work for you because of the demanding duties of their offices. In some cases, these people will have time to look up one specific item for you (a land grant, a deed record, a will, a military pension) if an overall index is available. Please don't ask them for detailed data, and please don't write them a long letter. If you do write them, enclose a long SASE, a check for $5 with the payee line left blank, and a brief request (no more than one-third page) for one specific item in an index or catalog. Ask them to use the check if there is a charge for their services or for copying, and if they do not have the time to look themselves, that they hand the check and your letter to a researcher who can do the work. The MSA operates their correspondence facility somewhat differently, so please see the last paragraph of the section in Chapter 3 for details.

4. Format of county listings

In the next 24 sections (5 through 28), you will find listings of major records in MD counties and in Baltimore City. Most of the records are governmental, but a number of important private records are given. In addition, libraries in the towns and cities are shown because they are valuable sources of information.

Please take a look at a couple of the county sections which follow (say, sections 5 and 8 which deal with Allegany and Baltimore Counties). First, the name of the county (or Baltimore City) is given, then the date on which it was created or established, along with the parent county or counties from which it came (or an indication that it was original). This is followed by the name and zip code of the present county seat. After this, you will find some notes regarding losses of county records, and sometimes a reference to a detailed guide book. Second, you will see a listing of national records which should be sought for the county. A detailed notice on censuses is included. Remember that the alphabetical symbols stand for: E (early pre-1790 lists), R (regular federal censuses), I(federal industrial or manufacturing censuses), P (Revolutionary War pensioners census), A (agricultural censuses), M (mortality censuses), S (slaveholder censuses), and C (Civil War Union veterans censuses). After the census listings, you are referred to appropriate sections in Chapter 2 where these national records are discussed. And you are reminded that most of them can be borrowed from AGLL, NA, and FHL (through FHC).

Third, state and colonial records which are pertinent to the county are set forth. Again, reference is made to the sections of Chapter 2 where each is discussed in detail. You are reminded that many of the records can be borrowed from MSA on microfilm, and that some are available from FHL (through FHC). Fourth, the numerous non-governmental records that should be sought for research in the county are reviewed, and you are told the sections in Chapter 2 where detailed discussions appear. You are also prompted to recall that microfilms of some of these records can be borrowed from FHL (through FHC).

Fifth, the next underlined heading informs you about the county records which are available in MSA. You must recognize that some of the record categories cover a fairly diverse set of records. For example, county [circuit] court records can include abstracts, adoptions, appeals, births, bonds, censuses, chattels, civil cases, claims, contracts, criminal cases, divorces, equity cases, judgments, land, licenses, liens, marriages, naturalizations, plats, taxes, and various dockets. Similarly, orphans' court records may include accounts, administrations, certificates of freedom, estates, guardianships, inventories, oaths, papers, petitions, releases, and wills. At the end of the listings you are asked to look at the following volume by Papenfuse and others:
__E. C. Papenfuse and others, A GUIDE TO GOVERNMENT RECORDS AT
   THE MSA, The Archives, Annapolis, MD, latest issue.
In it, you will find detailed listings of the county's records at the MSA. Further, the volume also tells you which of them are on microfilm and therefore can be borrowed on interlibrary loan.

Sixth, the general types of county records available at FHL are shown. These microfilmed materials may be borrowed through FHC. Details on the records and code numbers that you need to order them are given in the Locality Section of the FHL Catalog which is held by every FHC. Seventh, a selection of records which have been published is given. Included are histories and atlases (before 1900). These publications are available in MHS, MSLL, FHL, and LGL, and may be located by looking under the county in the catalogs of the named repositories. Some of them have been microfilmed by FHL and may therefore be borrowed through FHC.

Eighth, you will next see listings of early church records which are available. Details are given in the following volume, which also refers to many other church records:

__E. A. Kanely, DIRECTORY OF MD CHURCH RECORDS, Family Line Publications, Silver Spring, MD, 1987.

In this same paragraph, there is a reminder of how to locate manuscripts in the MHS which are pertinent to the county. The two basic reference works to the vast collection at MHS are those by Pedley and by Cox and Sullivan:

__A. J. M. Pedley, THE MANUSCRIPT COLLECTIONS OF THE MHS, The Society, Baltimore, MD, 1968.

__R. J. Cox and L. E. Sullivan, GUIDE TO THE RESEARCH COLLECTIONS OF THE MHS, The Society, Baltimore, MD, 1981.

Finally, the last paragraph names for you the society or societies in or near the county which have genealogical interests, and the repository or repositories where local materials may be found. Telephone numbers are provided for the latter.

Now, a couple of remarks about these listings are in order. The listings are not complete, but are meant mainly to guide you to the availability of the most genealogically appropriate records. Many others will be found in Papenfuse, which it is essential to use. Records listed above do not include any series which begins after 1900, since most genealogists are working on ancestors who lived before this time. When a set of inclusive dates is given, such as (1817–1903), it does not necessarily mean that every year is included; there may be a few gaps.

5. ALLEGANY COUNTY

Created 1789 from Washington County. County seat: Cumberland, MD 21502. Court house fire in 1893, some marriage, a few naturalization, court, deed and mortgage records lost. Marriage records reconstituted from newspapers.

National records: Census (1800R, 1810R, 1820RI, 1830R, 1840RP, 1850RAIMS, 1860RAIMS, 1870RAIM, 1880RAIM, 1890C, 1900R, 1910R). See these sections in Chapter 2: (6) Census, (11) Court, (15) Emigration and emigration, (25, 26, 27) Military, (29) Naturalization, (33) Tax. Microfilms available from AGLL, NA, FHL(FHC).

State and colonial records: Census (Pre–1790E). See these sections of Chapter 2: (4) Birth, (6) Census, (10) Colonial, (11) Court, (13) Death, (14) Divorce, (15) Emigration and Immigration, (21) Land, (23) Marriage, (24, 25, 26, 27) Military, (29) Naturalization, (33) Tax, (34) Will and probate. Many microfilms available from MSA, some from FHL(FHC).

Non–governmental records: See these sections of Chapter 2: (2) Bible, (3) Biographies, (5) Cemetery, (7) Church, (8) City directories, (9) City and county histories, (10) Colonial, (12) DAR, (15) Emigration and

immigration, (16) Ethnic, (17) Gazetteers, maps, and atlases, (18) Genealogical indexes and compilations, (19) Genealogical periodicals, (20) Genealogical and historical societies, (22) Manuscripts, (28) Mortuary, (30)
Newspapers, (31) Published US indexes, (32) Regional publications. Some
microfilms available from FHL(FHC).

County records in MSA [microfilms can be borrowed on interlibrary
loan]: county [circuit] court (1791–1954), equity (1815–1926), estate
(1789–1964), guardian (1793–1867), land (1791–1987), marriage
(1791–1914), naturalization (1845–1904), orphans' court (1791–1963),
plats (1792–1943), tax (1793), will (1790–1964). See Papenfuse for
details on these records and on which ones are available on interlibrary
loan.

County records in FHL [microfilms can be borrowed through FHC]:
estate (1790–1855), guardian (1793–1867), land (1791–1850), marriage (1791–1865), will (1790–1850). Many church records also. See
the FHL Catalog – Locality Section for details on these microfilm county
holdings and for other records on microfilm which can borrowed through
FHC.

Published records [MHS, MSLL, FHL, LGL]: biography (1898), court
(1788–1812), land (1788–95), marriage (1791–1847), Methodist (1792–
1813), miscellaneous (1787–1921), newspaper (1811–15, 1820–30,
1864–67), pioneers, Presbyterian (1810–1950), tax (1804–12), wills
(1784–1960). Histories by Scharf in 1882, Thomas in 1923, and Steg-
maier in 1976.

Early church records: Catholic (1791), Lutheran (1794). Manuscripts in MHS: See indexes under Allegany County in Pedley (324) and
Cox (281).

Society: Genealogical Society of Allegany County, PO Box 3103, La
Vale, MD 21504. Repository: Allegany County Library, 31 Washington St.,
Cumberland, MD 21502, Tel: 1–(301)–777–1200.

---

6. ANNE ARUNDEL COUNTY

Created 1650 as an original county.
County seat Annapolis, MD 21404.
Fire in 1704, most records destroyed.
Land records partly reconstituted.

National records: Census
(1790R, 1800R, 1810R, 1820RI, 1830R, 1840RP, 1850RAIMS, 1860
RAIMS, 1870RAIM, 1880RAIM, 1890C, 1900R, 1910R). See these
sections in Chapter 2: (6) Census, (11) Court, (15) Emigration and emigration, (25, 26, 27) Military, (29) Naturalization, (33) Tax. Microfilms available from AGLL, NA, FHL(FHC).

State and colonial records: Census (Pre-1790E). See these sections of Chapter 2: (4) Birth, (6) Census, (10) Colonial, (11) Court, (13)
Death, (14) Divorce, (15) Emigration and Immigration, (21) Land, (23) Marriage, (24, 25, 26, 27) Military, (29) Naturalization, (33) Tax, (34) Will and
probate. Many microfilms available from MSA, some from FHL(FHC).

Non–governmental records: See these sections of Chapter 2: (2) Bible, (3) Biographies, (5) Cemetery, (7) Church, (8) City directories, (9) City and county histories, (10) Colonial, (12) DAR, (15) Emigration and immigration, (16) Ethnic, (17) Gazetteers, maps, and atlases, (18) Genealogical indexes and compilations, (19) Genealogical periodicals, (20) Genealogical and historical societies, (22) Manuscripts, (28) Mortuary, (30) Newspapers, (31) Published US indexes, (32) Regional publications. Some microfilms available from FHL(FHC).

County records in MSA [microfilms can be borrowed on interlibrary loan]: birth (1804–77, 1898–1931), bonds (1841–1965), County [circuit] court (1703–1945), death (1865–80, 1899–1930), divorce (1908–84), equity (1851–1980), estate (1777–1980), guardian (1777–1966), indenture (1795–1919), land (1653–1977), marriage (1777–1933), naturalization (1899–1980), orphans' court (1777–1980), plats (1799–1967), tax (1827–49, 1876–1918), will (1777–1980). See Papenfuse for details on these records and on which ones are available on microfilm loan.

County records in FHL [microfilms can be borrowed through FHC]: guardian (1777–1893), land (1653–1880), marriage (1777–86, 1840–50), orphans' court (1777–1853), will (1777–1917). Many church records also available. See the FHL Catalog – Locality Section for details on these microfilm county holdings and for other records on microfilm which can be borrowed through FHC.

Published records [MHS, MSL, FHL, LGL]: biography (1905), cemetery, Episcopal (1682–), estate (1788–98), marriage (1810–45, 1840–51), Methodist, militia (1812–14), mortality census (1850–80), pioneers, Quaker, rent rolls (1705–24), wills (1777–1918). Histories by Riley in 1905, by Warfield in 1905, and Bradford in 1977. Atlas: 1878.

Early church records: Episcopal (1663), Quaker (1655). Manuscripts in MHS: See indexes under Anne Arundel County and Annapolis in Pedley (324) and Cox (282).

Society: Anne Arundel Genealogical Society, PO Box 221, Pasadena, MD 21122. Repositories: MSA, 350 Rowe Blvd., Annapolis, MD 21401, Tel: 1-(301)-974-3915; MSLL, 361 Rowe Blvd., Annapolis, MD 21401, Tel: 1-(301)-974-3345; Public Library of Annapolis and Anne Arundel County, 5 Harry S. Truman Parkway, Annapolis, MD 21401.

7. BALTIMORE CITY

Created 1851 as a separate government unit from Baltimore County. Baltimore City had been the county seat of Baltimore County since 1768 and the records of the county were there. When Baltimore City was split off, the seat of Baltimore County was moved to Towson. However, the pre-1851 Baltimore County records were kept in Baltimore City. For detailed treatment of research, see R. W. Barnes, GUIDE TO RESEARCH IN BALTIMORE CITY AND COUNTY, Family Line Publications, Westminster, MD,

1989; W. G. LeFurgy, THE RECORDS OF A CITY, A GUIDE TO THE BALTI-MORE CITY ARCHIVES, City Archives and Records Management Office, Baltimore, MD, 1984.

National records: Census (1790R, 1800R, 1810R, 1820RI, 1830R, 1840RP, 1850RAIMS, 1860RAIMS, 1870RAIM, 1880RAIM, 1890C, 1900R, 1910R). See these sections of Chapter 2: (6) Census, (11) Court, (15) Emigration and immigration, (25, 26, 27) Military, (29) Naturalization, (33) Tax. Microfilms available from AGLL, NA, FHL(FHC).

State and colonial records: Census (Pre–1790E). See these sections of Chapter 2: (4) Birth, (6) Census, (10) Colonial, (11) Court, (13) Death, (14) Divorce, (15) Emigration and immigration, (21) Land, (23) Marriage, (24, 25, 26, 27) Military, (29) Naturalization, (33) Tax, (34) Will and probate. Many microfilms available from MSA, some from FHL(FHC).

Non–governmental records: See these sections of Chapter 2: (2) Bible, (3) Biographies, (5) Cemetery, (7) Church, (8) City directories, (9) City and county histories, (10) Colonial, (12) DAR, (15) Emigration and immigration, (16) Ethnic, (17) Gazetteers, atlases, and maps, (18) Genealogical indexes and compilations, (19) Genealogical periodicals, (20) Genealogical and historical societies, (22) Manuscripts, (28) Mortuary, (30) Newspapers, (31) Published US indexes, (32) Regional publications. Some microfilms available from FHL(FHC).

City records in MSA [microfilms can be borrowed through interlibrary loan]: birth (1875–1941), city circuit courts (1853–1984), city court (1821–1982), city court of common pleas (1851–1974), city court of oyer and terminer (1789–1816), city criminal court (1851–1977), city records index (1756–1938)–VERY VALUABLE, city superior court (1851–1982), death (1874–1972), equity (1853–1982), estate (1666–1973), guardian (1777–1976), indentures (1810–1916), land (1832–1981), marriage (1851–1935), naturalizations (1827–1933), orphans' court (1777–1970), plat (1785–1900), tax (1799–1825), voters (1838–39), will (1789–1970). See Papenfuse for details on these records and on which ones are available on microfilm loan.

City records in FHL [microfilms can be borrowed through FHC]: See Baltimore County listings in the next section. Many church records also available. See the FHL Catalog – Locality Section for details on these microfilm county holdings and for other records on microfilm which can be borrowed through FHC.

Published records [MHS, MSLL, FHL, LGL]: Catholic, cemetery, citizens (1807), city directories (1752, 1796–present), commissioners (1797–1813), Episcopal, newspaper (1796–1816), Quaker, tax (1798–1808). See Baltimore County listings in the next section. Histories by Griffith in 1824, Richardson in 1871, Scharf in 1874 and 1881, Howard in 1889, and Hollander in 1893. Atlases: 1877, 1878, 1898.

Early church records: Quaker (1649), Episcopal (1694). Manuscripts in MHS: See indexes under Baltimore City and Baltimore County in Pedley (325–28) and Cox (381).

Societies: MD Genealogical Society, 201 W. Monument St., Baltimore, MD 21201; MD Historical Society, Genealogy Committee, 201 W. Monument St., Baltimore, MD 21201; Jewish Historical Society of MD, 15 Lloyd St., Baltimore, MD 21202. Repositories: Baltimore City Archives, 211 East Pleasant St., Baltimore, MD 21202, Tel 1-(301)-396-4863; Baltimore Sun Library, 501 N. Calvert St., Baltimore, MD 21278, Tel 1-(301)-332-6253; Jewish Historical Society of MD Library, 1330 Dillon Heights Ave., Baltimore, MD 21202, Tel 1-(301)-732-6400; Peabody Collection of the Eisenhower Library of Johns Hopkins University, 17 E. Mt. Vernon Place, Baltimore, MD21202, Tel 1-(301)-659-8197; MHS, 201 W. Monument St., Baltimore, MD 21201, Tel 1-(301)-685-3750; Enoch Pratt Free Library, 400 Cathedral St., Baltimore, MD 21201, Tel 1-(301)-396-5430; United Methodist Historical Society Library, 2200 St. Paul St., Baltimore, MD 21218, Tel 1-(301)-889-4458; Baltimore Hebrew College Library, 5800 Park Heights Ave., Baltimore, MD 21215.

8. BALTIMORE COUNTY

Created 1659/60 as an original county. County seat Towson, MD 21204. Pre-1851 records remain in Baltimore City when it was split off in 1851. Court house fire in 1835, essentially no records lost. For detailed treatment of research, see R. W. Barnes, GUIDE TO RESEARCH IN BALTIMORE CITY AND COUNTY, Family Line Publications, Westminster, MD, 1989.

National records: Census (1790R, 1800R, 1810R, 1820RI, 1830R, 1840RP, 1850RAIMS, 1860RAIMS, 1870RAIM, 1880RAIM, 1890C, 1900R, 1910R). See these sections of Chapter 2: (6) Census, (11) Court, (15) Emigration and immigration, (25, 26, 27) Military, (29) Naturalization, (33) Tax. Microfilms available from AGLL, NA, FHL(FHC).

State and colonial records: Census (Pre-1790E). See these sections of Chapter 2: (4) Birth, (6) Census, (10) Colonial, (11) Court, (13) Death, (14) Divorce, (15) Emigration and immigration, (21) Land, (23) Marriage, (24, 25, 26, 27) Military, (29) Naturalization, (33) Tax, (34) Will and probate. Many microfilms available from MSA, some from FHL(FHC).

Non-governmental records: See these sections of Chapter 2: (2) Bible, (3) Biographies, (5) Cemetery, (7) Church, (8) City directories, (9) City and county histories, (10) Colonial, (12) DAR, (15) Emigration and immigration, (16) Ethnic, (17) Gazetteers, atlases, and maps, (18) Genealogical indexes and compilations, (19) Genealogical periodicals, (20) Genealogical and historical societies, (22) Manuscripts, (28) Mortuary, (30) Newspapers, (31) Published US indexes, (32) Regional publications. Some microfilms available from FHL(FHC).

County records in MSA [microfilms can be borrowed through interlibrary loan]: birth (1865-83), county [circuit] court (1682-1985), equity (1851-1984), estate (1666-1969), guardian (1777-1981), indenture (1794-1913), land (1653-1988), marriage (1777-1954), naturalizations

(1796-1918), orphans' court (1777-1977), plat (1729-1958), tax (1699-1773, 1804-24, 1828-66, 1872-1943), will (1666-1981). See Papenfuse for details on these records and on which ones are available on microfilm loan.

County records in FHL [microfilms can be borrowed through FHC]: estate (1666-1852), guardian (1777-1852), land (1653-1849), marriage (1777-1851), orphans' court (1777-1850), will (1666-1851). Many church records also available. See the FHL Catalog – Locality Section for details on these microfilm county holdings and for other records on microfilm which can be borrowed through FHC.

Published records [MHS, MSLL, FHL, LGL]: administrations (1776-1800), biography (1881, 1897, 1912, 1916), cemetery, county directory (1879), Episcopal (1689-), estate (1666-1720), families (1659-1850), guardian (1770-1875), inhabitants (1658-1800), land (1727-62), Lutheran, marriage (1651-56, 1659-1746, 1777-99, 1823-26), Methodist, militia (1812-14), newspaper (1796-1816, 1837-64), Quaker, rent rolls (1700-07), Revolutionary War (1775-83), tax (1692, 1694-95, 1699-1706, 1783, 1798), will (1659-1850). Histories by Scharf in 1881, Hall in 1912, Bonnett in 1916, and Brooks in 1979 and 1988. Atlases: 1877, 1878, 1898.

Early church records: Quaker (1649), Episcopal (1694). Manuscripts in MHS: See indexes under Baltimore County in Pedley (327) and Cox (284).

Societies: Baltimore County Genealogical Society, PO Box 10085, Towson, MD 21204; Catonsville Historical Society, Genealogy Section, 1824 Frederick Road, Catonsville, MD 21701. Repositories: See listings under Baltimore City in previous section; Genealogical Periodicals Library, 709 E. Main St., Middletown, MD 21769, Tel 1-(301)-371-6293; Baltimore County Public Library, 320 York Road, Towson, MD 21204, Tel 1-(301)-296-8500.

9. CALVERT COUNTY

Created 1654 as an original county. County seat Prince Frederick, MD 20678. Some records lost when county seat was moved in 1725. Some records lost in court house fire 1748. Court house burned by British in 1814, some records probably lost. Court house fire 1882, almost all records destroyed. Duplicates of land records which were sent to the state government are available for 1787-1817, 1863-67, 1873-82.

National records: Census (1800R, 1810R, 1820RI, 1830R, 1840RP, 1850RAIMS, 1860RAIMS, 1870RAIM, 1880RAIM, 1890C, 1900R, 1910R). See these sections of Chapter 2: (6) Census, (11) Court, (15) Emigration and immigration, (25, 26, 27), Military, (29) Naturalization, (33) Tax. Microfilms available from AGLL, NA, FHL(FHC).

State and colonial records: Census (Pre–1790E). See these sections of Chapter 2: (4) Birth, (6) Census, (10) Colonial, (11) Court, (13) Death, (14) Divorce, (15) Emigration and immigration, (21) Land, (23) Marriage, (24, 25, 26, 27) Military, (29) Naturalization, (33) Tax, (34) Will and probate. Many microfilms available from MSA, some from FHL(FHC).

Non–governmental records: See these sections of Chapter 2: (2) Bible, (3) Biographies, (5) Cemetery, (7) Church, (8) City directories, (9) City and county histories, (10) Colonial, (12) DAR, (15) Emigration and immigration, (16) Ethnic, (17) Gazetteers, atlases, and maps, (18) Genealogical indexes and compilations, (19) Genealogical periodicals, (20) Genealogical and historical societies, (22) Manuscripts, (28) Mortuary, (30) Newspapers, (31) Published US indexes, (32) Regional publications. Some microfilms available from FHL(FHC).

County records in MSA [microfilms can be borrowed through interlibrary loan]: birth (1898–1923), county [circuit] court (1847–1984), death (1898–1932), equity (1882–1976), estate (1882–1982), guardian (1882–1983), land (1840–1987), marriage (1812–1958), naturalizations (1812–1958), orphans' court (1882–1983), plat (1883–1988), will (1882–1988). See Papenfuse for details on these records and on which ones are available on microfilm loan.

County records in FHL [microfilms can be borrowed through FHC]: Practically no county governmental records, but many church records are available. See the FHL Catalog – Locality Section for details on these microfilm county holdings and for other records on microfilm which can be borrowed through FHC.

Published records [MHS, MSLL, FHL, LGL]: cemetery, family (1670–1929), land (very early), militia (1812–14), newspaper (1659–1850). History by Stein in 1976.

Early church records: Quaker (1662). Manuscripts in MHS: See indexes under Calvert County in Pedley (332) and Cox (290).

Society: Calvert County Historical Society, Genealogy Section, PO Box 300, Prince Frederick, MD 20678. Repositories: Calvert County Public Library, Prince Frederick, MD 20678, Tel 1–(301)–535–0291; Calvert Marine Museum Library, Solomons, MD 20688, Tel 1–(301)–326–2042.

10. CAROLINE COUNTY

Created 1773 from Dorchester and Queen Anne's Counties. County Seat Denton, MD 21629. No recorded fires, but losses of some administrative and levy court records, and all the unbound early papers of the county court.

National records: Census (1790R, 1800R, 1810R, 1820RI, 1830R, 1840RP, 1850RAIMS, 1860RAIMS, 1870RAIM, 1880RAIM, 1890C, 1900R, 1910R). See these sections of Chapter 2: (6) Census, (11) Court,

(15) Emigration and immigration, (25, 26, 27) Military, (29) Naturalization, (33) Tax. Microfilms available from AGLL, NA, FHL(FHC).

State and colonial records: Census (Pre–1790E). See these sections of Chapter 2: (4) Birth, (6) Census, (10) Colonial, (11) Court, (13) Death, (14) Divorce, (15) Emigration and immigration, (21) Land, (23) Marriage, (24, 25, 26, 27) Military, (29) Naturalization, (33) Tax, (34) Will and probate. Many microfilms available from MSA, some from FHL(FHC).

Non–governmental records: See these sections of Chapter 2: (2) Bible, (3) Biographies, (5) Cemetery, (7) Church, (8) City directories, (9) City and county histories, (10) Colonial, (12) DAR, (15) Emigration and immigration, (16) Ethnic, (17) Gazetteers, atlases, and maps, (18) Genealogical indexes and compilations, (19) Genealogical periodicals, (20) Genealogical and historical societies, (22) Manuscripts, (28) Mortuary, (30) Newspapers, (31) Published US indexes, (32) Regional publications. Some microfilms available from FHL(FHC).

County records in MSA [microfilms can be borrowed through interlibrary loan]: birth (1865–84), bonds (1877–1938), county [circuit] court (1774–1986), estate (1679–1970), guardian (1774–1983), indenture (1774–77, 1794–1853), land (1774–1986), marriage (1774–1928), naturalizations (1853), orphans' court (1785–1955), plat (1774–1955), tax (1781, 1830, 1841, 1866–1917, 1918–74), will (1685–1984). See Papenfuse for details on these records and on which ones are available on microfilm loan.

County records in FHL [microfilms can be borrowed through FHC]: estate (1679–1856), guardian (1787–1857), land (1774–1851), marriage (1774–1865), orphans' court (1785–1866), will (1685–1866). Many church records also available. See the FHL Catalog – Locality Section for details on these microfilm county holdings and for other records on microfilm which can be borrowed through FHC.

Published records [MHS, MSLL, FHL, LGL]: cemetery, chancery court (1815–63), church (1776–1825), Episcopal (1752–), land (1774–1895), marriage (1774–1825), newspaper (1830–74), plats (early), vital records (1850–80), wills (1680–1817). Histories by Noble in 1918, Cochrane in 1920, and Clark in 1969. Atlas: 1877.

Early church records: Episcopal (1749), Quaker (1755), Methodist (1785). Manuscripts in MHS: See indexes under Caroline County in Pedley (332) and Cox (291).

Nearest Societies: See Dorchester and Talbot County listings in sections following this one. Repository: Caroline County Public Library, 100 Market St., Denton, MD 21629, Tel 1–(301)–479–1343.

11. CARROLL COUNTY

Created 1837 from Baltimore and Frederick Counties. County seat Westminster, MD 21157. No record losses. For detailed research information, see H. G. Lanham, A GUIDE TO GENEALOGICAL

RESEARCH IN CARROLL COUNTY, Carroll County Genealogical Society, Westminster, MD, 1984.

National records: Census (1840RP, 1850RAIMS, 1860RAIMS, 1870RAIM, 1880RAIM, 1890C, 1900R, 1910R). See these sections of Chapter 2: (6) Census, (11) Court, (15) Emigration and immigration, (25, 26, 27) Military, (29) Naturalization, (33) Tax. Microfilms available from AGLL, NA, FHL(FHC).

State and colonial records: See these sections of Chapter 2: (4) Birth, (6) Census, (10) Colonial, (11) Court, (13) Death, (14) Divorce, (15) Emigration and immigration, (21) Land, (23) Marriage, (24, 25, 26, 27) Military, (29) Naturalization, (33) Tax, (34) Will and probate. Remember that Carroll County is a post-colonial county. Many microfilms available from MSA, some from FHL(FHC).

Non-governmental records: See these sections of Chapter 2: (2) Bible, (3) Biographies, (5) Cemetery, (7) Church, (8) City directories, (9) City and county histories, (10) Colonial, (12) DAR, (15) Emigration and immigration, (16) Ethnic, (17) Gazetteers, atlases, and maps, (18) Genealogical indexes and compilations, (19) Genealogical periodicals, (20) Genealogical and historical societies, (22) Manuscripts, (28) Mortuary, (30) Newspapers, (31) Published US indexes, (32) Regional publications. Some microfilms available from FHL(FHC).

County records in MSA [microfilms can be borrowed through interlibrary loan]: county [circuit] court (1842-1988), equity (1837-1988), estate (1837-1987), guardian (1838-65), land (1837-1988), marriage (1837-1914), orphans' court (1837-1962), plat (1842-1951), tax (1844-1974), will (1837-1987). See Papenfuse for details on these records and on which ones are available on microfilm loan.

County records in FHL [microfilms can be borrowed through FHC]: estate (1837-53), guardian (1838-65), land (1837-50), orphans' court (1837-52), will (1837-53). Many church records also available. See the FHL Catalog – Locality Section for details on these microfilm county holdings and for other records on microfilm which can be borrowed through FHC.

Published records [MHS, MSLL, FHL, LGL]: cemetery, indentures (1837-1927), Lutheran (1784-1863), marriage (1837-99), names of citizens, newspaper (l831-46), pioneers, Reformed (1812-66), tax (1798). Histories by Scharf in 1882, Lynch in 1939, and Warner in 1976. Atlas: 1877.

Early church records: Quaker (1730), Brethren (1737), Reformed (1754), Lutheran (1754), Presbyterian (1763), Episcopal (1771), Baptist (1791). Manuscripts in MHS: See indexes under Carroll County and Westminster in Pedley (333, 387) and Cox (291, 350).

Society: Carroll County Genealogical Society, 50 E. Main St., Westminster, MD 21157. Repository: Carroll County Public Library, 50 E. Main St., Westminster, MD 21157, Tel 1-(301)-848-4250.

12. CECIL COUNTY

Created 1674 from Kent County. County seat Elkton, MD 21921. Some record losses, perhaps due to the British carrying the records off in 1777, and only a partial recovery of them. Sizable record losses later, probably in 1940 when records were moved to a new court house. For detailed research information, see D. M. McCall and L. E. Alexander-Porter, GENEALOGICAL RESEARCH GUIDE FOR CECIL COUNTY, The Authors, Elkton, MD, 1983.

National records: Census (1790R, 1800R, 1810R, 1820RI, 1830R, 1840RP, 1850RAIMS, 1860RAIMS, 1870RAIM, 1880RAIM, 1890C, 1900R, 1910R). See these sections of Chapter 2: (6) Census, (11) Court, (15) Emigration and immigration, (25, 26, 27) Military, (29) Naturalization, (33) Tax. Microfilms available from AGLL, NA, FHL(FHC).

State and colonial records: Census (Pre-1790E). See these sections of Chapter 2: (4) Birth, (6) Census, (10) Colonial, (11) Court, (13) Death, (14) Divorce, (15) Emigration and immigration, (21) Land, (23) Marriage, (24, 25, 26, 27) Military, (29) Naturalization, (33) Tax, (34) Will and probate. Many microfilms available from MSA, some from FHL(FHC).

Non-governmental records: See these sections of Chapter 2: (2) Bible, (3) Biographies, (5) Cemetery, (7) Church, (8) City directories, (9) City and county histories, (10) Colonial, (12) DAR, (15) Emigration and immigration, (16) Ethnic, (17) Gazetteers, atlases, and maps, (18) Genealogical indexes and compilations, (19) Genealogical periodicals, (20) Genealogical and historical societies, (22) Manuscripts, (28) Mortuary, (30) Newspapers, (31) Published US indexes, (32) Regional publications. Some microfilms available from FHL(FHC).

County records in MSA [microfilms can be borrowed through interlibrary loan]: birth (1865-91, 1898-1927), county [circuit] court (1683-1988), death (1898-1931), estate (1670-1988), guardian (1778-1982), indenture (1794-1869), land (1674-1984), marriage (1777-1977), orphans' court (1777-1964), plat (1831-1967), will (1674-1976). See Papenfuse for details on these records and on which ones are available on microfilm loan.

County records in FHL [microfilms can be borrowed through FHC]: estate (1674-1859), guardian (1778-1859), land (1674-1850), marriage (1777-1885), orphans' court (1777-1850), will (1674-1853). Many church records also available. See the FHL Catalog - Locality Section for details on these microfilm county holdings and for other records on microfilm which can be borrowed through FHC.

Published records [MHS, MSLL, FHL, LGL]: accounts (1717-76), Bible, biography (1897), Catholic, cemetery, Episcopal (1687-), land patents marriage (1777-1840, 1865-85) militia (1812-14), newspaper (1822-30, also some later), Quaker (1680-1889), Revolutionary War (1775-83). Histories by Johnston in 1881, Miller in 1949, County Directors in 1956, and Gifford in 1974. Atlas: 1877.

Early church records: Quaker (1679), Episcopal (1693). Manuscripts in MHS: See indexes under Cecil County and Elkton in Pedley (332, 342) and Cox (292–301).

Society: Cecil County Genealogical Society, PO Box 11, Charlestown, MD 21814. Repository: Cecil County Public Library, 301 Newark Ave., Elkton, MD 21921, Tel 1–(301)–398–0914.

13. CHARLES COUNTY

Created 1658 as an original county. County seat La Plata, MD 20646. Court proceedings and many papers lost in 1746 fire at clerk's house where they had been taken. Records partly reconstituted. Court house burned 1892, many important records saved, but heavy losses of loose papers, and of administrative and financial records.

National records: Census (1790R, 1800R, 1810R, 1820RI, 1830R, 1840RP, 1850RAIMS, 1860RAIMS, 1870RAIM, 1880RAIM, 1890C, 1900R, 1910R). See these sections of Chapter 2: (6) Census, (11) Court, (15) Emigration and immigration, (25, 26, 27) Military, (29) Naturalization, (33) Tax. Microfilms available from AGLL, NA, FHL(FHC).

State and colonial records: Census (Pre–1790E). See these sections of Chapter 2: (4) Birth, (6) Census, (10) Colonial, (11) Court, (13) Death, (14) Divorce, (15) Emigration and immigration, (21) Land, (23) Marriage, (24, 25, 26, 27) Military, (29) Naturalization, (33) Tax, (34) Will and probate. Many microfilms available from MSA, some from FHL(FHC).

Non–governmental records: See these sections of Chapter 2: (2) Bible, (3) Biographies, (5) Cemetery, (7) Church, (8) City directories, (9) City and county histories, (10) Colonial, (12) DAR, (15) Emigration and immigration, (16) Ethnic, (17) Gazetteers, atlases, and maps, (18) Genealogical indexes and compilations, (19) Genealogical periodicals, (20) Genealogical and historical societies, (22) Manuscripts, (28) Mortuary, (30) Newspapers, (31) Published US indexes, (32) Regional publications. Some microfilms available from FHL(FHC).

County records in MSA [microfilms can be borrowed through interlibrary loan]: birth (1654–1706), county [circuit] court (1658–1984), death (1654–1706), estate (1665–1980), guardian (1788–1981), land (1658–1988), marriage (1654–1706, 1865–1941), orphans' court (1777–1964), plat (1697–1984), will (1665–1981). See Papenfuse for details on these records and on which ones are available on microfilm loan.

County records in FHL [microfilms can be borrowed through FHC]: estate (1673–1852), guardian (1790–1823), land (1658–1886), marriage (1654–1706), orphans' court (1791–1853), will (1665–1947). Many church records also available. See the FHL Catalog – Locality Section for details on these microfilm county holdings and for other records on microfilm which can be borrowed through FHC.

Published records [MHS, MSLL, FHL, LGL]: cemetery, emigration and immigration (1650–1720), Episcopal (1729–), militia (1812–14), newspaper (1844–54), vital records (1654–1726), will (1744–72). Histories by Klapthor in 1958 and Brown in 1976.

Early church records: Episcopal (1666). Manuscripts in MHS: See indexes under Charles County and La Plata in Pedley (334, 357) and Cox (292, 318).

Nearest Societies: See societies listed under Calvert, Prince George's, and St. Mary's Counties. Repositories: Charles County Community College, Learning Resource Center, Mitchell Rd., La Plata, MD 20646, Tel 1-(301)-934-2251; Charles County Public Library, La Plata, MD 20646, Tel 1-(301)-934-9001.

14. DORCHESTER COUNTY

Created 1669 from Somerset and Talbot Counties. County seat Cambridge, MD 21613. Some early record gaps, possibly due to poor record keeping. Court house fire in 1852, many records destroyed, chiefly those of the orphans' court. Reconstitution of the records not too successful.

National records: Census (1790R–partial, 1800R, 1810R, 1820RI, 1830R, 1840RP, 1850RAIMS, 1860RAIMS, 1870RAIM, 1880 RAIM, 1890C, 1900R, 1910R). See these sections of Chapter 2: (6) Census, (11) Court, (15) Emigration and immigration, (25, 26, 27) Military, (29) Naturalization, (33) Tax. Microfilms available from AGLL, NA, FHL(FHC).

State and colonial records: Census (Pre–1790E). See these sections of Chapter 2: (4) Birth, (6) Census, (10) Colonial, (11) Court, (13) Death, (14) Divorce, (15) Emigration and immigration, (21) Land, (23) Marriage, (24, 25, 26, 27) Military, (29) Naturalization, (33) Tax, (34) Will and probate. Many microfilms available from MSA, some from FHL(FHC).

Non–governmental records: See these sections of Chapter 2: (2) Bible, (3) Biographies, (5) Cemetery, (7) Church, (8) City directories, (9) City and county histories, (10) Colonial, (12) DAR, (15) Emigration and immigration, (16) Ethnic, (17) Gazetteers, atlases, and maps, (18) Genealogical indexes and compilations, (19) Genealogical periodicals, (20) Genealogical and historical societies, (22) Manuscripts, (28) Mortuary, (30) Newspapers, (31) Published US indexes, (32) Regional publications. Some microfilms available from FHL(FHC).

County records in MSA [microfilms can be borrowed through interlibrary loan]: county [circuit] court (1690–1987), equity (1811–1976), estate (1688–1987), guardian (1770-76, 1852–1949), land (1669–1984), marriage (1780–1841, 1851–1941), orphans' court (1843–1961), plat (1717–1874), tax (1831–1911), will (1688–1987). See Papenfuse for details on these records and on which ones are available on microfilm loan.

County records in FHL [microfilms can be borrowed through FHC]: estate (1688–1856), land (1669–1851), marriage (1780–1841, 1851–80), will (1688–1899). Many church records also available. See the FHL

Catalog – Locality Section for details on these microfilm county holdings and for other records on microfilm which can be borrowed through FHC.

Published records [MHS, MSLL, FHL, LGL]: Bible (1617–1969), cemetery, church (1751–1825), early settlers, Episcopal (1743–), land (1669–1852), Methodist (1855–66), newspaper (1830–55), will (1669–1825). Histories by Jones in 1902, 1925, and 1966, Ruelle in 1969, and Mowbray in 1987. Atlas: 1877.

Early church records: Episcopal (1737). Manuscripts in MHS: See indexes under Dorchester County and Cambridge in Pedley (332, 340) and Cox (290, 299).

Society: Dorchester County Historical Society, 1058 Taylors Island Road, Cambridge, MD 21613. Repositories: Dorchester County Public Library, 303 Gay St., Cambridge, MD 21613, Tel 1–(301)–7331.

15. FREDERICK COUNTY

Created 1748 from Baltimore and Prince George's Counties. County seat Frederick, MD 21701. Two major court house fires, one in 1842, another in 1861. However, very few records lost. For a detailed treatment of research, see D. V. Russell, FREDERICK COUNTY RESEARCH GUIDE, Catoctin Press, Middletown, MD, 1987.

National records: Census (1790R, 1800R, 1810R, 1820RI, 1830R, 1840RP, 1850RAIMS, 1860RAIMS, 1870RAIM, 1880RAIM, 1890C, 1900R, 1910R). See these sections of Chapter 2: (6) Census, (11) Court, (15) Emigration and immigration, (25, 26, 27) Military, (29) Naturalization, (33) Tax. Microfilms available from AGLL, NA, FHL(FHC).

State and colonial records: Census (Pre-1790E). See these sections of Chapter 2: (4) Birth, (6) Census, (10) Colonial, (11) Court, (13) Death, (14) Divorce, (15) Emigration and immigration, (21) Land, (23) Marriage, (24, 25, 26, 27) Military, (29) Naturalization, (33) Tax, (34) Will and probate. Many microfilms available from MSA, some from FHL(FHC).

Non–governmental records: See these sections of Chapter 2: (2) Bible, (3) Biographies, (5) Cemetery, (7) Church, (8) City directories, (9) City and county histories, (10) Colonial, (12) DAR, (15) Emigration and immigration, (16) Ethnic, (17) Gazetteers, atlases, and maps, (18) Genealogical indexes and compilations, (19) Genealogical periodicals, (20) Genealogical and historical societies, (22) Manuscripts, (28) Mortuary, (30) Newspapers, (31) Published US indexes, (32) Regional publications. Some microfilms available from FHL(FHC).

County records in MSA [microfilms can be borrowed through interlibrary loan]: birth (1865–73), bonds (1877–1945), county [circuit] court (1748–1988), death (1865–81, 1898–1915), equity (1807–1987), estate (1748–1988), guardian (1792–1982), indenture (1794–1931), land (1748–1988), marriage (1778–1915), naturalizations (1785–1836, 1854–1958), orphans' court (1748–1988), plat (1793–1982), tax

(1793-1841, 1852-1974), will (1745-1981). See Papenfuse for details on these records and on which ones are available on microfilm loan.

County records in FHL [microfilms can be borrowed through FHC]: estate (1748-1853), guardian (1792-1853), land (1748-1851), marriage (1778-97), will (1745-1854). Many church records also available. See the FHL Catalog - Locality Section for details on these microfilm county holdings and for other records on microfilm which can be borrowed through FHC.

Published records [MHS, MSLL, FHL, LGL]: biography (1898), Catholic, cemetery, Episcopal (1711-), family, German, inhabitants (1765-75), Lutheran (1743-1840), marriage (1778-1839), Moravian (1759-1871), naturalization (1799-1850), pioneers, Quaker. Histories by Scharf in 1882 and Williams in 1910 and 1967. Atlas: 1873.

Early church records: Episcopal (1711), Evangelical Lutheran (1730), Reformed (1742), Evangelical Reformed (1746), Lutheran (1754), Moravian (1759). Manuscripts in MHS: See indexes under Frederick County and Frederick in Pedley (345) and Cox (305). Do not forget the Holdcraft Collection available on microfilm from FHL(FHC).

Society: Frederick County Genealogical Society, 1133 Apple Tree Court, Frederick, MD 21701. Repository: Frederick County Public Library, 110 E. Patrick St., Frederick, MD 21701, Tel 1-(301)-694-1613.

16. GARRETT COUNTY

Created 1872 from Allegany County. County seat Oakland, MD 21550. No notable record losses.

National records: Census (1870 RAIM, 1880RAIM, 1890C, 1900R, 1910R). See these sections of Chapter 2: (6) Census, (11) Court, (15) Emigration and immigration, (25, 26, 27) Military, (29) Naturalization, (33) Tax. Microfilms available from AGLL, NA, FHL(FHC).

State and colonial records: Census (Pre-1790E). See these sections of Chapter 2: (4) Birth, (6) Census, (10) Colonial, (11) Court, (13) Death, (14) Divorce, (15) Emigration and immigration, (21) Land, (23) Marriage, (24, 25, 26, 27) Military, (29) Naturalization, (33) Tax, (34) Will and probate. Remember that Garrett County is a post-colonial county. Many microfilms available from MSA, some from FHL (FHC).

Non-governmental records: See these sections of Chapter 2: (2) Bible, (3) Biographies, (5) Cemetery, (7) Church, (8) City directories, (9) City and county histories, (10) Colonial, (12) DAR, (15) Emigration and immigration, (16) Ethnic, (17) Gazetteers, atlases, and maps, (18) Genealogical indexes and compilations, (19) Genealogical periodicals, (20) Genealogical and historical societies, (22) Manuscripts, (28) Mortuary, (30) Newspapers, (31) Published US indexes, (32) Regional publications. Some microfilms available from FHL (FHC).

County records in MSA [microfilms can be borrowed through interlibrary loan]: Bonds (1884-1959), county [circuit] court (1870-1988), equity (1878–83), estate (1872–1980), guardian (1873–1976), land (1872–1988), marriage (1873–1957), orphans' court (1872–1980), plat (1852–1956), will (1873–1988). See Papenfuse for details on these records and on which ones are available on microfilm loan.

County records in FHL [microfilms can be borrowed through FHC]: Some church and other non–governmental records available. See the FHL Catalog – Locality Section for details on these microfilm county holdings and for other records on microfilm which can be borrowed through FHC.

Published records [MHS, MSLL, FHL, LGL]: biography (1898), Catholic, cemetery, pioneers, will (1872–1960). Histories by Scharf in 1882 and Schlosnagle in 1978.

Early church records: Lutheran (1854). Manuscripts in MHS: See indexes under Garrett County in Pedley (346) and Cox (306).

Nearest Society: See listing under Allegany County. Repository: Ruth Enlow Library of Garrett County, 6 N. Second St., Oakland, MD 21550; Tel 1–(301)–334–3996.

---

17. HARFORD COUNTY

Created 1773 from Baltimore County. County seat Bel Air, MD 21014. Court house fire in 1858. Probate and court records unharmed, but losses of records of county administration and commissioners. Some early losses of court records may have occurred between creation of the county and the building of the first court house (1791).

National records: Census (1790R, 1800R, 1810R, 1820RI, 1830R, 1840RP, 1850RAIMS, 1860RAIMS, 1870RAIM, 1880RAIM, 1890C, 1900R, 1910R). See these sections of Chapter 2: (6) Census, (11) Court, (15) Emigration and immigration, (25, 26, 27) Military, (29) Naturalization, (33) Tax. Microfilms available from AGLL, NA, FHL (FHC).

State and colonial records: Census (Pre–1790E). See these sections of Chapter 2: (4) Birth, (6) Census, (10) Colonial, (11) Court, (13) Death, (14) Divorce, (15) Emigration and immigration, (21) Land, (23) Marriage, (24, 25, 26, 27) Military, (29) Naturalization, (33) Tax, (34) Will and probate. Many microfilms available from MSA, some from FHL (FHC).

Non–governmental records: See these sections of Chapter 2: (2) Bible, (3) Biographies, (5) Cemetery, (7) Church, (8) City directories, (9) City and county histories, (10) Colonial, (12) DAR, (15) Emigration and immigration, (16) Ethnic, (17) Gazetteers, atlases, and maps, (18) Genealogical indexes and compilations, (19) Genealogical periodicals, (20) Genealogical and historical societies, (22) Manuscripts, (28) Mortuary, (30) Newspapers, (31) Published US indexes, (32) Regional publications. Some microfilms available from FHL (FHC).

County records in MSA [microfilms can be borrowed through interlibrary loan]: county [circuit] court (1774–89), death (1898–1909), equity (1803–1971), estate (1774–1968), guardian (1773–1984), land (1774–1989), marriage (1782–1886), orphans' court (1772–1984), plat (1790–

1952), survey (1658–1894), will (1774–1976). See Papenfuse for details on these records and on which ones are available on microfilm loan.

County records in FHL [microfilms can be borrowed through FHC]: estate (1774–1868), guardian (1773–1902), land (1774–1850), marriage (1774–1886), will (1774–1948). Many church records also available. See the FHL Catalog – Locality Section for details on these microfilm county holdings and for other records on microfilm which can be borrowed through FHC.

Published records [MHS, MSLL, FHL, LGL]: Bible, biography (1897), cemetery, directory (1879), Episcopal (1681–1951), family, militia (1812–14), mortuary, newspaper (1882–99), orphans' court (1778–1800), Quaker (1738–), Revolutionary War (1775–83), tax (1778, 1783), will (1774–1960). Histories by Preston in 1901, Mason in 1940 and 1955, and Wright in 1967.

Early church records: Quaker (1680), Episcopal (1681). Manuscripts in MHS: See indexes under Harford County and Bel Air in Pedley (328, 350) and Cox (286, 309).

Societies: Harford County Genealogical Society, PO Box 15, Aberdeen, MD 21001. Repositories: Harford Community College, Learning Resources Center, 401 Thomas Run Rd., Bel Air, MD 21014, Tel 1–(301)–836–4316; Harford County Library, 1221 Brass Mill Road, Belcamp, MD 21017, Tel 1–(301)–272–4348.

---

18. HOWARD COUNTY

Created 1851 from Anne Arundel County. County seat Ellicott City, MD 21043. A legislative act of 1838 designated the area now occupied by Howard County as the Howard District of Anne Arundel County. The district began keeping some records of its own as early as 1840. There have been no notable losses of records.

National records: Census (1860RAIMS, 1870RAIM, 1880 RAIM, 1890C, 1900R, 1910R). See these sections of Chapter 2: (6) Census, (11) Court, (15) Emigration and immigration, (25, 26, 27) Military, (29) Naturalization, (33) Tax. Microfilms available from AGLL, NA, FHL (FHC).

State and colonial records: Census (Pre–1790E). See these sections of Chapter 2: (4) Birth, (6) Census, (10) Colonial, (11) Court, (13) Death, (14) Divorce, (15) Emigration and immigration, (21) Land, (23) Marriage, (24, 25, 26, 27) Military, (29) Naturalization, (33) Tax, (34) Will and probate. Recall that Howard County is a post–colonial county. Many microfilms available from MSA, some from FHL (FHC).

Non–governmental records: See these sections of Chapter 2: (2) Bible, (3) Biographies, (5) Cemetery, (7) Church, (8) City directories, (9) City and county histories, (10) Colonial, (12) DAR, (15) Emigration and immigration, (16) Ethnic, (17) Gazetteers, atlases, and maps, (18) Genealogical indexes and compilations, (19) Genealogical periodicals, (20) Genealogical and historical societies, (22) Manuscripts, (28) Mortuary, (30)

Newspapers, (31) Published US indexes, (32) Regional publications. Some microfilms available from FHL (FHC).

County records in MSA [microfilms can be borrowed through interlibrary loan]: county [circuit] court (1840-1968), equity (1840-1980), estate (1840-1983), guardian (1840-1975), land (1839-1989), marriage (1840-1985), orphans' court (1840-1979), plat (1851-1949), tax (1851-1974), will (1840-1979). See Papenfuse for details on these records and on which ones are available on microfilm loan.

County records in FHL [microfilms can be borrowed through FHC]: estate (1840-73), guardian (1840-1942), land (1840-50), orphans' court (1840-49), will (1840-62). Many church records also available. See the FHL Catalog – Locality Section for details on these microfilm county holdings and for other records on microfilm which can be borrowed through FHC.

Published records [MHS, MSLL, FHL, LGL]: biography (1905), cemetery, Episcopal (1711-), founders, genealogical records, Presbyterian, will (1840-1950). Histories by Warfield in 1905 and Stein in 1972. Atlas: 1878.

Manuscripts in MHS: See indexes under Howard County and Ellicott City in Pedley (342, 353) and Cox (301, 313).

Societies: Howard County Genealogical Society, PO Box 74, Columbia, MD 21045. Repository: Howard County Library, 10375 Little Patuxent Pkwy., Columbia, MD 21044, Tel 1-(301)-997-8000.

19. KENT COUNTY

Created about 1642 as an original county. County seat Chestertown, MD 21620. Some early record losses because of poor custodial action. Court house fire in 1720, but destruction of records was minimal. A number of the earlier records decayed badly, but transcripts of many were made; others were lost. In spite of all of this, a sizable proportion of Kent County's records survive.

National records: Census (1790R, 1800R, 1810R, 1820RI, 1830R, 1840RP, 1850RAIMS, 1860RAIMS, 1870RAIM, 1880RAIM, 1890C, 1900R, 1910R). See these sections of Chapter 2: (6) Census, (11) Court, (15) Emigration and immigration, (25, 26, 27) Military, (29) Naturalization, (33) Tax. Microfilms available from AGLL, NA, FHL (FHC).

State and colonial records: Census (Pre-1790E). See these sections of Chapter 2: (4) Birth, (6) Census, (10) Colonial, (11) Court, (13) Death, (14) Divorce, (15) Emigration and immigration, (21) Land, (23) Marriage, (24, 25, 26, 27) Military, (29) Naturalization, (33) Tax, (34) Will and probate. Many microfilms available from MSA, some from FHL (FHC).

Non-governmental records: See these sections of Chapter 2: (2) Bible, (3) Biographies, (5) Cemetery, (7) Church, (8) City directories, (9) City and county histories, (10) Colonial, (12) DAR, (15) Emigration and immigration, (16) Ethnic, (17) Gazetteers, atlases, and maps, (18) Genealogical indexes and compilations, (19) Genealogical periodicals, (20) Genealogical and historical societies, (22) Manuscripts, (28) Mortuary, (30) Newspapers, (31) Published US indexes, (32) Regional publications. Some microfilms available from FHL (FHC).

County records in MSA [microfilms can be borrowed through interlibrary loan]: birth (1865–73), bonds (1694–1782), county [circuit] court (1648–1851), estate (1664–1984), guardian (1778–1985), indenture (1694–1829), land (1648–1988), marriage (1796–1852), orphans' court (1803–1963), plat (1703–1946), tax (1841–51, 1867–73), will (1669–1983). See Papenfuse for details on these records and on which ones are available on microfilm loan.

County records in FHL [microfilms can be borrowed through FHC]: county [circuit] court, estate (1664–1850), guardian (1794–1860), land (1648–1869), marriage (1796–1866), will (1669–1948). Many church records also available. See the FHL Catalog – Locality Section for details on these microfilm county holdings and for other records on microfilm which can be borrowed through FHC.

Published records [MHS, MSLL, FHL, LGL]: Bible, cemetery, church (1648–1825), early genealogical data, Episcopal (1650–), marriage (1796–1850), Methodist (1825–1975), military (1775), Quaker, will (1642–1960). Histories by Hanson in 1876, Usilton in 1916 and 1980, and Howell in 1931. Atlas: 1877.

Early church records: Episcopal (1650), Quaker (1698). Manuscripts in MHS: See indexes under Kent County and Chestertown in Pedley (334, 356) and Cox (292, 317).

Societies: See listing under Cecil County. Repositories: Kent County Public Library, 408 High St., Chestertown, MD 21620, Tel 1-(301)-778-3636; Washington College Library, Washington Ave., Chestertown, MD 21620, Tel 1-(301)-778-2800.

20. MONTGOMERY COUNTY

Created 1776 from Frederick County. County seat Rockville, MD 20850. No notable record losses.

National records: Census (1790R, 1800R, 1810R, 1820RI, 1840RP, 1850RAIMS, 1860RAIMS, 1870RAIM, 1880RAIM, 1890C, 1900R, 1910R). See these sections of Chapter 2: (6) Census, (11) Court, (15) Emigration and immigration, (25, 26, 27) Military, (29) Naturalization, (33) Tax. Microfilms available from AGLL, NA, FHL (FHC). For detailed research information, see E. M. V. Clark, GUIDE TO THE RECORDS OF MONTGOMERY COUNTY, Family Line Publications, Westminster, MD, 1989.

State and colonial records: Census (Pre-1790E). See these sections of Chapter 2: (4) Birth, (6) Census, (10) Colonial, (11) Court, (13) Death, (14) Divorce, (15) Emigration and immigration, (21) Land, (23) Marriage, (24, 25, 26, 27) Military, (29) Naturalization, (33) Tax, (34) Will and probate. Many microfilms available from MSA, some from FHL (FHC).

Non–governmental records: See these sections of Chapter 2: (2) Bible, (3) Biographies, (5) Cemetery, (7) Church, (8) City directories, (9) City and county histories, (10) Colonial, (12) DAR, (15) Emigration and immigration, (16) Ethnic, (17) Gazetteers, atlases, and maps, (18) Genealogical indexes and compilations, (19) Genealogical periodicals, (20) Genealogical and historical societies, (22) Manuscripts, (28) Mortuary, (30) Newspapers, (31) Published US indexes, (32) Regional publications. Some microfilms available from FHL (FHC).

County records in MSA [microfilms can be borrowed through interlibrary loan]: birth (1865–99), bonds (1898–1962), county [circuit] court (1777–1977), death (1898–1947), equity (1800–1968), estate (1777–1978), guardian (1844–1988), land (1777–1986), marriage (1798–1839, 1865–1910), orphans' court (1779–1966), plat (1777–1963), tax (1839–97), will (1777–1985). See Papenfuse for details on these records and on which ones are available on microfilm loan.

County records in FHL [microfilms can be borrowed through FHC]: estate (1777–1855), guardian (1844–1855), land (1777–1863), orphans' court (1779–1855), tax (1777, 1783), will (1777–1851). Many church records also available. See the FHL Catalog – Locality Section for details on these microfilm county holdings and for other records on microfilm which can be borrowed through FHC.

Published records [MHS, MSLL, FHL, LGL]: biography (1879, 1898), Catholic, cemetery, Episcopal (1792–), marriage (1798–1898), newspaper (1855–99), pioneers, Presbyterian, will (1776–1850). Histories by Boyd in 1879, Scharf in 1882, Farquhar in 1962, and Sween in 1984. Atlas: 1879.

Early church records: Episcopal (1711), Quaker (1736). Manuscripts in MHS: See indexes under Montgomery County in Pedley (365) and Cox (326).

Societies: Genealogical Club of the Montgomery County Historical Society, 103 West Montgomery Ave., Rockville, MD 20850. Repositories: Montgomery County Department of Libraries, 97 Maryland Ave., Rockville, MD 20850, Tel 1–(301)–217–7165; Montgomery County Historical Society Library, 103 West Montgomery Ave., Rockville, MD 20850, Tel 1–(301)–762–1492; Takoma Park MD Library, 101 Philadelphia Ave., Takoma Park, MD 20912, Tel 1–(301)–270–1717.

21. PRINCE GEORGE'S COUNTY

Created 1696 from Calvert and Charles Counties. County seat Upper Marlboro, MD 20870. No notable record losses.

National records: Census (1790R, 1800R, 1810R, 1820RI, 1840RP, 1850RAIMS, 1860RAIMS, 1870RAIM, 1880RAIM, 1890C,

1900R, 1910R). See these sections of Chapter 2: (6) Census, (11) Court, (15) Emigration and immigration, (25, 26, 27) Military, (29) Naturalization, (33) Tax. Microfilms available from AGLL, NA, FHL (FHC).

State and colonial records: Census (Pre-1790E). See these sections of Chapter 2: (4) Birth, (6) Census, (10) Colonial, (11) Court, (13) Death, (14) Divorce, (15) Emigration and immigration, (21) Land, (23) Marriage, (24, 25, 26, 27) Military, (29) Naturalization, (33) Tax, (34) Will and probate. Many microfilms available from MSA, some from FHL (FHC).

Non-governmental records: See these sections of Chapter 2: (2) Bible, (3) Biographies, (5) Cemetery, (7) Church, (8) City directories, (9) City and county histories, (10) Colonial, (12) DAR, (15) Emigration and immigration, (16) Ethnic, (17) Gazetteers, atlases, and maps, (18) Genealogical indexes and compilations, (19) Genealogical periodicals, (20) Genealogical and historical societies, (22) Manuscripts, (28) Mortuary, (30) Newspapers, (31) Published US indexes, (32) Regional publications. Some microfilms available from FHL (FHC).

County records in MSA [microfilms can be borrowed through interlibrary loan]: birth (1865-67, 1898-1982), bonds (1739-1952), county [circuit] court (1696-1975), death (1865-66), equity (1819-24, 1852-1972), estate (1696-1987), guardian (1725-1988), indenture (1777-1881), land (1696-1983), marriage (1777-1923), naturalizations (1777-1845, 1865-1910), orphans' court (1777-1987), plat (1835-1972), tax (1780-1850, 1861-1919), will (1697-1984). See Papenfuse for details on these records and on which ones are available on microfilm loan.

County records in FHL [microfilms can be borrowed through FHC]: estate (1696-1948), guardian (1725-1858), land (1696-1884), marriage (1777-1886), orphans' court (1777-1948), will (1697-1948). Many church records also available. See the FHL Catalog – Locality Section for details on these microfilm county holdings and for other records on microfilm which can be borrowed through FHC.

Published records [MHS, MSLL, FHL, LGL]: biography (1947), cemetery, church (1686-1885), court (1696-99), Episcopal (1686-), free blacks (1806-63), land (1702-17), marriage (1777-1886), Methodist (1840-80), militia (1812-14), oaths of fidelity (1778), orphans' court (1696-1750), probate (1696-1900), tax (1828), War of 1812, will (1696-1900). Histories by Bowie in 1947, Watson in 1962, Hienton in 1972, and Van Horn in 1976. Atlas: 1878.

Early church records: Episcopal (1686). Manuscripts in MHS: See indexes under Prince George's County and Upper Marlboro in Pedley (371, 385) and Cox (332-33).

Societies: Prince George's County Genealogical Society, 12207 Tulip Grove Drive, PO Box 819, Bowie, MD 20715. Repositories: University of MD Libraries, College Park, MD 20742, Tel 1-(301)-454-3011; Prince George's County Memorial Library, 6532 Adelphi Rd., Hyattsville, MD 20782, Tel 1-(301)-699-3500; US Bureau of the Census Library, FB3, Room 2449, Suitland, MD 20233, Tel 1-(301)-763-5040; National

Archives, Washington National Records Center, 4205 Suitland, Suitland, MD 20409, Tel 1-(301)-763-7000; Takoma Park MD Library, 101 Philadelphia Ave., Takoma Park, MD 20912, Tel 1-(301)-270-1717.

22. QUEEN ANNE'S COUNTY

Created 1706 from Talbot, Dorchester, and Kent Counties. County seat Centreville, MD 21617. No notable record losses, except for a few court proceedings.

National records: Census (1790R, 1800R, 1810R, 1820RI, 1840RP, 1850RAIMS, 1860RAIMS, 1870RAIM, 1880RAIM, 1890C, 1900R, 1910R). See these sections of Chapter 2: (6) Census, (11) Court, (15) Emigration and immigration, (25, 26, 27) Military, (29) Naturalization, (33) Tax. Microfilms available from AGLL, NA, FHL (FHC).

State and colonial records: Census (Pre-1790E). See these sections of Chapter 2: (4) Birth, (6) Census, (10) Colonial, (11) Court, (13) Death, (14) Divorce, (15) Emigration and immigration, (21) Land, (23) Marriage, (24, 25, 26, 27) Military, (29) Naturalization, (33) Tax, (34) Will and probate. Many microfilms available from MSA, some from FHL (FHC).

Non-governmental records: See these sections of Chapter 2: (2) Bible, (3) Biographies, (5) Cemetery, (7) Church, (8) City directories, (9) City and county histories, (10) Colonial, (12) DAR, (15) Emigration and immigration, (16) Ethnic, (17) Gazetteers, atlases, and maps, (18) Genealogical indexes and compilations, (19) Genealogical periodicals, (20) Genealogical and historical societies, (22) Manuscripts, (28) Mortuary, (30) Newspapers, (31) Published US indexes, (32) Regional publications. Some microfilms available from FHL (FHC).

County records in MSA [microfilms can be borrowed through interlibrary loan]: birth (1865-81), bonds (1778-1835, 1860-69), county [circuit] court (1709-1987), estate (1707-1979), guardian (1778-1924), land (1706-1987), marriage (1817-1927), orphans' court (1778-1963), plat (1831-1950), tax (1820-60), will (1706-1987). See Papenfuse for details on these records and on which ones are available on microfilm loan.

County records in FHL [microfilms can be borrowed through FHC]: estate (1707-1857), guardian (1778-1864), land (1706-1873), orphans' court (1778-1857), will (1706-1857). Many church records also available. See the FHL Catalog - Locality Section for details on these microfilm county holdings and for other records on microfilm which can be borrowed through FHC.

Published records [MHS, MSLL, FHL, LGL]: Bible, Catholic, church (1726-1825), Episcopal (1694-), marriage (1763-1845). History by Emory in 1950. Atlas: 1877.

Early church records: Episcopal (1694). Manuscripts in MHS: See indexes under Queen Anne's County and Centreville in Pedley (333, 372) and Cox (292, 333).

Societies: See society listed under Talbot County. Repository: Queen Anne's County Free Library, 121 S. Commerce St., Centreville, MD 21617, Tel 1-(301)-758-0980.

23. ST. MARY'S COUNTY

Created 1637 as the original county of MD. County seat Leonardtown, MD 20650. Some records lost in 1768 in fire at deputy clerk's house where they were being kept. Fire in 1831 consumed practically all county court records. Efforts to reconstitute land records not too successful. Many probate and other orphans' court records survived, but some were lost.

National records: Census (1790R, 1800R, 1810R, 1820RI, 1840-RP, 1850RAIMS, 1860RAIMS, 1870RAIM, 1880RAIM, 1890C, 1900R, 1910R). See these sections of Chapter 2: (6) Census, (11) Court, (15) Emigration and immigration, (25, 26, 27) Military, (29) Naturalization, (33) Tax. Microfilms available from AGLL, NA, FHL (FHC).

State and colonial records: Census (Pre-1790E). See these sections of Chapter 2: (4) Birth, (6) Census, (10) Colonial, (11) Court, (13) Death, (14) Divorce, (15) Emigration and immigration, (21) Land, (23) Marriage, (24, 25, 26, 27) Military, (29) Naturalization, (33) Tax, (34) Will and probate. Many microfilms available from MSA, some from FHL (FHC).

Non-governmental records: See these sections of Chapter 2: (2) Bible, (3) Biographies, (5) Cemetery, (7) Church, (8) City directories, (9) City and county histories, (10) Colonial, (12) DAR, (15) Emigration and immigration, (16) Ethnic, (17) Gazetteers, atlases, and maps, (18) Genealogical indexes and compilations, (19) Genealogical periodicals, (20) Genealogical and historical societies, (22) Manuscripts, (28) Mortuary, (30) Newspapers, (31) Published US indexes, (32) Regional publications. Some microfilms available from FHL (FHC).

County records in MSA [microfilms can be borrowed through interlibrary loan]: birth (1865-67), county [circuit] court (1777-1981), equity (1851-1981), estate (1674-1976), guardian (1779-1984), indenture (1794-1908), land (1777-1989), marriage (1794-1976), naturalizations (1833-1918), orphans' court (1777-1964), plat (1828-1948), tax (1793-1917), will (1658-1967). See Papenfuse for details on these records and on which ones are available on microfilm loan.

County records in FHL [microfilms can be borrowed through FHC]: county [circuit] court (1658-66, 1807-41), estate (1782-1959), guardian (1787-1912), land (1781-1930), marriage (1794-1940), orphans' court (1801-52), will (1658-1946). Many church records also available. See the FHL Catalog – Locality Section for details on these microfilm county holdings and for other records on microfilm which can be borrowed through FHC.

Published records [MHS, MSLL, FHL, LGL]: Catholic, deaths (1634–1900), emigration (1790–1810), Episcopal (1692–), free blacks (1850, 1860), inhabitants (1639–1724), marriage (1634–1900), militia (1812–14). Histories by Fenwick in 1955 and Hammett in 1977.

Early church records: Catholic (1637), Episcopal (1692). Manuscripts in MHS: See indexes under St. Mary's County in Pedley (375) and Cox (337).

Society: St. Mary's County Genealogical Society, General Delivery, Callaway, MD 20620. Repositories: St. Mary's County Historical Society Library, Leonardtown, MD 20650, Tel 1–(301)–475–2467; St. Mary's County Memorial Library, Route 1, Leonardtown, MD 20650, Tel 1–(301)–475–2846; St. Mary's College of MD Library, St. Mary's City, MD 20686, Tel 1–(301)–862–0257.

24. SOMERSET COUNTY

Created 1666 as an original county. County seat Princess Anne, MD 21853. Early moves resulted in some loose papers and administrative records. Practically all records were saved in a court house fire of 1831.

National records: Census (1800R, 1810R, 1820RI, 1830R, 1840RP, 1850RAIMS, 1860RAIMS, 1870RAIM, 1880RAIM, 1890C, 1900R, 1910R). See these sections of Chapter 2: (6) Census, (11) Court, (15) Emigration and immigration, (25, 26, 27) Military, (29) Naturalization, (33) Tax. Microfilms available from AGLL, NA, FHL (FHC).

State and colonial records: Census (Pre–1790E). See these sections of Chapter 2: (4) Birth, (6) Census, (10) Colonial, (11) Court, (13) Death, (14) Divorce, (15) Emigration and immigration, (21) Land, (23) Marriage, (24, 25, 26, 27) Military, (29) Naturalization, (33) Tax, (34) Will and probate. Many microfilms available from MSA, some from FHL (FHC).

Non–governmental records: See these sections of Chapter 2: (2) Bible, (3) Biographies, (5) Cemetery, (7) Church, (8) City directories, (9) City and county histories, (10) Colonial, (12) DAR, (15) Emigration and immigration, (16) Ethnic, (17) Gazetteers, atlases, and maps, (18) Genealogical indexes and compilations, (19) Genealogical periodicals, (20) Genealogical and historical societies, (22) Manuscripts, (28) Mortuary, (30) Newspapers, (31) Published US indexes, (32) Regional publications. Some microfilms available from FHL (FHC).

County records in MSA [microfilms can be borrowed through interlibrary loan]: birth (1649–1720, 1865–94), bonds (1815–1930), county [circuit] court (1666–1983), death (1649–1720), equity (1816–1983), estate (1678–1977), guardian (1778–1938), indenture (1797–1909), land (1665–1989), marriage (1649–1720, 1796–1966), orphans' court (1778–1960), plat (1722–1955), tax (1723–59, 1783–1822, 1852–

1917), will (1664-1984). See Papenfuse for details on these records and on which ones are available on microfilm loan.

County records in FHL [microfilms can be borrowed through FHC]: estate (1664-1948), guardian (1778-1850), land (1665-1850), marriage (1796-1832), orphans' court (1778-1948), will (1664-1850). Many church records also available. See the FHL Catalog - Locality Section for details on these microfilm county holdings and for other records on microfilm which can be borrowed through FHC.

Published records [MHS, MSLL, FHL, LGL]: cemetery, church (1648-1825), constables' lists, county [circuit] court (1675-77), Episcopal (1695-1887), land, marriage (1796-1871), newspaper (1835-40), Presbyterian (1672-), rent rolls (1663-1723), surveys, tax (1739, 1783), vital records (1666-1720), voter (1865), will (1664-1955). Histories by Torrence in 1935 and the Board of Education in 1955. Atlas: 1877.

Early church records: Episcopal (1734), Presbyterian (1759). Manuscripts in MHS: See indexes under Somerset County and Princess Anne in Pedley (371, 379) and Cox (333, 341-42).

Society: Lower Shore Genealogical Society, 1133 Somerset Avenue, Princess Anne, MD 21853. Repositories: Somerset County Library, 1 South Beechwood St., Princess Anne, MD 21853, Tel 1-(301)-651-0852; University of MD - Eastern Shore, Frederick Douglas Library, Princess Anne, MD 21853, Tel 1-(301)-651-2200.

25. TALBOT COUNTY

Created 1661/62 from Kent County. County seat Easton, MD 21601. Various causes have resulted in some record losses, but much survives, fortunately including land and probate records. Some record losses prior to 1936 by basement water seepage.

National records: Census (1790R, 1800R, 1810R, 1820RI, 1830R, 1840RP, 1850RAIMS, 1860RAIMS, 1870RAIM, 1880RAIM, 1890C, 1900R, 1910R). See these sections of Chapter 2: (6) Census, (11) Court, (15) Emigration and immigration, (25, 26, 27) Military, (29) Naturalization, (33) Tax. Microfilms available from AGLL, NA, FHL (FHC).

State and colonial records: Census (Pre-1790E). See these sections of Chapter 2: (4) Birth, (6) Census, (10) Colonial, (11) Court, (13) Death, (14) Divorce, (15) Emigration and immigration, (21) Land, (23) Marriage, (24, 25, 26, 27) Military, (29) Naturalization, (33) Tax, (34) Will and probate. Many microfilms available from MSA, some from FHL(FHC).

Non-governmental records: See these sections of Chapter 2: (2) Bible, (3) Biographies, (5) Cemetery, (7) Church, (8) City directories, (9) City and county histories, (10) Colonial, (12) DAR, (15) Emigration and immigration, (16) Ethnic, (17) Gazetteers, atlases, and maps, (18) Genealogical indexes and compilations, (19) Genealogical periodicals, (20) Genealogical and historical societies, (22) Manuscripts, (28) Mortuary, (30) microfilms available from FHL(FHC).

County records in MSA [microfilms can be borrowed through interlibrary loan]: birth (1657-91), bonds (1874-1939), county [circuit] court (1662-1976), death (1865-67, 1898-1926), equity (1854-1953), estate (1664-1974), guardian (1790-1981), indenture (1794-1920), land (1662-1989), marriage (1657-91, 1794-1965), naturalizations (1878-1929), orphans' court (1664-1946), plat (1721-1949), tax (1786-1896), will (1665-1986). See Papenfuse for details on these records and on which ones are available on microfilm loan.

County records in FHL [microfilms can be borrowed through FHC]: estate (1664-1960), guardian (1790-1879), land (1662-1850), will (1665-1900). Many church records also available. See the FHL Catalog - Locality Section for details on these microfilm county holdings and for other records on microfilm which can be borrowed through FHC.

Published records [MHS, MSLL, FHL, LGL]: cemetery, church (1648-1825), Episcopal (1672-), indentures (1794-1920), land (1702-90), marriage (1657-91, 1738-51, 1794-1850), Quaker, will (1744-53). Histories by Tilgham in 1915 and Preston in 1983. Atlas: 1877.

Early church records: Quaker (1664), Episcopal (1672). Manuscripts in MHS: See indexes under Talbot County and Easton in Pedley (341, 382) and Cox (300, 344).

Society: Upper Shore Genealogical Society of MD, PO Box 275, Easton, MD 21601. Repositories: Talbot County Free Library, 100 W. Dover St., Easton, MD 21601, Tel 1-(301)-822-1626; Chesapeake Bay Maritime Museum Library, St. Michaels, MD 21663, Tel 1-(301)-745-2916.

26. WASHINGTON COUNTY

Created 1776 from Frederick County. County seat Hagerstown, MD 21740. Court house fire in 1871, some record losses, especially loose papers. However, most county court, commissioners, and probate records survived.

National records: Census (1790R, 1800R, 1810R, 1820RI, 1830R, 1840RP, 1850RAIMS, 1860RAIMS, 1870RAIM, 1880RAIM, 1890C, 1900R, 1910R). See these sections of Chapter 2: (6) Census, (11) Court, (15) Emigration and immigration, (25, 26, 27) Military, (29) Naturalization, (33) Tax. Microfilms available from AGLL, NA, FHL (FHC).

State and colonial records: Census (Pre-1790E). See these sections of Chapter 2: (4) Birth, (6) Census, (10) Colonial, (11) Court, (13) Death, (14) Divorce, (15) Emigration and immigration, (21) Land, (23) Marriage, (24, 25, 26, 27) Military, (29) Naturalization, (33) Tax, (34) Will and probate. Many microfilms available from MSA, some from FHL (FHC).

Non-governmental records: See these sections of Chapter 2: (2) Bible, (3) Biographies, (5) Cemetery, (7) Church, (8) City directories, (9) City and county histories, (10) Colonial, (12) DAR, (15) Emigration and immigration, (16) Ethnic, (17) Gazetteers, atlases, and maps, (18) Genealogical indexes and compilations, (19) Genealogical periodicals, (20) Genealogical and historical societies, (22) Manuscripts, (28) Mortuary, (30) Newspapers, (31) Published US indexes, (32) Regional publications. Some microfilms available from FHL(FHC).

County records in MSA [microfilms can be borrowed through interlibrary loan]: birth (1865-67, 1898-1926), bonds (1868-1914), county [circuit] court (1777-1984), death (1865-67, 1898-1926), equity (1815-1918), estate (1751-1942), guardian (1786-1968), indenture (1794-1917), land (1777-1989), marriage (1799-1984), orphans' court (1777-1964), plat (1786-1965), tax (1803-04), will (1749-1989). See Papenfuse for details on these records and on which ones are available on microfilm loan.

County records in FHL [microfilms can be borrowed through FHC]: estate (1777-1863), guardian (1786-1872), land (1777-1860), marriage (1799-1860), orphans' court (1777-1863), will (1777-1863). Many church records also available. See the FHL Catalog – Locality Section for details on these microfilm county holdings and for other records on microfilm which can be borrowed through FHC.

Published records [MHS, MSLL, FHL, LGL]: biography (1898), cemetery, Civil War, Episcopal (1768-), Methodist (1801-), newspaper (1786-1837), pioneers, Reformed (1766-),   Histories by Scharf in 1882, Williams in 1906, and the Board of Education in 1938. Atlas: 1877.

Early church records: Lutheran (1747), Reformed (1766), Episcopal (1768). Manuscripts in MHS: See indexes under Washington County and Hagerstown in Pedley (349, 388) and Cox (308, 350).

Nearest Societies: See listings under Frederick and Allegany Counties. Repository: Washington County Free Library, 100 S. Potomac St., Hagerstown, MD 21740, Tel 1-(301) 739-3250.

27. WICOMICO COUNTY

Created 1867 from Somerset and Worcester Counties. County seat Salisbury, MD 21801. No notable record losses.

National records: Census (1870RAIM, 1880RAIM, 1890C, 1900R, 1910R). See these sections of Chapter 2: (6) Census, (11) Court, (15) Emigration and immigration, (25, 26, 27) Military, (29) Naturalization, (33) Tax. Microfilms available from AGLL, NA, FHL (FHC).

State and colonial records: Census (Pre-1790E). See these sections of Chapter 2: (4) Birth, (6) Census, (10) Colonial, (11) Court, (13) Death, (14) Divorce, (15) Emigration and immigration, (21) Land, (23) Marriage, (24, 25, 26, 27) Military, (29) Naturalization, (33) Tax, (34) Will and probate. Many microfilms available from MSA, some from FHL(FHC). Please note that Wicomico County is a post-colonial county.

Non–governmental records: See these sections of Chapter 2: (2) Bible, (3) Biographies, (5) Cemetery, (7) Church, (8) City directories, (9) City and county histories, (10) Colonial, (12) DAR, (15) Emigration and immigration, (16) Ethnic, (17) Gazetteers, atlases, and maps, (18) Genealogical indexes and compilations, (19) Genealogical periodicals, (20) Genealogical and historical societies, (22) Manuscripts, (28) Mortuary, (30) Newspapers, (31) Published US indexes, (32) Regional publications. Some microfilms available from FHL(FHC).

County records in MSA [microfilms can be borrowed through interlibrary loan]: bonds (1877–1983), county [circuit] court (1868–1989), equity (1867–1984), estate (1867–1989), land (1867–1989), marriage (1868–1981), naturalizations (1879–1975), orphans' court (1867–1989), plat (1867–1964), tax (1866–1916), will (1867–1989). See Papenfuse for details on these records and on which ones are available on microfilm loan.

County records in FHL [microfilms can be borrowed through FHC]: Many church records available. See the FHL Catalog – Locality Section for details on these microfilm holdings and for other records on microfilm which can be borrowed through FHC.

Published records [MHS, MSLL, FHL, LGL]: cemetery, church (1726–1825), Episcopal (1709–1889), land (1666–1810). Histories by Torrence in 1935, Bailey in 1967, and Corddry in 1981. Atlas: 1877.

Early church records: Episcopal (1676), Presbyterian (1759). Manuscripts in MHS: See indexes under Wicomico County and Salisbury in Pedley (376, 388) and Cox (337, 351).

Society: Lower Delmarva Genealogical Society, PO Box 3602, Salisbury, MD 21801. Repositories: Salisbury State University Library, Camden and College Aves., Salisbury, MD 21801, Tel 1–(301)–543–6130; Wicomico County Free Library, 122–126 S. Division St., Salisbury, MD 21801, Tel 1–(301)–749–3612.

28. WORCESTER COUNTY

Created 1742 from Somerset County, County seat Snow Hill 21863. Courthouse fires in 1834 and 1893. Sizable losses of records resulted. Most probate and land records survived, but losses were sustained in loose papers, orphans' court proceedings, county court judgements, levy court records, and commissioners' records.

National records: Census (1790R, 1800R, 1810R, 1820RI, 1830R, 1840RP, 1850RAIMS, 1860RAIMS, 1870RAIM, 1880RAIM, 1890C, 1900R, 1910R). See these sections of Chapter 2: (6) Census, (11) Court, (15) Emigration and immigration, (25, 26, 27) Military, (29) Naturalization, (33) Tax. Microfilms available from AGLL, NA, FHL(FHC).

State and colonial records: Census (Pre–1790E). See these sections of Chapter 2: (4) Birth, (6) Census, (10) Colonial, (11) Court, (13) Death, (14) Divorce, (15) Emigration and immigration, (21) Land, (23) Marriage, (24, 25, 26, 27) Military, (29) Naturalization, (33) Tax, (34) Will and probate. Many microfilms available from MSA, some from FHL(FHC).

Non-governmental records: See these sections of Chapter 2: (2) Bible, (3) Biographies, (5) Cemetery, (7) Church, (8) City directories, (9) City and county histories, (10) Colonial, (12) DAR, (15) Emigration and immigration, (16) Ethnic, (17) Gazetteers, atlases, and maps, (18) Genealogical indexes and compilations, (19) Genealogical periodicals, (20) Genealogical and historical societies, (22) Manuscripts, (28) Mortuary, (30) Newspapers, (31) Published US indexes, (32) Regional publications. Some microfilms available from FHL(FHC).

County records in MSA [microfilms can be borrowed through interlibrary loan]: birth (1865–89), county [circuit] court (1769–1989), equity (1818–1985), estate (1667–1963), guardian (1787–1941), indenture (1794–1851), land (1742–1989), marriage (1795–1917), orphans' court (1777–1963), plat (1793–1981), tax (1880–88), will (1666–1983). See Papenfuse for details on these records and on which ones are available on microfilm loan.

County records in FHL [microfilms can be borrowed through FHC]: estate (1688–1851), guardian (1824–46), land (1742–1868), orphans' court (1777–1850), will (1666–1850). Many church records also available. See the FHL Catalog – Locality Section for details on these microfilm county holdings and for other records on microfilm which can be borrowed through FHC.

Published records [MHS, MSLL, FHL, LGL]: cemetery, church (1726–1825), estate (1783–90), land (1666–1810), marriage (1795–1865), newspaper (1835–40), probate (1694–1742), tax (1783), will (1666–1851). Histories by the Board of Education in 1956 and Truitt in 1977. Atlas: 1877.

Early church records: Episcopal (1722). Manuscripts in MHS: See indexes under Worcester County and Snow Hill in Pedley (379, 389) and under Worcester County in Cox (353).

Nearest Society: See listing under Wicomico County in the previous section. Repository: Worcester County Library, 307 N. Washington St., Snow Hill, MD 21863, Tel 1–(301)–632–2600.

Key to Abbreviations

A	=	Agricultural census records
AGLL	=	American Genealogical Lending Library
B	=	Baltimore police census
BCA	=	Baltimore City Archives (Baltimore)
C	=	Civil War Union veterans census
DAR	=	Daughters of the American Revolution
E	=	Early census-like lists
FHC	=	Family History Center(s)
FHL	=	Family History Library (Salt Lake City)
FHLC	=	Family History Library Catalog
I	=	Industrial census records
IGI	=	International Genealogical Index
LGL	=	Large genealogical libraries
LL	=	Local library(ies) in MD
LR	=	Local repositories
M	=	Mortality census records
MHS	=	MD Historical Society (Baltimore)
MSA	=	MD State Archives (Annapolis)
MSLL	=	MD State Law Library (Annapolis)
NA	=	National Archives (Washington)
NARB	=	National Archives, Regional Branch(es)
P	=	Revolutionary War pensioner census
R	=	Regular census records
RL	=	Regional library(ies) in MD
S	=	Slaveholder census
SASE	=	Long, self-addressed, stamped envelope

Books by George K. Schweitzer

CIVIL WAR GENEALOGY. A 78-paged book of 316 sources for tracing your Civil War ancestor. Chapters include [I]: The Civil War, [II]: The Archives, [III]: National Publications, [IV]: State Publications, [V]: Local Sources, [VI]: Military Unit Histories, [VII]: Civil War Events.

GEORGIA GENEALOGICAL RESEARCH. A 235-paged book containing 1303 sources for tracing your GA ancestor along with detailed instructions. Chapters include [I]: GA Background, [II]: Types of Records, [III]: Record Locations, [IV]: Research Procedure and County Listings (detailed listing of records available for each of the 159 GA counties).

HANDBOOK OF GENEALOGICAL SOURCES. A 217-paged book describing all major and many minor sources of genealogical information with precise and detailed instructions for obtaining data from them. 129 sections going from adoptions, archives, atlases---down through gazetteers, group theory, guardianships---to War of 1812, ward maps, wills, and WPA records.

KENTUCKY GENEALOGICAL RESEARCH. A 154-paged book containing 1191 sources for tracing your KY ancestor along with detailed instructions. Chapters include [I]: KY Background, [II]: Types of Records, [III]: Record Locations, [IV]: Research Procedure and County Listings (detailed listing of records available for each of the 120 KY counties).

MARYLAND GENEALOGICAL RESEARCH. A 208-paged book containing 1176 sources for tracing your MD ancestor along with detailed instructions. Chapters include [I]: MD Background, [II]: Types of Records, [III]: Record Locations, [IV]: Research Procedure and County Listings (detailed listing of records available for each of the 23 MD counties and for Baltimore City).

MASSACHUSETTS GENEALOGICAL RESEARCH. A 279-paged book containing 1709 sources for tracing your MA ancestor along with detailed instructions. Chapters include [I]: MA Background, [II]: Types of Records, [III]: Record Locations, [IV]: Research Procedure and County-Town-City Listings (detailed listing of records available for each of the 14 MA counties and the 351 cities-towns).

NEW YORK GENEALOGICAL RESEARCH. A 240-paged book containing 1426 sources for tracing your NY ancestor along with detailed instructions. Chapters include [I]: NY Background, [II]: Types of Records, [III]: Record Locations, [IV]: Research Procedure and NY City Record Listings (detailed listing of records available for the 5 counties of NY City), [V]: Record Listings for Other Counties (detailed listing of records available for each of the other 57 NY counties).

NORTH CAROLINA GENEALOGICAL RESEARCH. A 172-paged book containing 1233 sources for tracing your NC ancestor along with detailed instructions. Chapters include [I]: NC Background, [II]: Types of Records, [III]: Record Locations, [IV]: Research Procedure and County Listings (detailed listing of records available for each of the 100 NC counties).

PENNSYLVANIA GENEALOGICAL RESEARCH. A 225-paged book containing 1309 sources for tracing your PA ancestor along with detailed instructions. Chapters include [I]: PA Background, [II]: Types of Records, [III]: Record Locations, [IV]: Research Procedure and County Listings (detailed listing of records available for each of the 67 PA counties).

REVOLUTIONARY WAR GENEALOGY. A 110-paged book containing 407 sources for tracing your Revolutionary War ancestor. Chapters include [I]: Revolutionary War History, [II]: The Archives, [III]: National Publications, [IV]: State Publications, [V]: Local Sources, [VI]: Military Unit Histories, VII: Sites and Museums.

SOUTH CAROLINA GENEALOGICAL RESEARCH. A 190-paged book containing 1107 sources for tracing your SC ancestor along with detailed instructions. Chapters include [I]: SC Background, [II]: Types of Records, [III]: Record Locations, [IV]: Research Procedure and County Listings (detailed listing of records available for each of the 47 SC counties and districts).

TENNESSEE GENEALOGICAL RESEARCH. A 136-paged book containing 1073 sources for tracing your TN ancestor along with detailed instructions. Chapters include [I]: TN Background, [II]: Types of Records, [III]: Record Locations, [IV]: Research Procedure and County Listings (detailed listing of records available for each of the 96 TN counties).

VIRGINIA GENEALOGICAL RESEARCH. A 187-paged book containing 1273 sources for tracing your VA ancestor along with detailed instructions. Chapters include [I]: VA Background, [II]: Types of Records, [III]: Record Locations, [IV]: Research Procedure and County Listings (detailed listing of records available for each of the 100 VA counties and 41 major cities).

WAR OF 1812 GENEALOGY. A 69-paged book of 289 sources for tracing your War of 1812 ancestor. Chapters include [I]: History of the War, [II]: Service Records, [III]: Bounty Land and Pension Records, [IV]: National and State Publications, [V]: Local Sources, [VI]: Military Unit Histories, VII: Sites and Events.

All of the above books may be ordered from Dr. George K. Schweitzer at the address given on the title page. Or send a long SASE for a FREE descriptive leaflet on any or all of the books.